PROBLEMS OF EVIL AND THE POWER OF GOD

Why do bad things happen, even to good people? If there is a God, why aren't God's existence and God's will for humans more apparent? And if God really does miracles for some people, why not for others? This book examines these three problems of evil – suffering, divine hiddenness, and unfairness if miracles happen as believers claim – to explore how different ideas of God's power relate to the problem of evil.

Keller argues that as long as God is believed to be all-powerful, there are no adequate answers to these problems, nor is it enough for theists simply to claim that human ignorance makes these problems insoluble. Arguing that there are no good grounds for the belief that God is all-powerful, Keller instead defends the understanding of God and God's power found in process theism and shows how it makes possible an adequate solution to the problems of evil while providing a concept of God that is religiously adequate.

ASHGATE PHILOSOPHY OF RELIGION SERIES

Series Editors

Paul Helm, King's College, University of London, UK
Jerome Gellman, Ben-Gurion University of the Negev, Israel
Linda Zagzebski, University of Oklahoma, USA

The *Ashgate Philosophy of Religion* series spans many critical debates, and presents new directions and new perspectives in contemporary research and study within the philosophy of religion. This series presents books by leading international scholars in the field, providing a platform for their own particular research focus to be presented within a wider contextual framework. Offering accessible, stimulating new contributions to each topic, this series will prove of particular value and interest to academics, graduate, postgraduate and upper-level undergraduate readers world-wide focusing on philosophy, religious studies and theology, sociology or other related fields.

Titles in the series include:

Religion and Morality
William J. Wainwright

God and the Nature of Time
Garrett J. DeWeese

Rationality and Religious Theism
Joshua L. Golding

God and Realism
Peter Byrne

Religious Diversity
A Philosophical Assessment
David Basinger

Mystical Experience of God
A Philosophical Inquiry
Jerome Gellman

Problems of Evil and the Power of God

JAMES A. KELLER
Wofford College, USA

ASHGATE

Published by
Ashgate Publishing Limited
Gower House
Croft Road
Aldershot
Hampshire GU11 3HR
England

Ashgate Publishing Company
Suite 420
101 Cherry Street
Burlington, VT 05401-4405
USA

Ashgate website: http://www.ashgate.com

British Library Cataloguing in Publication Data
Keller, James A.
  Problems of evil and the power of God. – (Ashgate philosophy of religion series)
  1. Good and evil – Religious aspects – Christianity 2. God – Attributes
  I. Title
  231.8

Library of Congress Cataloging-in-Publication Data
Keller, James A.
  Problems of evil and the power of God / James A. Keller.
    p. cm. – (Ashgate philosophy of religion series)
  Includes index.
    ISBN-13: 978-0-7546-5808-5 (hardcover: alk. paper) 1. Theodicy. 2. Good and evil–
Religious aspects–Christianity. 3. God (Christianity)–Omnipotence. 4. Process theology.
I. Title.

  BT160.K45 2007
  231'.8–dc22

2006031845

ISBN 978-0-7546-5808-5

Printed and bound in Great Britain by MPG Books Ltd, Bodmin, Cornwall.

For William P. Alston

Contents

Preface

My concern with the problem of evil goes back to my graduate school days. At the time I was becoming increasingly dissatisfied with the evangelical Christianity that had shaped my faith in college. Not only did what evangelicals and other traditional theists (my term for those who believe that God is omnipotent, omniscient, and all-good) say seem to me to be an inadequate explanation of why God permits the evil that occurs, but so did their explanations of why God's existence and will were not more clear and why it is not more clear what God has allegedly revealed in the Bible. (Think of the many still unresolved debates about what God has allegedly revealed in the Bible.) At the time, these were more feelings than well-thought-out arguments. For several years after graduate school I relegated these problems to the back burner. Then I began working on them systematically, presenting papers on various aspects of these problems. As I continued to reflect on these problems and examine the attempts by traditional theists to explain why the world exhibits these features, I became increasingly convinced of the inadequacy of their attempts to explain the problematic features – despite the ingenuity and subtlety of many of those who tried.

I also came to believe that claims about alleged miracles are important for whatever overall cogency traditional theism has, yet they also raise a nest of problems. Miracles, if they occur, would provide one kind of evidence that God is omnipotent – or at least that God has the power to unilaterally determine some creaturely states of affairs. And in the Christian tradition, alleged miracles have been cited as evidence of the revelatory status of certain individuals and events. Given the important roles that miracles could play and that are often claimed for them, I found it strange that the evidence for their occurrence is as weak as it is and that clear dramatic miracles are alleged to have occurred very seldom and in the experience of very few eyewitnesses. This line of reasoning led me to believe that the weakness of the evidence and the infrequency with which miracles are alleged to have occurred constitute still another problem of evil.

As I worked through each of the problems individually, I also saw tensions and possibly even inconsistencies among some of the explanations given for the problematic features. For example, often explanations of the unclarity of God's existence and God's will claim that such unclarity is important to allow for genuine faith and/or for the sort of moral development that John Hick calls soul-making. But if this unclarity is important, then why did God allegedly perform dramatic miracles for some people, such as showing the risen Christ to the apostles and certain other early Christians? Why didn't that preclude genuine faith and moral development on their parts?

While I was working through the foregoing issues, a new type of response to the problems of evil (particularly suffering and wicked actions) was being developed and refined by traditional theists: the claim that we humans should not expect to be able to understand or explain why the world has these problematic features. We should not expect to be able to do so because God is so much wiser and more knowledgeable than we are. I term this type of response the *ignorance defense*. It did not originate *de novo* in the past two decades, but in that time it has been stressed far more than any other time I know of.

While in graduate school and earlier in seminary, I gained my initial acquaintance with process theism, which I felt offers more promise as a way to respond to the problem of suffering and evil actions than does traditional theism. Charles Hartshorne and some others had written some short discussions of this problem from the perspective of process theism, but there were no book-length treatments of the problem. David Griffin provided one in his *God, Power, and Evil*, and then another one in his *Evil Revisited*, which was a response to various criticisms of his earlier work. Later, Marjorie Suchocki also provided a book-length treatment in *The End of Evil*. I was glad to see these treatments, and I learned much from them. But despite the many merits of these works, neither they nor any other work I am familiar with treated the other problems of evil from the perspective of process theism. It is my intention that this book will fill that gap.

It is a truism that the author of any philosophical work owes a debt to many people. The fact that this work had so long a period of germination makes the truism applicable to this work to a degree greater than most other works. I cannot begin to mention by name all those who have contributed to it, but some individuals and groups cannot be left unmentioned. In 1986 I attended an NEH Institute in the Philosophy of Religion, co-directed by William Alston and Alvin Plantinga. The speakers and the other participants greatly increased my understanding of issues in the philosophy or religion, including many discussed in this work, and they set an example of excellence I can only try to emulate. I want also to acknowledge the contributions made over the years by members of the Society for Philosophy of Religion. Many of the ideas and arguments developed in this work received preliminary formulation and discussion in that forum; the comments of respondents and those in attendance helped me greatly to refine what I said in this work. Several generations of students at Wofford College in my courses on the philosophy of religion and process philosophy have also contributed by their often searching questions and comments. In addition to people in these groups, I want to thank explicitly those who read and commented on earlier drafts of this work: Richard Creel, AK Anderson, Derek Malone-France, Frank Dilley, and Ashley Sherman Dunn. Most of all I want to express my thanks to William Alston, who not only read and commented on an earlier draft of this work and engaged in some extended exchanges about points in it, but who for many years has advised and encouraged me in many ways, though not even his sagacity and philosophical acumen could convince me that traditional theism offers a better perspective than process theism to respond to the problems of evil. I also want to thank Sarah Lloyd and her colleagues at Ashgate Publishing, who guided and helped in the process of manuscript preparation. Finally, I want to thank my wife Susan, who patiently bore with me, supported me, and loved me as I worked on this project.

James A. Keller
July 2007

CHAPTER 1

Introduction

Why do bad things happen? Why do they happen to good people? Why did this happen to me? To my family? Why do so many bad things happen? Why do such horribly bad things happen? Why does God let this thing (or such things) happen? In various ways these questions arise on the lips and in the hearts of thousands of people every day. The difficulty in answering them is a major source of perplexity among believers in theistic religions, and a major cause of non-belief among others. They are popular, lay expressions of what has been termed the problem of evil. In its scholarly formulation the problem is typically posed as something like the following question: if there is a God who is omnipotent, omniscient, and all-good, why is there evil (or so much evil, or so great evil)?

Unless it is just an expression of bewilderment with life and not a genuine question, in its various forms it presupposes some sort of a theistic context, even when it is raised by atheists. For it is a request for a reason why things happen, a purpose they serve, not for their scientific or commonsense causes. If a hurricane or an earthquake kills many people and someone asks, "Why did this happen?", that person is not asking for meteorological or geological information – information about the causes; rather, that person is asking what purpose this evil event served. And that purpose must be the purpose of some agent great enough to envisage and control the event. Only a divine being could have purposes and abilities large enough to make the question a sensible one. If there is no divine being, then there is no reason why bad things happen; they just do. We can seek their causes, we can be bewildered by them, but it is pointless to seek any purpose in them.

Of course, when the evil is something deliberately done by humans, the question of why this happened might refer to their purposes. But often theistic believers will wonder why God did not do something to prevent or alleviate the evil – and many atheists will raise the same question, as a reason for thinking there is no God. This is why events such as the Holocaust had such a great impact on the religious beliefs and religious faith of so many people. Clearly the Holocaust happened because of the evil choices and actions of some humans – humans who pursued evil purposes. But many people's faith in a God who is omnipotent, omniscient, and all-good was challenged or shattered as they wondered why God did not prevent this event. Other great evils perpetrated by humans – as well as those resulting from natural processes such as the weather and diseases – have challenged or shattered the faith of other people in such a God.

In light of the pervasiveness of the problem both among theistic believers and non-believers, it is not surprising that discussions of the problem abound both on a popular level and among scholars. In the latter context the great majority of the discussions employ or presuppose something like the scholarly formulation of the question given earlier. In so doing they presuppose that God should be understood to have the three characteristics mentioned earlier – that is, they presuppose that God is omnipotent, omniscient, and all-good. Because this way of conceiving of God is so widespread in scholarly discussions, in this work I will refer to those who hold it as *traditional theists*, and to their belief about God as *traditional theism*. Of course, atheists do not believe that a God of this sort exists, but generally this is the sort of God whose existence they deny.

One result of the widespread presupposition of traditional theism in discussions of the problem of evil has been to allow traditional theists to claim that even if the problem of evil might have the effect of making theism less probable than it might otherwise be, other considerations might more than offset this effect, making theism more probable than not. For example, arguments for the existence of God might be strong enough to offset the negative effect of the problem of evil. But these other considerations will have this effect only if they are arguments for *traditional* theism or traditional theism is the only viable form of theism. I believe that neither of these conditions is met. For example, the teleological argument does not require an omnipotent creator, and I will argue in Chapter 8 for another form of theism.

Another characteristic of the ongoing debate between traditional Christian theists and their atheistic or agnostic opponents has been the widespread tendency to incorporate into their theodicies other religious beliefs in addition to those constituting traditional theism. For example, they might use beliefs about God's purposes for human beings as part of their explanation of why God allows suffering. Or they might make use of belief in a life after death to provide a context in which some injustices not dealt with in life on earth will be rectified. Employing other beliefs in their theodicies is entirely proper, for no religious person believes simply that an omnipotent, omniscient, all-good being exists. Such a belief is always part of a larger set of beliefs that inform the person's religious life. And no one belief in the set can be evaluated adequately without reference to at least some of the other beliefs.

But however proper it is to expand in this way the beliefs that must be examined, it makes the task of evaluating a theodicy more complicated. It does so for at least two reasons. First, traditional theists do not agree completely on what these additional beliefs are. Even within a single religion, such as Christianity, traditional theists do not agree completely on these additional beliefs. For example, they do not agree on whether God knows all the details of the future, nor on whether some people will suffer eternal torment in hell. Second, if other beliefs are employed as part of a theodicy, then any full assessment of the theodicy will have to include an assessment of these other beliefs as well.

The broadening of attention from the defining beliefs of traditional theism to other religious beliefs has made the problem of evil more difficult for traditional Christian theists in ways that are often not discussed. Discussions of the problem of evil have focused on suffering, on the events in nature that cause suffering, and on human wickedness. But some of the additional beliefs employed in theodicies to respond to this problem of evil seem to imply that the world is worse than we should expect it to be in ways other than those considered in these discussions. For example, one of the common additional beliefs is that God desires humans to do God's will and to have fellowship with God. This belief leads one to expect that God's existence, God's having these desires, and God's will should be much clearer than they are. Other beliefs are that God has performed miracles that benefit some people, and that God loves all people. These beliefs lead one to expect that God would perform additional miracles that would benefit other people who are similar to the ones benefited by the miracles God has allegedly performed. I see both these issues as problems of evil, because in each case the world is worse than we should expect it to be if traditional theism and certain additional Christian beliefs are true. A relatively few traditional Christian theists have discussed the former problem, but almost none have discussed the latter. No one, so far as I know, has attempted to discuss all these problems in a single work. Such an undertaking would be valuable because, among other things, it would make it relatively easy to test for consistency in the responses traditional Christian theists give or might give to the three problems: suffering and evil human actions, the unclarity of God's existence and certain alleged truths about God, and anomalies in the pattern of alleged miracles.

In light of the foregoing characterization of discussions of the problem of evil, I can explain why I offer yet another book on this much-discussed problem and why my book includes the topics it does. First, it does consider a full-bodied theism – all the religious beliefs that seem relevant to a theodicy. This inclusion, however, comes at a cost: it looks only at the beliefs of one religion (Christianity), and even then it has to be selective, for Christians do not completely agree on many of their religious beliefs. In making my selection of beliefs to discuss, I have tried to focus on the most widely held beliefs, or on what I argue are the most plausible ones.

Second, it includes consideration of the three problems of evil delineated above. These form the topics of Chapters 2, 3, and 4 respectively. In each of these chapters I set forth the problem and I summarize and evaluate what traditional theists have said or might say to resolve the problem. In relation to each problem, I conclude that the theodicy offered by traditional Christian theists is inadequate or implausible.

Chapter 5 is devoted to another sort of response some traditional theists have given to the problems of evil, particularly to the problem of suffering and evil human actions, though it might be extended to the other problems I have delineated. This response, which has been given much attention in the last twenty or so years, centers on the claim that we humans should not expect to understand why God does many of the things God does. I term this line of argument the *ignorance defense*, and I conclude that it has some plausibility, but that its usefulness in relation to the problems of evil is limited.

My overall assessment of the theodicies and defenses offered by traditional Christian theists discussed in Chapters 2–5 is that their problems give us good reason to question the beliefs that constitute traditional theism. Of the three beliefs that constitute it, one seems to me particularly doubtful: the belief that God is omnipotent. Therefore, the next two chapters are concerned with assessing the grounds for this belief.

One possible ground is the belief that divine omnipotence is a revealed truth. Therefore, in Chapter 6 I discuss the issue of whether we have any good grounds to believe that there are any propositions that are clearly divinely certified to be revealed truths. I argue that we do not. This, incidentally, raises additional problems for traditional Christian theists. Since they believe that God could clearly certify certain propositions as revealed truths, the absence of such truths implies either that

God does not wish to clearly certify any propositions as revealed truths or that God could not (and therefore that their belief that God is omnipotent is false). Moreover, since there are no clearly divinely certified revealed truths, traditional theists cannot justify other beliefs used in their theodicies and discussions of God's power on the grounds that they are revealed truths. Chapter 7 examines grounds other than alleged revelations that have been or might be offered for the belief that God is omnipotent. I conclude that none of these grounds is adequate.

In light of the arguments in Chapters 6–7, the weakness of the theodicies and defenses in Chapters 2–5 assumes an even greater importance. For if there are no good grounds for one of the defining beliefs of traditional theism and the theodicies and defenses are themselves weak, then there seems to be no adequate reason to continue to believe that traditional theism is true. Many atheists might be content to stop at this point, thinking that once again traditional theism had been shown to be unjustified. But stopping here assumes that traditional theism is the only form of theism worth considering. In the final chapter I discuss another form of theism that I think offers a far better way for theists to respond to the problems of evil discussed in Chapters 2–4 and to the lack of clearly divinely certified revealed truths discussed in Chapter 6.

This form of theism is often termed *process theism*. It differs from traditional theism in many ways, but the most important way for this work is in its understanding of divine power. In Chapter 8 I expound the understanding of divine power in process theism and show how it solves the problems of evil discussed in Chapters 2–4. I also offer an explanation of the absence of clearly divinely certified revealed truths discussed in Chapter 6, and I argue that God's power, as process theists understand it, is adequate to fill all the legitimate religious aspirations involved in the reasons for thinking that God is omnipotent discussed in Chapter 7.

Thus, this book brings together within a single cover a range of issues that, as far as I know, has not hitherto been discussed in a single work: the three problems of evil, the ignorance defense, grounds for thinking that God is omnipotent, whether there are clearly divinely certified revealed truths, and a response from the perspective of process theism to the foregoing issues. The range of issues to which I am proposing a process theistic response is one of the features that distinguishes this work from earlier attempts to argue for the superiority of process theism to traditional theism in relation to the problem of evil.[1] The earlier discussions tended to focus exclusively on suffering and evil human actions (and not the other two problems), and did not evaluate all the grounds for traditional theists' belief in divine omnipotence.

This breadth, however, has an associated cost: many of my discussions of particular issues could profitably be pursued at greater length. I resisted the impulse to do so because my primary aim is to present and defend broadly a different framework for Christians to use in responding to the problems of evil; of course, they might also use this framework in thinking about other matters as well. In pursuing my primary aim I wanted to keep the main outlines of the argument clear and to avoid pursuing details in a depth that might distract from the overall argument.

I see our situation today as in some ways similar to times of revolutionary science as described by Thomas Kuhn in *The Structure of Scientific Revolutions*.[2] He spoke of situations in science when the anomalies (observations not easily accommodated under the scientific theories of the time) trouble some scientists enough to prompt them to look for and test alternative theories, while other scientists continue to think that the old theories are adequate and attempt to show that the old theories can explain the anomalies. If anything induces scientists to shift from the old approach to the new, or vice versa, it is not some re-examination of very fine details of particular experiments, but rather an overall comparison of the way things look from each perspective. Analogously, if anything will induce traditional Christian theists to shift to the perspective of process theism or some other alternative, or vice versa, I believe it will be not some re-examination in ever greater detail of some one issue in dispute, but rather an overall comparison of the way things look from both perspectives. This is why I say that neither those who believe that the old way (traditional Christian theism) is basically adequate and needs at most only minor adjustments nor their opponents will be persuaded by arguing disputed points in ever greater detail.

Therefore, I believe that showing the broad outlines of how a variety of issues look from a different perspective is a more useful approach than is pursuing many particular arguments in great detail. The latter approach is useful in other contexts, but in the present work I wish to focus on the main lines of the overall argument. By way of review, that argument has three main parts: the claim that there are serious problems with even the most plausible theodicies and defenses offered by traditional Christian theists (argued in Chapters 2–5); the claim that Christians have no adequate grounds for believing that God is omnipotent (argued in Chapters 6–7), and the claim that process theism does not generate the problems of evil, and it is religiously adequate (argued in Chapter 8).

However, I cannot close this introductory chapter without admitting explicitly that on the issues I discuss, like many issues in philosophy, we are far from a conclusive argument for any position, my own included. In this work I have tried to articulate the reasons that convince me that process theism provides a better way than does traditional theism for Christians today to think about the power of God and the problems of evil. Underlying those reasons is a conviction that the world is not as one would expect if traditional theism were true. I suspect that most people – including traditional theists – feel this discrepancy to some degree. That is one of the reasons why even traditional theists are troubled by the evils of the world and by the absence of clear indications of God's existence and will. Traditional Christian theists try to minimize the significance of this discrepancy by stating reasons why it is not as great as we might imagine, and reasons why any remaining discrepancy should not trouble us. Atheists, agnostics, and non-traditional Christian theists (like me) give reasons for thinking the discrepancy indicates a serious problem with the beliefs that generate it. The weakness of the grounds for at least one of those beliefs (that God is omnipotent) is, I will argue, another issue that traditional Christian theists must face.

All these issues defy easy resolution. People will inevitably differ on the weight they give to the various considerations and on how serious they judge various problems to be. Some will think it very important that their position accord with that of the majority of earlier Christians or with what they take to be the positions of various biblical writers and/or with historic Christian creeds; other Christians will not think one or more of these are important, and certainly atheists will not think any of them is important. Some people will find the evils of the world and the issue of God's relation to those evils to be burning questions, for which they must have some answers, and others will not. Some people will find themselves strongly convinced that a particular metaphysical scheme is the correct one, and others will not explicitly adhere to any. Differences on matters such as these will inevitably affect a person's judgment about the most adequate response to the problems of evil. As long as such differences obtain, it is unlikely that we will ever reach unanimous agreement, even among the adherents of a single religion such as Christianity, about the best response to the problems of evil. Nevertheless, I believe that dialog can help us move toward more adequate responses. I hope that this book makes a contribution to that dialog.

Notes

1. For example, there are fine presentations of a process theistic response to the problem of suffering and evil human actions as well as a critique of traditional theistic responses to that problem in David Ray Griffin, *God, Power, and Evil: A Process Theodicy* (Philadelphia, PA: The Westminster Press, 1976); idem, *Evil Revisited: Responses and Reconsiderations* (Albany, NY: State University of New York Press, 1991); and Marjorie Hewitt Suchocki, *The End of Evil: Process Eschatology in Historical Context* (Albany, NY: State University of New York Press, 1988).
2. Chicago, IL: University of Chicago Press, 1970.

CHAPTER 2

The Traditional Problem of Evil:
Suffering and Evil Actions

Most discussions of the problem of evil have been concerned with evil in the sense of the suffering of humans (and sometimes animals) and with the morally evil actions and intentions of human beings. Those defending traditional theism have attempted to show one or both of two things about the existence of these evils: propositions asserting their existence are not logically inconsistent with a proposition asserting the existence of a God of the sort traditional Christians believe exists, and their existence does not make unlikely (or render irrational) the belief that this sort of God exists. The alleged inconsistency is often called the logical problem of evil. In this chapter we will have relatively little concern with this problem, for I wish to try to determine what is the most plausible response for a Christian to make to evils of the sort considered in this chapter. Therefore, we will focus largely on the second issue, which is often termed the evidential problem of evil. One strategy for dealing with this second issue has been to try to provide reasons (explanations) why a God of this sort might cause or permit the existence of these evils. Another strategy has been to argue that human limitations make it irrational for us humans to expect to be able to discover the reason(s) God has. Our task in this chapter is to discuss and evaluate the explanations offered by those who follow the former strategy. Discussion and evaluation of the latter strategy will be deferred until Chapter 5.

In the past some explanations for evil have been advanced that are no longer regarded as plausible. One is the theory that natural evils (suffering caused by processes in nature, in contrast with moral evil, that caused by voluntary human actions) are really the work of one or more evil supernatural beings; we might call this the Satan hypothesis. Aside from certain biblical passages, there is no reason to think this hypothesis is true, and I will argue in Chapter 6 that the biblical writers had no supernatural source of information that might give us reason to accept anything they might say on this matter. Moreover, allowing evil spirits to have this much power over humans hardly seems like something an all-good being would do. Another theory is that God allows or imposes specific instances of suffering for specific purposes such as punishment or discipline; we will discuss this theory in Chapter 5. In this chapter we will focus on the explanation that is most common today.

Central to most contemporary explanations of the existence of moral evil is the idea that God permits evils so that humans will have the opportunity to develop in morally and religiously appropriate ways; John Hick calls this process of character development "soul-making." Humans must develop through their own choices, and this requires that they have free will. Therefore, God created human beings with a power of self-determination, a power to choose what they will do within the physical limitations of their bodies and environments. Because humans have free will, they have the power to choose to do evil as well as to do good. Because what they do is their choice, the responsibility for evil actions is theirs, not God's. Thus moral evil provides no grounds for questioning the power and goodness of God. This, in outline, is what is often termed the free-will defense.

What about natural evil? In so far as it involves the suffering of human beings, contemporary Christian traditional theists generally relate their explanations of natural evil to human moral development. They see natural evil as a consequence of natural laws operating in a universe that consists of various physical objects including human bodies; they claim that a system of natural laws is essential if it is to be possible for us humans to exercise any meaningful free choice. Only such a system makes it possible for us to have any idea what the consequences of our actions will be, and free actions are morally significant only if they are means whereby we can accomplish our goals. In particular, we can do helpful (or harmful) actions only if there are things we can manipulate to help (or harm) others; and we can do this in a way for which we are responsible only if the things have stable properties that enable us to know the consequences of various manipulations of these things. (Even helping or harming others by our speech requires the ability to manipulate some medium, typically the air, in order to communicate with others.) Moreover, natural evils present opportunities and motivations for us to act in ways that will develop our moral and spiritual virtues. This development and the consequent fellowship with God are what the free-will defense alleges are the purposes for which God created us as beings with free will.

Since this explanation of natural evil does fit so well with the free-will defense, we will focus the remainder of our discussion in this chapter on the combination of it and the free-will defense as the contemporary traditional Christian theists' explanation of evil. Our primary task in most of the rest of the chapter will be to state and evaluate some objections to this theory. But first we must comment on the concept of omnipotence and note one important issue on which contemporary Christian theists disagree, for it sometimes affects how they would respond to some objections and problems in this and the next three chapters.

The concept of omnipotence requires comment because it has been understood in different ways by traditional theists. However, we need not resolve their differences because for our purposes in this work it can be understood in a sense that is entailed by any definitions they have offered: the power to unilaterally determine or control all logically possible[1] creaturely states of affairs, *whether or not God chooses to exercise that power*.[2] Various proposed definitions of omnipotence entail this power, and for my purposes it does not matter whether the reverse entailment holds or whether omnipotence includes a greater power than this. (Descartes thought that it included the power to do what is logically impossible.) Thus the definition of traditional theism should be understood as the belief that God is omniscient and all-good and has at least the power to unilaterally determine or control all logically possible creaturely states of affairs. Because most traditional theists use "omnipotence" to characterize God's power, I will continue to use this term, but the reader should bear in mind the minimal definition of this term given above. It is sufficient to raise all the problems of evil.

The issue on which contemporary Christian traditional theists disagree that is important for this work is whether God knows the future actions of free creatures in any way that would be useful in deciding what to do in relation to them. Just knowing what the future actually will be is of no use, for nothing God could do would change a future God knows will occur. So what is required is knowledge of what free creatures will do in all possible circumstances; propositions formulating such knowledge are called counterfactuals of freedom, and knowledge of them is often called middle knowledge. Such knowledge would allow God to select the best way to achieve God's goals; it is providentially useful foreknowledge. For many issues to be discussed in this work, differences about whether God has such knowledge would not affect how traditional Christian theists would respond; where it would affect their response, we will note that. Now let us consider some objections to the theory that God permits or causes evil as part of a process intended to enable humans to develop in morally and religiously appropriate ways.

The Guilty Bystander Objection

The guilty bystander objection is based on the assumption that God is a witness to all that occurs and that God has the power to act in the world at any time and to prevent any particular event or action. When evil strikes close to home, this assumption is implicit in the question that seems to arise naturally in the minds of many believers, "Why did God let this happen?" It draws its poignancy from the feeling that many of us have when confronted by some evil occurrence, such as an act of child abuse or someone drowning, that we would have prevented if we could. According to traditional theists, there is no doubt that God observes the event, that God has the power to prevent it, and that (unlike us sometimes) God can prevent it at no personal risk or cost to Godself. In the words of William Hasker: "*God's capacity to control the detailed course of events is limited only by his self-restraint, not by any inability to do so.*"[3] God's failure to prevent such things seems to make God a guilty bystander to every evil event and action. I believe that this objection is central for most people for whom this problem of evil is a problem.

This objection is posed and explored in Bruce Russell's paper "The Persistent Problem of Evil."[4] In it he presents the following argument (123):

7. If God exists, then nothing happens which he should have prevented from happening.
8. If something happens that any moral agent should have prevented if he knew about it and could have prevented it without serious risk to himself or others, then something happens which God should have prevented from happening.
9. Something has happened that any moral agent should have prevented if he knew about it and could have prevented it without serious risk to himself or others.
10. Therefore, God does not exist.

To support point 9, Russell cites the case of a little girl who "had been raped, severely beaten over most of her body and strangled to death by the boyfriend" of her mother (123). This clearly is a case that satisfies point 9; moreover, other events that satisfy point 9 are legion, so there is no doubt that it is true. Nor can traditional theists question point 7 if God is good. So the only way to challenge this argument is to challenge point 8.

Russell considers two ways to challenge point 8. The first is to say that "it may be wrong of one person, but not wrong of someone else, to permit a person to be treated in a certain way, because the former, but not the latter, stands in a special relationship to the person in question" (124). Russell points out that God's relationship to humans has been likened to that of a parent to a child, and he rightly says that such a relationship would not justify permitting an act of the sort described in point 8. It may be objected that the parent–child relationship may not be the best model for the God–human relationship because a parent is not the creator of the child in the sense in which God is our creator. However, Christians have another basis for rejecting this challenge to point 8 based on God's being our creator. The basis, not mentioned by Russell, is their claim that God's attitude toward humans is fundamentally love. If love is God's basic attitude toward humans, then no other relationship would provide a basis for God to do less than an ordinarily good human would.

The second way to challenge point 8 considered by Russell is to claim that "differences in knowledge can determine differences in obligation" (124). Russell gives the example that a member of a primitive tribe might be obligated to try to prevent someone from cutting open a fellow member of the tribe, while an onlooker from a technological society who knows that the cutter is a surgeon would not be obligated to prevent the cutting. To rebut this challenge, Russell claims that to succeed against point 8, it must be based on the assumption that God knows some good that outweighs the evil and for the sake of which God does not prevent the evil. To counter this assumption, Russell argues that we have reason to believe that there are no outweighing goods in this incident.

His argument takes the form of rebutting suggestions about goods that might outweigh evils of the sort under consideration. From Richard Swinburne he gets the suggestion that the good is that humans will be able to make significant differences in the world by their free choices. From John Hick he gets the suggestion that humans will be able "to achieve the infinite good of *having become* morally and spiritually good persons through the exercise of their own free choices" (126, italics his). Russell agrees that the suggested goods are indeed goods, but he claims that they are not sufficiently good to justify someone in permitting the suffering of the little girl. The girl is suffering, without having consented, so that others may benefit. In effect, God is permitting her to be victimized for the sake of the good of another person. The claim that it is wrong for God to do so exemplifies what I term *the victimization objection*. It is the next objection we will consider, but before we do so, more must be said about the responses the theist might make when asked about the goods for the sake of which God permits evil events such as the one Russell discusses.

For one thing, Russell does not adequately represent Hick's suggestion. Russell's treatment of Hick (and of Swinburne, for that matter) suggests that he thinks of them as saying that the only person for whose sake God permits the evil is the boyfriend (or, more generally, the perpetrator). But Hick's position is more complex. Hick believes that God permits such evils so that all of us will have an opportunity to become morally and spiritually good persons, not only by refraining from doing such things, but also by trying to prevent others from doing them, by dealing with the victims, by dealing with the perpetrators, and by learning how to deal with suffering we innocently undergo. That is, in Hick's view, God permits us to act without divine interference[5] so that as a community as well as individuals we will learn to try to prevent evil and to heal its ravages. Of course, this way of construing Hick's view does not preclude raising the victimization objection, but it does indicate that the good envisaged is broader than Russell recognizes and often includes some good for the victim. Richard Swinburne adds what he regards as another very important good: the good of being of use to others. I will postpone discussing his suggestion till later in this chapter.

Let us return to the sort of considerations Hick raises, for he is far from alone in taking this larger view of the intended beneficiaries and benefits of God's restraint. If God were always to intervene to prevent one person from harming (or seriously harming) another, not only would individuals soon learn that it is fruitless to try to harm others, but the world would no longer present us with some important challenges: for example, the challenge of trying to help others such as our children to develop so that they do not do such things; that of trying to help others such as our friends continue to live in this way and to develop spiritually; that of helping others who have suffered evil; and that of trying to help evildoers reform. In a world of this sort, there would be no incentive for moral development. People could not do wrong to others, and there would be no occasion when others needed help. Of course, there could be natural evils, and a similar guilty bystander objection can be raised against God for not preventing them, but a similar line of argument can be used to show that it would frustrate human development if God were always to intervene to prevent natural evils. But even if God could not prevent all evils, could not God prevent many of them?

A powerful argument for a negative answer to this question is given by William Hasker in *Providence, Evil, and the Openness of God*.[6] Unlike many contributors to the debate about the adequacy of various theodicies, Hasker does not envisage God as considering in relation to each evil event whether the evil is outweighed by some good it makes possible. Instead, Hasker defends God's having a policy of (almost) never intervening with processes in nature and with the free choices of human beings. He does so by focusing on those instances of evil which are not necessary to achieve some good that outweighs the evil (or to prevent some greater evil); he calls each of these a *gratuitous evil*. He claims that gratuitous evils are not just consistent with traditional theism, but are to be expected. To support this claim, he considers the consequences of God's preventing all gratuitous evils. Consider first gratuitous evil arising from human choices. If all the evil that occurs is necessary for some greater good, then it cannot be obligatory for anyone to prevent it; if it were better that the evil be prevented, God would have done so. And if it became known that God is preventing all gratuitous evils, then most human motivation for preventing evil, refraining from evil, and alleviating suffering would be removed. (Some motivation might remain because some people might want to prevent an evil from happening to them or their loved ones even if it meant that someone else might be deprived of a greater good or suffer a greater evil.) Thus both the obligation and much of the motivation for humans to prevent or alleviate evil would be eliminated. To the extent that moral and spiritual growth consists in developing habits of acting in which one refrains from doing evil and helps those who are suffering unnecessarily, there would be no obligation and little motivation for such growth. Hasker describes this result by saying that *morality is undermined* (64–5). Therefore, the fundamental purpose for which God created humans on earth would be impossible to achieve.

Hasker responds to two attempts to use his argument itself to show that the evils are not gratuitous. One attempt notes that Hasker has shown that if God were to prevent all gratuitous evil, morality would be undermined. But the undermining of morality would be a very bad thing. So the evil is not gratuitous, since it is necessary for moral development. To this Hasker replies that though morality would be undermined if God prevented *all* gratuitous evils, it would not be undermined if God prevented *any one* instance of such evil. Therefore, each such instance is genuinely gratuitous (68). The other attempt claims that if God prevented the evil, a good would be prevented: the good that a morally significant free choice was made on this particular occasion. To this Hasker replies that there is no reason to think that the good that is a free choice outweighs any amount of evil produced by that choice and its consequences. He says that "we cannot for a moment suppose, for example, that the evil of a murder is outweighed by the intrinsic value of the freedom that enabled the agent to commit it" (84).

Hasker's argument has been formulated in terms of gratuitous moral evil, but he points out that a similar argument could be made in relation to gratuitous natural evil. The occurrence of natural evil makes possible many goods such as "knowledge, prudence, courage, foresight, cooperation and compassion" (74). If God were to prevent all gratuitous natural evils, this might have little effect on the attainment of the goods in question, "*so long as human beings did not know or suspect that God was doing this!*" (74, his italics). But, Hasker claims, keeping humans in this condition would require "in effect a massive 'disinformation campaign' on God's part, something which is surely morally dubious in itself" (74). Moreover, the more, accurate information humans have about God, the greater will be their tendency to derive from that information the (alleged) conclusion that God will prevent all gratuitous natural evil. But then God's purpose of leading humans to an accurate knowledge of God would undermine the purpose of keeping humans ignorant of God's preventing gratuitous natural evil (74).

It is noteworthy that an advocate of a version of the free-will defense should make these points about the inappropriateness of God's keeping humans in ignorance. For, as we will see in Chapter 3, it is typical of traditional theists who employ this defense also to claim that God deliberately hides Godself from humans. God allegedly does this for a good purpose: to make possible a free, uncoerced faith in God. But one could object to Hasker's argument by claiming that God's keeping humans in ignorance about God's preventing gratuitous evils also has a good purpose: to make possible the acquiring of the goods listed in the previous paragraph. Hasker does not present any argument to show that this good purpose would not justify God's keeping humans ignorant of a policy on God's part of preventing all gratuitous evils.

It is important to note that Hasker's argument that God should not prevent all gratuitous evils relies on the assumption that if God did prevent all of them, humans would know or believe that God is doing this. If they did not, they might well be motivated to prevent evils for which they could not envision any outweighing goods. Therefore, in evaluating his argument that God is not required to have a policy of preventing all gratuitous evil, we must bear in mind that an essential condition for the argument is that if God did have such a policy, humans would know or believe that God has it. Hasker gives no argument for this condition in relation to moral evil, and his argument for it in relation to natural evil may be inconsistent with a common explanation (mentioned above) of the fact that many things about God are not clear. For now, however, let us grant this condition. What follows with respect to gratuitous evil?

I do not think the consequences on human motivation would necessarily be as detrimental as Hasker argues. For at least many times some human(s) would have a moral obligation to do something about the evil situation; that God might intervene to prevent gratuitous evil they should have prevented but failed to prevent need not destroy their motivation to prevent the evil, particularly if they have developed into morally concerned people. Then they might realize that God is permitting some potentially gratuitously evil situation to develop in order to give them the chance to make a correct moral decision to prevent the occurrence. They might know that if they did not do the morally correct thing, God would prevent the evil, but they still would have failed to do their moral duty. The (assumed) fact that God would prevent evil they failed to prevent would decrease the harmful consequences of their failure (and in that way perhaps weaken their motivation), but it would not decrease their obligation, and it would not lessen their culpability for failing to meet their responsibility. Analogously, if I don't feed my children, the government will, so if I do not feed them – but could have – they will not go hungry, but I will have failed to meet a moral obligation.[7]

We have seen two possible problems with Hasker's argument for the necessity of gratuitous evils: the motivation provided by moral obligation even if God has the policy of preventing all gratuitous evils, and the necessity of the condition that if God has the policy of preventing all gratuitous evil humans not know or believe that God does. But even with these problems, his argument to show that God could not have a policy of preventing all gratuitous evils seems quite strong. But though God could not have the policy of preventing *all* gratuitous evils, could God have the policy of preventing some gratuitous evils? William Rowe answered this question by claiming that God should permit only members of the smallest subset of gratuitous evils adequate for humans to become morally responsible, but no more (68).

This claim seems implausible because it seems unlikely that this number could be determined with complete precision. Given the psychological differences that exist among humans, different amounts would be needed by different humans and perhaps by the same human at different times. Thus, there would be no one amount that is the minimum for everybody at all times. Moreover, Hasker accepts the view not only that humans are free, but that God does not know timelessly or in advance with complete certainty what humans will actually do and does not have middle knowledge. This provides a second reason why not even God could determine for all future humans the minimum amount of gratuitous evil needed to motivate moral development.

Nevertheless, even if God could not determine the precise amount needed, there are certainly amounts that are sufficient. So it would seem that God could prevent many gratuitous evils provided God allows a generous amount of such evils, including a sufficient margin to be sure there are enough evils that no one's development of moral responsibility is undermined by an insufficiency of gratuitous evils. Such a cautious policy might permit God to prevent some gratuitous evils, particularly if God does the prevention subtly. In the absence of exact knowledge of the amount of gratuitous evils necessary to sustain human motivation, it might seem that all we could do is note that it is possible that God could prevent some of them without our being able to say which or how many.

However, we should consider a possible argument against the claim that God should reduce the excessive gratuitous evils somewhat. Suppose that God were to consider eliminating some of those that could be eliminated without decreasing human motivation to achieve various goods. Of all the evils, which should God prevent? Would not preventing any involve some sort of favoritism? If God prevents one person's murder but not another's, would that not involve giving the former some favor the latter needed as much? This line of reasoning provides some support for God's adopting a policy of not preventing any instance of gratuitous evil *by the use of superior force*. The italicized phrase is crucial. If God prevents some moral evil by persuading the potential wrongdoer not to do the evil action, this would not conflict with God's purposes for that person (and for all people): to develop morally by choosing to do morally right actions. Throughout the discussion of the guilty bystander objection, we have been discussing whether God should prevent evil by using superior force. (It is implicit in traditional theists' treatment of natural evils that God could prevent them only by exerting superior force; the creatures that cause natural evils are not candidates to be persuaded not to cause that evil.) But note that this line of reasoning provides support for a policy only of total non-prevention. If one were to claim (as most traditional theists do) that God sometimes intervenes using superior force, as in a miracle, then questions could well be raised about the values underlying God's decision about when to intervene and when to refrain. We will discuss this issue in Chapter 4.

There is, however, at least one basis on which God could intervene without implying favoritism for those benefited: God might intervene to prevent the worst evils – those which result in the most widespread and debilitating suffering (or perhaps the greatest excess of suffering over the goods achieved by the suffering). Acting in relation to such evils does not imply that God cares more for the people who suffer in them than God cares for people who suffer in lesser evils. On the contrary, the basis for acting in relation to these rather than other evils is that God has equal concern (love) for everyone. If God has equal concern for everyone, then (assuming that God cannot prevent all gratuitous evils and achieve God's goals) God would be most strongly motivated to prevent or mitigate evils that cause the greatest suffering (or the greatest excess of evil over good consequences).

However, this proposed basis for God to decide when to intervene supports the conclusion that God never intervenes to prevent gratuitous evil by the use of superior force. For there is reason to think that God does not intervene to prevent the greatest evils (or evils with the greatest excess of evil over good consequences). In the twentieth century surely one such evil was the Holocaust. We have no reason to think that some divine intervention by the use of superior force mitigated the evil. The evil was about as great as was technologically and psychologically possible; its extent was limited only by the capabilities of humans and the physical instruments available to them. If that is so, then we have reason to believe that God did not intervene to mitigate it. Nor does it seem that the Holocaust has produced goods that significantly compensate for the evils it involved. (It might be replied that there might be goods unknown to us or whose connection with the Holocaust is unknown to us that significantly reduce or even eliminate the amount by which the evil in the Holocaust exceeds the goods it makes possible. I will consider this sort of response in Chapter 5 and argue that it is unlikely.) If God did not intervene to prevent or mitigate that evil, which was about as great as humans could accomplish, why should one think that God has intervened or would intervene to prevent or mitigate any evil?[8]

To claim that God would prevent some of these evils but not the greatest ones seems to involve attributing strange values to God. That God has in fact subtly prevented the greatest gratuitous evils is possible, but not likely. Given the catalog of evils about which we know (for example, the Holocaust, Stalin's terrorism, and mass starvations), it is hard even to imagine any greater evils that might have occurred in world history prior to 1945 that might be candidates for worse evils that God prevented. There are physical and perhaps psychological limits to the amount of evil that humans and nature are capable of inflicting on humans. Nor is there any evidence that God has, by superior force, prevented humans from developing the capacity to inflict ever greater evils. Since the Holocaust, humans have developed the capacity to wipe out virtually all human life on earth by nuclear and biological weapons. Throughout history prior to the Holocaust, as technology has developed, there have been a steady increase in human capacity to inflict ever greater evils and all too many instances in which humans exercise that capacity to the fullest.

It might be objected that expecting God to prevent the worst evils creates a slippery slope with no stopping point short of God's preventing all evils except those belonging to some minimal set. For no matter what evils might occur, if God prevented the worst, then others would become the worst in the resulting totality of all actual evils, and God should prevent them, and so on. However, my categorizing the worst evils as those that are as great as humans have the technological and psychological capacity to inflict gives a way to identify the worst evils other than their being the worst. There could be a world with many evils, but none that is as bad as it is technologically and psychologically possible for humans to inflict. In such a world one might think that God had prevented the worst evils; however, we do not live in such a world. The presence in our world of evils that are as great as humans could inflict gives us a reason to doubt that God prevents the worst evils.

One point Hasker makes might be understood as another sort of reply to my claim that God has not prevented the worst evils: "'events' ... such as the Holocaust, are of course not individual instances of moral evil but rather comprise many thousands, even millions, of individual decisions" (77–8, n. 23). In an obvious sense Hasker is correct that the events he mentions comprise many individual decisions, but there is also reason to call each *an event* because the decisions in each event of this sort are organized and interrelated, often in ways that not only crush the spirits of people involved, but also call into question the meaning and value of the larger historical process in which the decisions are embedded. This aspect of such events makes their prevention or mitigation by God more important than the prevention or mitigation of an equal number of unrelated equally evil individual acts. If God had prevented or greatly mitigated "events" such as these, that would significantly lessen the power of evil to call into question the value of existence without lessening our motivation to oppose evil. Even without these meaning-destroying events of vast scope, surely there is enough evil in the world to motivate people to develop morally. If not, those who lived before the events or who were ignorant of them could not have had adequate motivation to develop morally. That seems highly unlikely.

From the foregoing, it seems that the most morally defensible and empirically plausible response to the guilty bystander objection is that in order to make it possible for humans to develop morally and spiritually God has a policy of not preventing any evils by miraculous interventions. However, many traditional theists would find this position hard to accept because they believe that God has intervened miraculously to prevent or remedy some evils. In Chapter 4 we will explore the problems about divine justice raised by these alleged interventions. Now we will discuss an objection mentioned earlier, the victimization objection.

The Victimization Objection

The victimization objection claims that if, in order not to interfere with a person's free will, God does not prevent one person from deliberately harming another, then God has treated the second as a means for the development of the first. The good of the evildoer is thus valued above that of the innocent victim. For example, in order not to interfere with the freedom of child abusers, God does not intervene to prevent the beating, sexual abuse, and murder of innocent infants and young children, such as that described by Russell. In order not to interfere with the freedom of Hitler and other Nazis, God did not prevent the Holocaust. This is the objection that was powerfully expressed in Dostoevsky's *The Brothers Karamazov* when Ivan says to Alyosha:

> Imagine that you are creating a fabric of human destiny with the object of making men happy in the end, giving them peace and rest at last, but that it was essential and inevitable to torture to death only one tiny creature – that baby beating its breast with its fist, for instance – and to found that edifice on its unavenged tears, would you consent to be the architect on those conditions?[9]

Alyosha of course answers that he would not. The victimization objection charges that in order to attain, not the exalted goal of happiness and peace for everyone, but just the possibility of free action for one person, God permits one person to torture or in some way harm or kill another or even many others.

We have already noted that this way of posing the objection is unnecessarily restrictive in the way it understands who are the people for whose freedom and moral and spiritual development God refrains from intervening. If God were to intervene frequently to prevent people from harming others through free actions, then God would undermine or at least weaken the motivation of affected people to develop morally and spiritually. Thus God apparently follows a general policy of not intervening not only for the sake of those whose free action would be abridged if God intervened, but for the sake of all people.

Here we might note that the victimization objection might equally well be raised in relation to God's not preventing natural evils. For traditional theists might explain God's not intervening to help someone by saying (as we noted earlier) that humans need a stable natural order to make possible their moral and spiritual development. Then it might be objected that this explanation implies that God refrains from intervening to help some people for the sake of making possible the moral and spiritual development of others, and this seems to imply that God treats the former as means in relation to the latter. Again traditional theists might reply that the intended beneficiaries of God's policy are not just a few humans, but all humans. For if God were to intervene frequently to prevent natural evils, then humans would no longer have a stable natural order. Therefore, God refrains from frequently intervening to prevent natural evils that harm some people, not for the benefit of only a few people, but for the sake of all people, who need a stable natural order and whose moral and spiritual development would allegedly be undermined by its absence.

Thus the victimization objection can be raised in relation to both moral and natural evils. In relation to both, the traditional theist can give Hasker's reply that God's apparent general policy of non-intervention (whether with or without occasional exceptions) is followed for the sake of the all humans. But is this reply adequate? Does not this reply still leave one vulnerable to something like, but even worse than, Ivan's complaint? Are we not still building the edifice not even of human happiness, but of the possibility of human moral and spiritual development on the suffering not of one little girl, but of countless children and adults? Can more be said to defend God against the victimization objection?

One traditional theist, Eleonore Stump, has made a bold attempt to meet this challenge directly by claiming that all suffering is potentially beneficial to the person who suffers.[10] Though admitting that some general good (for example, the existence of free human actions) might be "the ultimate end for the sake of which God permits evil" (411), Stump goes on to say:

> It seems to me nonetheless that a perfectly good entity who was also omniscient and omnipotent must govern the evil resulting from the misuse of that significant freedom in such a way that the sufferings of any particular person are outweighed by the good which the suffering produces *for that person*; otherwise, we might justifiably expect a good God to prevent *that particular suffering*, either by intervening (in one way or another) to protect the victim, while still allowing the perpetrator his freedom, or by curtailing the freedom in some select cases. (411, italics hers)

Clearly, the good envisaged by Stump is not pleasure or freedom from suffering; rather, it is a greater possibility of redemption, which requires appropriate spiritual development. For Stump believes that non-voluntary suffering has primarily a pedagogical purpose: to bring humans to recognize their own sinfulness and their need for God. Each instance of suffering is such that if the sufferer responds appropriately to it, it will advance that purpose better than any alternative amount of suffering in that situation (including not suffering at all). Of course, people do not always respond appropriately, but their failure to do so is their own free choice and thus their own responsibility, not God's. Therefore, the victimization objection cannot be correctly lodged against God because God never permits one person to suffer simply for someone else's benefit.

Stump advances her proposal "with considerable diffidence" (410). Certainly, the proposal is strongly counterintuitive. It seems extremely implausible that the little girl mentioned by Russell had her possibility of responding appropriately to God maximized by being tortured and killed. She had no opportunity to respond in this life, so Stump is forced to postulate that the opportunity would come in another life. Moreover, those who suffer greatly as children but are not killed often grow up stunted by the experience, yet Stump's view implies that their opportunity for appropriate spiritual development is actually increased by their mistreatment. Another counterintuitive implication of Stump's proposal is that nothing really bad ever happens to a person. Stump herself agrees that her view has this implication and says that it is not implausible, but rather what we should "expect to follow from the assumption of a provident God."[11]

Her view also implies postulating a divine planning and control of all events, which seems hard to reconcile with believing that humans have free will in an incompatibilist sense, as Stump does.[12] It has this implication because it seems that who suffers and how much a person suffers often is the result of a "chance" coincidence of free actions and events in nature. The little girl happened to come downstairs when her mother's boyfriend was awake and yet still drunk and angry; if she had come downstairs at a slightly different time, she might not have been tortured and killed. If Stump's view were extended to natural evils – and I think the logic of her position suggests that it must be – we should note that often it seems a matter of "chance" who is in the wrong place at the wrong time and therefore becomes sick or is injured in some disaster. Yet Stump alleges that all these sufferings are potentially more beneficial to the sufferer than not suffering or suffering to a different degree at that time would be. Since we have no indication of frequent divine interventions preventing some events that would otherwise result in suffering that would not be potentially beneficial to the sufferer, somehow it must be that God does not have to intervene to prevent events that would involve non-beneficial suffering. How could this be unless God is exercising some sort of subtle control over these apparently chance events?

Another difficulty with this account arises when it is combined with the claim that God knows whether the person will eventually turn to God. If God knows that the person will not, then God knows that the suffering will have been in vain, even though it was permitted to increase the likelihood that the person would turn to God. But is it really possible to do something with a particular intention if one *knows for certain* (as Stump thinks God does) that the intention will not be fulfilled? Though not all traditional theists agree with Stump that God knows whether or not each instance of involuntary suffering will in fact result in spiritual growth, all traditional theists who claim that all involuntary suffering must maximize the sufferer's chances for spiritual growth have the other two problems. This may well prompt the traditional theist to ask whether there is another way to meet the victimization objection.

Thomas F. Tracy articulates another way that is worth exploring.[13] Tracy begins by noting that Ivan's objection contains two ambiguities:

1. Is the suffering and death a means to the achievement of the eternal harmony, or is it something that must be permitted to achieve the harmony?
2. Will the sufferers be included in, or excluded from, the eternal harmony?

Tracy next notes that standard free-will defenses claim that there is a morally sufficient reason why God permits evil. Even if the defenses are unwilling to claim that they can state God's reason for permitting evil, what they do say presupposes that certain conditions are met by God's reason. These include the following:

1. The existence of morally free creatures who perform morally good actions is an intrinsic good, and
2. God actualizes a world such that:
   a. W contains morally free creatures who freely do moral evil;
   b. There is a net balance of moral good over moral evil in W;
   c. It is not within God's power to actualize a world that contains as much moral good and less moral evil than that found in W;
   d. W contains no gratuitous evils, i.e., no evils that God can eliminate without thereby producing an equal or greater evil or eliminating a greater good.[14] (303–304)

This sort of defense assumes that the only moral condition on God's action pertains to the relative amounts of good and evil in the world that God actualizes. But Ivan's objection insists that there are moral limits on the *way* this overall good is achieved. (This is a common sort of deontological objection to consequentialist ethics, which focus on the overall balance of good and evil.) To meet this objection, Tracy adds a fifth subcondition for condition 2:

   e. None of the free creatures in W have lives that, through no fault of their own, are on balance an evil for them rather than a good. (315)

This condition assures that God is not responsible for any free creature's having a life that is on balance an evil for it. Tracy admits that under this condition God might actualize a world in which a person would suffer evils which, though they contribute to the greatest good overall, do not benefit that person. But he argues that this is not unjust, for no one has a right to claim that God must make one's life the best possible, particularly if doing so would mean a net increase of evil in the world. But it would be unjust if God actualized a world in which through no fault of one's own one's life had a net balance of evil over good.

Tracy points out that this principle makes it possible to escape Ivan's complaint not only against God's actualizing a world in which people suffer because of the evil actions of other free creatures, but also against God's actualizing a world in which there are natural laws whose operation results in a free creature's suffering. Again, it is necessary that these laws not have the result that through no fault of its own a free creature has a life that on balance is an evil for it rather than a good. But subject to this limitation, it is morally permissible for God to actualize a world in which the operation of natural laws results in a free creature's suffering more than what would be required to maximize (the possibility for) the greatest balance of good over evil in the life of that creature. Tracy also points out that it may be morally best for God to permit the occurrence of dysteleological evil because the consequences of God's preventing the evil would be worse than evil itself, though it would be better if the evil were not to occur or if some free creature were to prevent it (305). For example, suppose that God's preventing some evil would prevent some person from coming to faith in God, though some human's preventing the evil would not have this or any other bad consequence (other than frustrating the evil intentions of a wrongdoer). Or suppose that a human could have avoided being killed in an avalanche by freely choosing not to go hiking in a certain place at a certain time, but that God could not have prevented his being killed without violating the person's freedom or intervening in a miraculous way, which would have had other consequences worse than the death of the human.

Tracy has come up with a reasonable set of conditions to be used in answering the victimization objection. Of course, these meet the objection only if we live in a world that meets the conditions. Is it plausible to think that our world does? I am willing to grant conditions 1, 2a, 2b, and 2c. What of conditions 2d and 2e? The former will be considered later in this section and in the next section. At first glance, condition 2e seems unlikely. Consider that some people are born with painful birth defects and die very young after a brief life of intense suffering.

However, Richard Swinburne argues for another kind of good that would apply even in cases such as these: the good of being of use to others. He claims that "it is also a good thing to be of use, to help, to serve, either through freely exercising power in the right way, or through doing it naturally and spontaneously, or even by being used as the vehicle of a good purpose."[15] He adds that it is especially difficult for people in our cultural situation to see that helping is "an immense good for the helper" (101). Let us grant, at least for the sake of argument, that what he says are goods are indeed goods. But are they goods for the being who is of use? This is a crucial question because Swinburne agrees with Tracy that God has the right to permit one individual (including an animal) to suffer for the sake of others, but not to the extent that the individual's life as a whole is more bad than good. But he believes that "free will will not suffice for theodicy; and the other great good which I have stressed is the good of being of use. All the ways in which the suffering of A is beneficial to B are also beneficial for A – because A is privileged to be of use" (241). So it is crucial to his theodicy that the good of being of use is a good for the individual who is of use.

That it is a good for the one who is of use is easy to accept in instances of voluntary helping. But one does not need the category of being of use to understand why. Being of use through voluntary helping is the fulfillment of a good desire, and Swinburne says quite plausibly that the fulfillment of good desires is good for the individual who has them.

What about involuntary service? One plausible example mentioned by Swinburne is a "conscript killed in a just and ultimately successful war in defense of his country against a tyrannous aggressor" (102). (Note the way Swinburne has structured this example to create maximum sympathy with the conscript. He does not talk about conscripts who die in an unjust war, or a just but unsuccessful war.) As he says, relatives often comfort themselves by saying, "He died for a good cause." But, contrary to what Swinburne suggests, that does not mean that dying in this way is a good *for the one who died*. It is a good for the country or the society. Even if relatives say that he did not die in vain, that does not entail that they think it is good for him. It may indicate simply that their pain at their loss is somewhat lessened by their appreciation of the contribution it makes to some other good. Analogously, relatives of a murder victim may feel some comfort and feel that it is a good thing if the murderer is caught and punished. It is a good thing and it lessens their grief, but that does not entail that it is a good for the murderer.

In a footnote (102, n. 12) Swinburne mentions Greeks and Romans with no particular beliefs about rewards in an afterlife who believed that it is a good to die for their country. But this is not an apt comparison. People who believe that it is a good thing are people who do it voluntarily (or at least they voluntarily take the risk of dying for their country); thus they are examples in the category of voluntary service, not involuntary service. If those who believe it is a good thing to die for their country make this claim about others in their day who do not believe it, those others would exemplify involuntary service, but it is not clear that their claim entails that it is a good for those who died involuntarily as opposed to a good for the country or a good because the action exemplifies an ideal.

The other example Swinburne gives is the unemployed being compelled to work for some useful purpose rather than being allowed to be useless (his term). To make this example fit the category of involuntary service (rather than voluntary service), we have to assume that the unemployed in question would prefer not to do anything useful. But then one possible good of their being compelled to work might be a change in their values. This would be a good for them, but it is not the good of being of use, so we must not consider it in relation to the example. Suppose that one way in which their values changed was that they came to value being of use. Then they would no longer have to be compelled to work; their work would now be voluntary. This change in values would presumably be good for them, and so would their subsequent work. But there is no reason to think that their work prior to this change in values was a non-instrumental good for them. So it is not a good for them that they are forced to be of service. It may be a good for society and for the fulfillment of some ideals, but their being of involuntary service to others is not a non-instrumental good for them.

Therefore, the goods achieved by involuntary service are not goods for those who provide the service. Even less are the goods in Swinburne's third category – goods achieved by undergoing involuntary experiences – goods for those who undergo them. It is a good if the death of an accident victim leads to reforms that prevent or reduce such accidents in the future. But that does not entail that it is a good for the victim to be of use in this way. Some of Swinburne's other examples strike me as simply monstrous. He discusses the slave trade of the eighteenth century, saying that it provided numerous examples of particularly horrendous evils that might provoke even callous immoral people to moral reform (245). Even if this is so, to say (as Swinburne does) that it was a *good for the slaves* to be of use in this way is totally implausible. Using Swinburne's reasoning one would also conclude that it was a *good for the victims* of Nazi medical experiments and the Tuskegee syphilis study to be of use in these ways. I believe that to say that it is a good for them is not just false; it is monstrously wrong. Swinburne disagrees. At this point it may seem as though he and I simply have unresolvably different moral intuitions. However, I have tried to argue against his idea of a generalized good of being of use through both voluntary actions and involuntary actions and experiences. I agree that goods may be achieved through both kinds of being of use, but I have claimed that only voluntary service brings a good for the one who serves. And because voluntary service can be a good for the server simply due to its being an instance of the fulfillment of a good desire, the value of voluntary service for the server provides no reason to think that involuntary service or involuntary experiences that produce good are also good for the one who is of use in either of these ways.

If I am right that being of involuntary use is (even just sometimes) not a good for the one who is of use, this would raise a very significant problem for Swinburne's defense of God's right to permit (or even to cause) people to suffer to achieve or to make it possible to achieve other goals of God. For Swinburne's basic principle is roughly this: God has a right to permit a being to suffer somewhat (to have a worse life than it otherwise would) only if that suffering is a morally permissible way to achieve goals (or to make possible the achieving of goals) whose goodness outweighs the suffering. But it is proper for God to permit a being to suffer only "somewhat" – only to such an extent that the being's life as a whole remains good for the being. Swinburne could claim that God provides the possibility for every human to have a life that is more good than bad by providing the possibility of an afterlife filled with good things. But if Swinburne's theodicy of human suffering is to be adequate, it must pass two more tests: permitting the evils must be the only morally permissible means for God to make possible the logically necessary conditions for the possibility of the goods that allegedly justify the evils, and the goods must be good enough to outweigh the evils. I will accept Swinburne's arguments that the first condition is met with regard to various *types* of evils and goods. For example, one cannot have the possibility of helping others unless they need help; one cannot have the possibility of free decisions and actions with important consequences unless there is the possibility of decisions and actions with bad consequences. But that does not entail that every *token* of this type is justified. Some evils may be so great that no goods that they make possible outweigh them. Evils of the sort that Marilyn McCord Adams called horrendous evils,[16] particularly those that involve large numbers of people (such as the Holocaust), are plausible examples of evils so great that no goods they make possible outweigh them.

The problem, once again, is with the great number and intensity of tokens of actual bad states of various types. It is highly implausible to think that permitting the slave trade of the eighteenth century or the Holocaust was the only morally permissible way that God could bring about a logically necessary condition of some goods that outweigh the bad states involved in the slave trade and the Holocaust. If it were, then there would have to be some particular goods (tokens of goods, not types) for which the bad states involved in these two horrendous evils are logically necessary conditions. I find this very implausible because the goods Swinburne mentions – free will, knowledge, being responsible for others, and being of voluntary service – all had very significant tokens prior to the slave trade and the Holocaust. Throughout human history it has (presumably) been possible for humans to achieve what Swinburne regards as the greatest goods (a right relation to God and appropriate moral development). Therefore, the greatest evils of particular times (or knowledge of these evils) cannot be necessary for the greatest goods. The tokens of evil in earlier times were sufficient to allow people to exercise significant free will and undergo the sort of moral development that would determine their eternal destiny. These are what theists typically regard as the greatest goods. If people could achieve them prior to (and thus without) the slave trade and the Holocaust, it is very implausible to think that there are any (token) outweighing goods for which these evils are logically necessary conditions.

There are wider implications of the problems with Swinburne's principle that God has a right to permit a being to suffer somewhat (that is, to have a worse life than it otherwise would) only if that suffering is a morally permissible way to achieve goals (or to make possible the achieving of goals) whose goodness outweighs the suffering. Something like this principle is widely accepted in the theodicies of Christian traditional theists; it is implied by Tracy's condition 2d because 2d requires that there is no way God can increase the excess of good over evil in this world. But we have seen that it is likely that the worst tokens of various types of evils cannot be justified by Swinburne's principle. Our earlier discussion revealed that it is unlikely that each can be justified individually as necessary for the possibility or actuality of a greater good. Thus it is unlikely that Tracy's condition 2d is met; the next section gives an additional reason for thinking is not met. Therefore, just as we saw in the previous section, probably the most plausible response by traditional Christians to the victimization objection is to claim that God has the policy of not preventing any evils; such a policy requires accepting that some innocent victims will suffer. However, their suffering is not the means whereby some good is achieved; it is only something that must be permitted if humans are to have the opportunity to develop morally and spiritually. Note that Hasker's theodicy does not include the acceptance of Tracy's condition 2d, nor does Hasker commit himself to condition 2e.

As for condition 2e, our argument also reveals that if being of involuntary use is not an additional good for the one who is of use, then the only way in which this condition can be met is if there is an afterlife in which people may experience goods that outweigh any suffering in this life, as Tracy suggests (311). Tracy is correct in claiming that this is a traditional belief among Christians. Whether there is good reason to hold it is a matter we will discuss in Chapters 7 and 8. For now, we will label it at most a possible way in which condition 2e is met.

The Defective Creation Objection

The defective creation objection claims that the world could be better by containing fewer evils or more goods than this one, and in some proposals could do this without threatening to undermine morality. In support of this claim some people have tried to suggest that we can imagine a world that operates by somewhat different natural laws and has a better balance of good and evil. For example, one might suggest that all animal life could be vegetarian, thus eliminating the suffering associated with animals preying on other animals. However, suggestions of this sort are not convincing because they are inevitably incomplete. They are suggestions about how some features or natural laws might be changed, but they do not specify a complete set of features and natural laws, so we cannot gain a complete conception of what life would be like in a world operating in accordance with the suggested natural laws. Therefore, we cannot begin to determine whether there would be a better balance of good over evil in the new world than in this one. (For example, if all the animals in the world were vegetarians, one wonders what would keep their populations in check so as to mitigate overcrowding and mass starvation subsequent upon overgrazing.) Moreover, humans are not competent to compare the overall balance of good and evil in our world with the balance in a world with different natural laws.

A more plausible case for the defective creation objection can, however, be constructed if we content ourselves with more modest changes in our world and no different laws of nature. This would be more within human competence to compare. Of course, traditional theists could still claim that even small differences might entail other differences that are so many or so non-obvious that humans would not be competent to compare the two worlds. How plausible this claim is would depend on the differences in question. Let us consider a specific proposal.

One proposal along this line was made by Evan Fales.[17] He points out that humans vary in many qualities, including their aggressiveness, intelligence, and sensitivity to others. Though the behavior affected by each of these factors is modified by environmental and cultural factors, differences in our genetic endowments do affect our behavior. Having a particular genetic endowment that disposes us to act in particular ways cannot be inconsistent with free will, or we would have no free will. But an omnipotent God could modify the genetic endowment of some humans so that they are less aggressive, more intelligent, and more sensitive to others. The result would be humans who are as free as they now are, but there would be considerably less harm imposed by humans on other humans than there now is and more help rendered to those in need.

If a world has the same natural laws as our world but people are genetically disposed to be as kind and gentle as the kindest and gentlest among us now, it is hard to imagine any reason why such a world would not contain less evil than ours. It would contain fewer instances of people hurting other people. It might contain the same amount of natural evil, but more of the consequences of that evil would be responded to in a helpful way. And this supposed world would not differ from the actual world to such an extent that we should be concerned that the differences we listed might (causally or logically) entail other changes that would counterbalance the gains we noted with losses we have not thought of. Thus if humans are competent to assess the worlds that would result from modest proposals such as Fales's, it seems plausible to claim that an omnipotent God could have made a world that has less suffering and less moral evil than ours and that is nevertheless still suitable to provide opportunities and challenges for human moral development. Moreover, it seems that God could do all this without sacrificing any greater good or incurring any greater evil. If this conclusion is correct, then the defective world objection is sustained, providing another reason to reject Tracy's condition 2d.[18]

Though the defective world objection is effective against an argument such as Tracy's, Hasker's theodicy might seem to present a stronger reply to it. For Hasker might point out that it is simply a way of reducing the number and severity of some gratuitous evils. But Hasker could not challenge it on the grounds that it would undermine morality because there is no possibility that we would be aware that God has done this. Fales's proposal does not eliminate all gratuitous evils, for humans would still have their free will and the possibility of making significant moral choices, and natural evil would still occur. Nor would this proposal raise problems about God's fairness because everyone with worse genes would be improved, and all humans would benefit from the improvement. So Hasker would have to rely heavily on the claim that God is strongly committed to a policy of not intervening; he might ask why should God prevent these gratuitous evils and not some others? This question, while appropriate within the framework of Hasker's theodicy, makes even more problematic any claims that Hasker, like many traditional Christians makes, to the effect that God has sometimes intervened. As I will discuss in Chapter 4, one can ask about those purported interventions the same question Hasker might about what Fales proposes: why should God prevent these evils and no others?

The Animal Suffering Objection

The final objection we will discuss in this chapter is that arising from animal suffering. This aspect of the problem of evil has been considered much less frequently than human suffering. Most discussions of the problem of suffering focus on the latter and ignore the former. Swinburne's theodicy is an exception, but it fails because of the inadequacy of his argument that being of involuntary service to others is a good for the involuntary servant. And the few replies along more traditional lines seem even less adequate in relation to animal suffering than in relation to human suffering. The soul-making theodicy claims that God gives humans free will and creates the stable natural conditions in which they exercise it in order to make possible human moral development. This moral development is intended to (and, according to some such as John Hick, will certainly) culminate in humans' attaining a blissful everlasting life. It is the possibility (or certainty) of this blissful culmination that justifies the pain suffered in the process. But Western theists usually have not held out even the possibility of a blissful afterlife for animals. In that case, what would justify their suffering?

These reflections lead one to conclude that traditional theists' reply to the problem of animal suffering must appeal to considerations different from those used in connection with human suffering, and that is usually what is done. One consideration is that animal suffering is very different from human suffering because animals lack memory of past sufferings and anticipation of future[19] sufferings and of their own deaths.[20] Because they lack memories of past pains, their present painful experiences are not haunted and exacerbated by such memories (though I would add that they also cannot be mitigated by memories of past joys). Thus they suffer only physical pain, and their liability to physical pain generally promotes their well-being, for it motivates them to try to escape whatever conditions are causing them pain or discomfort, be it threat from another animal or hunger or the weather. Moreover, even if most animals die violent deaths rather than die of "natural causes" in old age, that may be beneficial to the individual animal, given that it does not anticipate the future. Therefore, the animal has no plans that are cut short by its death, nor does it foresee and fear its own death. Thus most animals live most of their lives in relatively good health. (If they are not in good health, either they get better soon or they die.)

But, as Hick points out, this realization raises the question of why there are animals at all. If animals have no everlasting destiny, why did God create them? In reply, some Christians have appealed to the "principle of plenitude." The divine nature expresses itself by bringing into existence creatures with a great variety of different natures. Creatures of all different types contribute to the "harmonious perfection of the whole" (350). Hick, however, advances another suggestion. He proposes that having an animal realm from which humans evolved contributes to humans' epistemic distance from God: "Seeing himself as related to the animals and as, like them, the creature of a day, made out of the dust of the earth, man is set in a situation in which the awareness of God is not forced upon him but in which the possibility remains open to him of making his own free response to his unseen Maker" (351). One might object to Hick that this proposal envisages God as creating a very vast stage for a limited company. Perhaps because he realizes this, he goes on to say that the realm of the subhuman may play other roles in the intentions of God (353).

What shall we say about these suggestions? Hick's claim that the subhuman realm contributes to our epistemic distance from God is certainly true, but is it an adequate reason for the existence of subhuman animals? At a minimum it would be so only if his theory about the need for epistemic distance between humans and God were satisfactory, but we will see in the next chapter that it is problematic. Moreover, since there are other factors that contribute to epistemic distance, the subhuman animal realm might not be necessary for this purpose. However, Hick does not insist that this is the only purpose those animals have. The idea that it is appropriate for God to create a great variety of kinds of beings would be acceptable provided that the resulting system is not morally questionable, but the issue here is precisely whether or not the system is morally questionable. The principle of plenitude does not address that issue.

A different reason for the creation of animals might be that the animals gain the opportunity for the experiences that constitute their lives, brief though their lives be. But if there are some animals whose lives on the whole have more bad than good experiences, is it not morally objectionable for God to create those particular animals? This is the animal analog to the victimization objection. Notice that an analog to Tracy's response is not possible here for those theists who deny that animals are or have selves that could enjoy an afterlife.[21] However, such theists might object that the question itself makes no sense. If animals have no sense of self and no sense of their lives as a whole, then it makes no sense from the animal's perspective to talk of its life as consisting of more misery than happiness; that sort of a summation is something we humans may make in relation to an animal, but the animal itself is not aware of the total. Even if we accept the claim that animals have no sense of self, at least two responses can be made. First, even if the animal does not make a summation, it still suffers at times, and we can ask why God permits it to suffer. Second, we humans can make the summation. If we do, we must conclude that it is very implausible to think that no animals have lives on earth that contain more bad than good; there are just too many animals for this not to happen at least occasionally. Moreover, there are cases in which it seems highly plausible to think that animals have lives of this sort. One example that strongly suggests that not all animals have a life that is more good than bad is provided by pelican chicks.[22] Typically white pelicans lay two eggs, the second about two days after the first. The second egg hatches about two days after the first, and the younger chick is deprived of food by the older one, often pushed out of the nest, and soon dies of hunger or exposure or at the hands of predators. The younger chick is a back-up chick. The second chick will receive adequate parental attention only if the first chick dies very young. Since this usually does not happen, most second white pelican chicks have lives that are very short and unpleasant. It is very plausible to conclude that most of them have lives that are more bad than good. It is inconceivable that none of them do. Thus, unless their being of use as a back-up chick is a good for them (and I have argued that being of use through involuntary experience is not), then there are clear cases of animals whose lives are more bad than good. If it does not impugn the goodness of God to create (or permit the existence of) animals whose lives include more bad than good, why think (as Tracy and many other theists do) that it would call into question the goodness of God if there were humans whose lives, through no fault of their own, include more bad than good? If it would not, then it would no longer be necessary to postulate a life after death to make it possible for all humans to have a life that includes more good than bad. (Of course, there may be other reasons to believe that there is life after death; I am just pointing out that this would no longer be one.)

We might also question the claim that no nonhuman animals are (or have) selves and that none have a sense of their lives as continuing things. Both Hick and Lewis admit that probably some of the higher mammals are selves and have a sense of themselves as continuing things.[23] Hick does not discuss the problems raised for his view if there are such animals. Lewis will consider attributing to such animals an afterlife, but only in relation to humans. Would this entail that a resurrected animal would spend eternity in hell if the animal's master did?

In addition to these difficulties in the details, an even more severe problem is that both thinkers seem to postulate an absolute difference between human and subhuman animals and then admit that there are probably exceptions. That is, they both begin by claiming that subhuman animals have no sense of self and no memory of earlier events, but then they admit that probably a few higher animals do. But if this is so, then it seems as though there should be an afterlife for these animals as much as for humans, though Hick does not say so. Lewis admits this, but claims that these animals, even the non-domesticated ones, have an afterlife only in relation to humans (126–31). Furthermore, it seems implied by Hick's account that for animals selfhood is not a quality which belongs to every member of a species, but only to certain ones. If it belonged to every member, then they would be as much persons as humans are, a conclusion Hick does not draw. If it belongs to only certain animals in a species, one wonders why. Thus the (probable) existence of animals with a sense of self constitutes an awkward loose end for the accounts we have discussed that attempt to justify the existence and suffering of animals.

Therefore we must place a question mark over the adequacy of the justification of animal suffering (and animal existence) offered by such accounts. This question mark is likely to apply to any account that traditional Christians might offer. Those accounts typically presuppose the spiritual uniqueness of humans and therefore attempt to justify animal suffering (and existence) using very different considerations from those used in justifying human suffering. We have seen serious problems with the attempts we considered. But if, as seems probable, there are animals with at least a rudimentary sense of self, this creates problems for the presupposition of the spiritual uniqueness of humans. Of course, the strength of this line of argument against traditional theistic justifications of the suffering of animals depends on the strength of our evidence for the existence of animals with at least a rudimentary sense of self. We cannot review this evidence here. Instead, I will simply remark that those who share Hick's and Lewis's conviction that there probably are such animals will find that this conviction adds to the problem of animal suffering in the theodicies provided by traditional Christian theists.

Conclusion

Let us review the primary conclusions that have emerged in the discussion of these objections. First, within the assumptions of the free-will defense, it is implausible to think that God permits each specific evil to make possible some outweighing good, but it is reasonable to hold that God could not prevent all gratuitous evil and still achieve God's goals for humans unless humans did not know or believe that God is following this policy. If God were following this policy, whether humans would know or believe that God is doing so would depend on the amount of evil that God is preventing and how God is doing it; we have seen reason to believe that if it were a great deal, then human motivation to develop morally and spiritually would probably be lessened though not by as much as Hasker suggests. It would be possible for God to eliminate some gratuitous evils, though then there might arise a problem of arbitrariness as God decided which evils to prevent. The most obvious way to avoid this problem would be for God to intervene to prevent the greatest evils, but there is reason to believe that God has not done so. Thus it seems that the most reasonable position for the traditional theist to adopt in relation to the guilty bystander, victimization, and defective world objections is to say that God has adopted the policy of not preventing any gratuitous evils. However, taking this position might be difficult for many traditional Christian theists, for many are committed to the view that God has intervened by working miracles to prevent or remedy certain evils. But we will see in Chapter 4 that this position on miracles raises serious problems about the justice of God's actions towards humans.

There does not seem to be a good response within traditional theism to the animal suffering objection, but reflection on this objection does suggest the possibility that it might be consistent with God's perfect goodness that some animals have lives that contain more evil than good. If it is consistent, then not only is the animal suffering objection weakened, but perhaps it is also consistent with divine goodness that some humans, through no fault of their own, have lives with more evil than good. This is an issue to which we will return in Chapter 8.

In this chapter we have been discussing the traditional problem of evil: suffering and human wickedness. But I believe there are at least two other problems of evil: divine hiddenness and certain issues about miracles. These will be the topics of the next two chapters. After these we will consider one other important sort of defense for the traditional Christian theist: to claim that we should not expect to be able to understand why God permits the evils that occur. This defense, which I term the ignorance defense, will be the topic of Chapter 5.

Notes

1. I add the phrase "logically possible" to cover suggestions such as the claim that it would not be logically possible for God to cause a person to freely choose to do something. According to this claim, if the action is freely chosen, God could not cause the person to choose it. But God could cause the person to do the action, though not to do it freely, and in this sense control the creaturely state of affairs. Thus, both omnipotence and the power to unilaterally determine all the logically possible details that occur in the universe include the power to cause a person to do something, though perhaps not freely.

2. In the words of Steven T. Davis, "God has the power totally to control all events and things but does not use it" ("Critique by Stephen T. Davis," *Encountering Evil: Live Options in Theodicy*, new edn., ed. Stephen T. Davis [Louisville, KY: Westminster John Knox Press, 2001], p. 136).

3. *God, Time, and Knowledge* (Ithaca, NY: Cornell University Press, 1989), p. 196, italics his.

4. *Faith and Philosophy* 6/2 (April 1989): 123. In discussion of Russell's argument, page numbers in parentheses refer to this article.

5. Hick does think that God is trying to motivate us to develop morally and spiritually, but it is not clear whether Hick also thinks that God occasionally intervenes (by doing a miracle) to prevent or ameliorate some evil. As we will see in Chapter 4, theists who affirm that God has done some miracles have some significantly different problems in their theodicy than do theists who deny that God has done any miracles.

6. New York: Routledge, 2004. In the discussion of Hasker's argument, page numbers in parentheses refer to this work.

7. I owe this example to Richard Creel.

8. In a conversation, William Hasker criticized my proposed basis for God's decision about intervening. Hasker claimed instead that God would intervene to prevent those evils which God had some particular reason to prevent. The problem with Hasker's alternative is the difficulty of conceiving of reasons that God might have that would not involve some sort of favoritism (for example, helping one person but not helping another very similar person in a very similar situation). In Chapter 4 we will explore the problems about favoritism raised by claims that God intervenes in the created order by superior force to help some people but not others who are similar.

9. Trans. Constance Garnett, *Great Books of the Western World*, 2nd edn., vol. 52 (Chicago, University of Chicago Press, 1990), pt. II, bk. V, ch. 4, p. 133.

10. "The Problem of Evil," *Faith and Philosophy* 4/2 (October 1985): 392–423. Page numbers in parentheses in the discussion of Stump's view refer to this article.

11. "Providence and the Problem of Evil," *Christian Philosophy*, ed. Thomas P. Flint (Notre Dame, IN: University of Notre Dame Press, 1990), p. 69.

12. Ibid., p. 72.

13. "Victimization and the Problem of Evil: A Response to Ivan Karamazov," *Faith and Philosophy* 9/3 (July 1992): 301–19. Page references in the discussion of Tracy's position refer to this article.

14. In Tracy's article, the last condition is labeled with a prime, for reasons that do not concern us in this work.

15. *Providence and the Problem of Evil* (Oxford: Clarendon Press, 1998), p. 101. In the discussion of Swinburne, page numbers in parentheses refer to this work.

16. She defines them as "evils the participation in which (that is, the doing or suffering of which) constitutes prima facie reason to doubt whether the participant's life could (given their inclusion in it) be a great good to him/her on the whole"; *Horrendous Evils and the Goodness of God* (Ithaca, NY: Cornell University Press, 1999), p. 26.

17. "Should God Not Have Created Adam?" *Faith and Philosophy* 9/2 (April 1992): 193–209.

18. I accept the claim that there is no best possible world, for no matter how good a world God creates or how great the excess of good over evil, it is always possible to make that world better or to create a greater excess of good over evil. But this claim is of no help to Tracy, for it is one of his conditions that the world contains "no evils that God can eliminate without thereby producing an equal or greater evil or eliminating a greater good." The defective world objection holds against Tracy and against any theodicy that takes as a necessary condition the impossibility of God's improving the excess of good over evil by eliminating some particular evil. That there is no best possible world is no reason to think that any particular world could not contain a greater excess of good over evil if some particular evil were eliminated by God.

19. "Future" in the sense of something beyond what is suggested by their current environment. An animal may fear when confronted by a predator in its environment, but it does not (according to the view under discussion) fear the pain that a predator might inflict next week.

20. The discussion of animal suffering in this section is based largely on ideas in John Hick, *Evil and the God of Love* (New York: Harper and Row, 1966), pp. 345–53, and C.S. Lewis, *The Problem of Pain* (London: Collins Fontana Books, 1961), ch. 9. In the discussion of Hick's and Lewis's ideas about animal suffering, page numbers in parentheses refer to these works.

21. According to this view, because of the lack of memory and anticipation and perhaps because of other reasons as well, animals are not individuals in the sense in which humans are. In the animal there occurs a series of experiences, but there is no "I" that unifies the experiences, that owns them as "my experiences." Therefore, Lewis concludes that resurrecting an animal, for example a newt, would be pointless: "It would not recognize itself as the same newt; the pleasant sensations of any other newt that lived after its death would be just as much, or just as little, a recompense for its earthly sufferings (if any) as those of its resurrected – I was going to say 'self,' but the whole point is that the newt probably has no self" (125).

22. My discussion of the plight of baby pelican chicks is based on that in Jay McDaniel's book *Of God and Pelicans* (Louisville, KY: Westminster John Knox Press, 1989), pp. 19–20.

23. Hick speaks of the "occasional animal genius" (350), and Lewis speaks of a "real, though doubtless rudimentary, selfhood in the higher animals, and especially in those we tame" (126). (Both deny that we can be certain that any animals have – or are – selves, but also both seem to think it more likely than not.)

CHAPTER 3

Another Problem of Evil: Divine Hiddenness

Most people, including most theists, agree that even if God exists, it is not clear that God exists, what God's nature is, and what God's will is regarding human actions and attitudes. (In this chapter I will refer to this last topic more briefly as *God's will*.) Many people, including many moral and intelligent people, do not believe that there is a God; even many theists would say that the existence, nature, and will of God are not clear to them, and that their convictions on these items are at least in part matters of faith. Admittedly, this is not the whole story; some theists do claim that at least some of these matters are clear at least to some people. I will not dispute that some people claim that these things are clear to them. Perhaps they are, but even theists who claim this often disagree with each other about the allegedly clear matters. But in this chapter I wish to discuss why these matters are not clear to more people, indeed to everyone, or virtually everyone. More particularly, I will examine reasons theists do or might give to explain this lack of clarity: that is, I will look only at explanations that assume that God exists. (Of course, if there is no God, the explanation for the lack of clarity is obvious.) Drawing upon a term from the Western theistic tradition, I will refer to the fact that these matters are not clear to many people as *the hiddenness of God* (though without any implication that the hiddenness is or is not intended by the hidden one). The aim of this chapter, then, is to discuss reasons theists do or might offer to explain the hiddenness of God.

The problem of divine hiddenness has not been discussed nearly as much as the first problem of evil, though some religious writings do contain expressions of anguish or perplexity about it. After quoting some of these writings, Thomas Morris says that the problem of divine hiddenness may be "at least as great a[n intellectual] problem, if not a greater problem, for theism" than is the problem of evil (that is, the problem of suffering and moral evil).[1] I share this opinion. As I will explain in this chapter, it seems to me that there are very good reasons why, if traditional theism is true, we should expect God to be less hidden; moreover, the explanations offered by traditional theists for divine hiddenness are, I will argue, far from adequate. (Some Christians might admit that God is indeed hidden apart from some sort of special revelation, but they would add that God has given us a revelation in the Bible. However, I will argue in Chapter 6 that the Bible also does not give us any clear revelation.)

The problem of the hiddenness of God has significant similarities to the traditional problem of evil discussed in the previous chapter. In both problems, a serious question arises because certain attributes typically ascribed to God by traditional Christian theists lead one to expect the world to exhibit some feature that it does not exhibit (or at least does not appear to exhibit), or the world not to exhibit some feature that it does exhibit (or at least appears to exhibit). In the traditional problem of evil, the feature in question is suffering, human and probably also animal. If God is omnipotent, omniscient, and all-good, then one might expect no suffering, or at least much less than actually occurs. In the problem of the hiddenness of God, the feature of the world that seems puzzling, if God exists, is the absence of clear indications of the existence, nature, and will of God. If God is omniscient, omnipotent, and all-good, and if God loves humans and desires them to associate with God and do God's will, as Christian and many other theists have claimed, then one might expect that God would provide to humans clear indications of God's existence and of God's will for humans, and of at least certain aspects of God's nature. In relation to each problem, many theists have responded by trying to offer reasons why we should not expect the world to be other than it is – or at least to appear to us humans to be other than it appears.

Moreover, the problem of the hiddenness of God is not just similar in structure to the traditional problem of evil; the two problems contribute to each other. One major reason why God's existence and aspects of God's nature are not clear is that the world contains so much evil. The evil in the world contributes to making the world, in John Hick's term, "religiously ambiguous" – that is, roughly, a world in which it is not clear whether the beliefs central to theistic religions are true or false. In this way, the evil in the world contributes to the hiddenness of God. On the other hand, the hiddenness of God is a significant contributor to evil in the world. Because humans often do not know what the right thing to do is (and they would know it if the existence and will of God were clear), the hiddenness of God's will is an important reason why people do inappropriate or wrong actions, actions that cause suffering, and fail to do actions that prevent or alleviate suffering. (Admittedly it is not the only reason – sometimes people do what they believe is morally wrong – but it is a reason.) Disputes about the nature and/or will of God have sometimes been the occasion for war, religious persecution, and other sorts of divisions, such as those over religiously mixed marriages, all of which cause considerable human suffering. (Even if it is wrong for humans to go to war over disagreements about God or to engage in religious persecution or to be alienated over religious differences, nevertheless they would have no occasion to do so if these matters were so clear to everyone that there would be no disagreement.) Moreover, theists often claim that faith in God contributes directly to a fuller human life, so it seems that they should think that the absence of faith would make life poorer. Because the hiddenness of God hinders awareness of God, it contributes to a poorer human life for many people. In at least these ways, the hiddenness of God causes or contributes to human suffering and thus is a part of the problem of evil. Indeed, as something that causes or contributes to suffering, divine hiddenness is itself evil. We have already discussed the traditional problem of evil; in this chapter we will prescind from the suffering that the hiddenness of God may occasion and focus on explanations of the hiddenness of God that do not consider it as a cause or occasion of suffering.

The Hiddenness of God and Divine Transcendence

In a recent paper Robert McKim discusses the hiddenness of God's existence and nature (but not of God's will).[2] I find helpful his way of categorizing proposed theistic explanations of the hiddenness of God, and I will adopt it for this chapter. He suggests (145–46) that these explanations focus on (1) divine transcendence, (2) human defectiveness, and (3) the appropriateness of divine hiddenness for achieving certain of God's goals. He cautions (145) that theists should be wary of using the first if they believe that eventually (typically, in some future state) God will be less hidden. If it is God's nature that renders God hidden from human beings now, then God will remain hidden as long as God has that nature and humans are human. That God will always be as hidden as God is now is an implication that most Western theists have not been willing to accept. A few, however, have been, so we might consider that option briefly.

Those who have been willing to accept this are to be found largely in the mystical tradition of Christianity and of other religions. These believers might try to explain God's hiddenness in terms of God's transcendence. They might well succeed in part. For example, God's transcendence might enable them to explain why humans do not understand God as well as they understand, say, other humans. However, it would not enable them to explain why God's will is so hidden. Though the divine nature may be forever obscure to humans, there is no reason to think that God's will for human actions and attitudes must be intrinsically obscure. Even if God's transcendence were such as to make it impossible for humans to figure out by themselves what God's will for them is, there is no reason to think that divine transcendence *per se* would make it impossible for God to clearly reveal God's will for humans.

However, if God is such that personalistic categories such as *act* and *will* are not appropriate to use in relation to God, then there would be no point to asking why God does not do this or that. This way of understanding divine transcendence does enable its advocates to explain divine hiddenness. If God's nature is such that God's existence and nature cannot be made more clear to humans and if it is not appropriate to speak of God's willing or acting, then God's hiddenness is fully compatible with the existence of God. This approach also solves the traditional problem of evil, for if God is not a personal being who wills and acts, then there is no problem understanding why God does not act to prevent or eliminate evil.

Nevertheless, despite these advantages of this approach, the two features that confer them also have made it objectionable to many Christians. First, if the hiddenness of God is a result of the nature of God, then it is a permanent condition. This, as noted above, conflicts with a belief that at some time in the future at least some humans will see and know God far more clearly than any now do. Second, if God is thought of and understood in an impersonal way, then one cannot understand how humans could have personal relationships with God. I find the first less convincing than the second. As will be argued in Chapter 6, there are good reasons to doubt that any human, including the biblical writers, could know that we will some day know God in a way qualitatively better than the way we know God now.

However, the second reason I find far more telling. Of all the features of the way God is addressed, spoken of, and understood by biblical writers, none is more pervasive or more central than that of thinking of God as a being with whom humans can have personal relationships. God is said to love, command, forgive, entreat, guide, and encourage human beings. God's relationship with humans is pictured in terms of a covenant and is expressed in terms of the analogy of king and subjects, husband and (often unfaithful) wife, parent and (often rebellious) child. To be sure, my own understanding of the nature of the authority of the Bible and of the inspiration of its writers does not involve ascribing divinely certified status to anything the writers say, so anything they say may be questioned. But if one tries to question this feature of their faith, on what basis will one do so? Not on the basis of a contrary, impersonal way to think and speak of God also employed by at least some biblical writers, for there is no such way. If any understanding of God as impersonal is to have a basis plausible to Christians, that basis would have to be either (1) severe tensions between conceiving God as personal and other important Christian beliefs, or (2) more general philosophical considerations, not anything found in the Bible itself. I share with most Christians the belief that there is no good basis of either type. For all these reasons, it is not surprising that conceiving God as impersonal has not found wide acceptance among Christians, so I will not give further consideration to views that explain the hiddenness of God in terms of divine transcendence and impersonality.

The Hiddenness of God and Human Defectiveness

The second type of explanations of the hiddenness of God identified by McKim focuses on human defectiveness, either as the cause of God's hiddenness (for it renders humans unable to see clear indications of God) or as the occasion of God's hiddenness (for it provides a reason for God to hide Godself from us). Within the Christian tradition, the former sort of explanation is employed by those who stress heavily what they call "the noetic effects of sin": sin so distorts human beings that they hate the things of God and are unable to perceive their truth and beauty. Only the regenerating work of the Holy Spirit is sufficient to restore to humans the ability to perceive God in the world and in the Bible. The radical defectiveness attributed to humans by this explanation, however, makes virtually impossible any fair direct assessment of it. For if humans are radically defective, that very defectiveness may well make it (almost) impossible for them to perceive their own defectiveness. Thus, a simple denial of the alleged defectiveness almost certainly begs the question.

But perhaps there are more indirect reasons for doubting that human defectiveness is the cause of God's hiddenness. If it were, then one would expect that spiritual improvement would be accompanied by God's becoming less hidden. Does this occur? Within a given religious tradition, it does often happen that spiritual progress as defined by that tradition is accompanied by claims that certain things about God have become more clear to believers. But believers do not always make such claims. And even when they do, it remains a fact that adherents of various traditions do not necessarily (or even typically) move toward agreement in what they claim is increasingly clear about God. This is true not only of differences among adherents of different religions, such as Christianity and Islam, but also of differences among adherents of various traditions (or sub-traditions) within one religion – for example, different groups of Christian fundamentalists. Thus, if spiritually developed adherents of various traditions (or sub-traditions) all claim that the things said about God in their own traditions have become increasingly clear to them, those in at least all but one tradition are mistaken in their claim. Things may *seem* clearer to members of each group, but in all except at most one group the members are simply gaining greater clarity about false beliefs. Thus, the apparent increase in clarity is almost certainly deceptive. We would need some very clear reason to accept the claim of any one group to be the one that has truly gotten it right.

I think the foregoing shows that offering human defectiveness as the cause of divine hiddenness has its problems, even if it cannot be decisively refuted. There is, moreover, another feature of such explanations that should be noted. On traditional assumptions about God's power, it would be possible for God to overcome the blindness caused by human defectiveness, either by repairing the defect or by making things about God even more obvious, or both. That things about God remain unclear indicates that those who rely on this sort of explanation finally have to rely as well on arguments that it is appropriate for God to allow humans to remain blinded by their defectiveness – and indeed (for those who are not in the tradition, if any, that correctly conceives God), to remain blinded even when they adopt what seems to them and to many others to be a sincere and morally disciplined attempt to follow God. The same consideration also shows that those who see human defectiveness as the occasion (rather than the cause) of God's being hidden are also relying on the implicit claim that it is appropriate for God to hide Godself because of human defectiveness.

The Hiddenness of God as Appropriate because of Human Defectiveness

Arguments based on the alleged appropriateness of God's being hidden include those which claim that it is appropriate because of some defectiveness in humans, and those which claim it is appropriate because of some good at which God aims. (This is not to suggest that no explanation can employ both of these reasons – the good aimed at may, for example, be in whole or in part the removal of human defectiveness – but I still think that it is helpful to make the distinction.) We will look first at explanations that base the appropriateness on some human defectiveness.

Suppose it is alleged that human sinfulness makes humans blind to God and makes it appropriate for God to leave humans in their blindness as a punishment for their sinfulness. (Something like this might be at least part of the Apostle Paul's point in Rom 1:18–25.) Such an explanation can succeed only if the sole purpose of this punishment is retribution, for none of the other recognized purposes of punishment apply (reform the wrongdoer, protect the innocent, and deter future wrongdoing).[3] Because the punishment simply makes God less clear but otherwise imposes no suffering of which the person is aware, it provides no motivation to do what is right or avoid doing what is wrong. Therefore, it will not contribute to that person's reform; indeed, it would seem to make reform less likely. Nor does this punishment tend to prevent future repetition of the crime (of ignoring and therefore not obeying

God), for God's hiddenness only makes it easier for the person to continue to ignore God. Nor would it help to protect others from future wrongdoing by the one from whom God is hidden, for God's being hidden does not physically restrain the wrongdoer (as prisons do), and it provides the wrongdoer with no reason to refrain from wrongdoing. Moreover, there is no possibility of its serving to deter anyone because the purported fact that sinful behavior will result in God's becoming hidden has not been clearly spelled out to humans in advance. Yet if no purpose other than retribution could be served by God's permitting wrongdoers to remain blind to God, then if God is hidden as a punishment for human sin, then the sole purpose of this punishment is retribution – and not a very effective retribution, for the wrongdoer is not aware of it.

Some theists – I am one – believe that it is inappropriate to attribute to God any punishment that has a *solely* retributive purpose. Several considerations support this belief. First, as an analogy, consider that loving parents disciplining their child may impose some punishment with a partially retributive purpose, but the purpose would never be solely retributive; they would want to reform the child and deter future wrongdoing. Moreover, they would have given the child advance warning of the consequences of doing the thing for which the punishment is imposed, but one aspect of divine hiddenness is that humans have not been clearly warned that divine hiddenness will result from human sinfulness. Second, God's permitting humans to remain blind to God certainly does not seem to be a loving way to treat the people from whom God hides Godself. To see why I make this claim, return to the analogy of the loving parents. It *may* be that the punishment itself will make the child angry and thus tend to motivate disobedience, but the punishment would be set in a context that the child perceives as one of love and acceptance. However, God's being hidden is not set in a context perceived by humans as one of love and acceptance; God's hiddenness is itself part of the context. Third, attributing a solely retributive purpose to God's permitting humans to remain blind to God makes it more difficult for people to do the very thing that God allegedly most wants people to do: to come to faith in and love for God.[4] Therefore, attributing this purpose to God's punishing people by permitting them to remain blind to indications of God implies an inconsistency between God's actions and God's alleged aims. For these reasons, claiming (or implying) that some divine hiddenness is a punishment and has a solely retributive purpose seems inconsistent with the claim that God loves humans. For if God loves humans, God would want them to develop in positive ways, but punishing them by permitting them to be blind to indications of God is likely to hinder rather than to further their positive development.

So let us try a different approach. Suppose it is alleged that what makes it appropriate for God to leave humans blind to things about God is the danger that if they knew these things, they would be able to manipulate God. For example, if humans knew what God would do in response to various human actions, they would be able to get God to do just what they wanted by acting in the appropriate way.[5] However, I do not see this as a danger. If God is as most theists conceive God, then God's responses would be related to human motivations rather than to human actions. (In biblical language, God looks at people's hearts, not at their outward behavior.) Therefore, no human could manipulate God simply by performing some external action (such as praying some prayer or going through some ritual), for no such action would be the sort of thing required to evoke a particular divine response. Could a human generate the required motivation and thereby manipulate God? This is very unlikely, for people cannot generate motivations at will as they can perform actions. But even if a person could eventually generate some desired motivation, the motivation required by God would be certainly be one that makes manipulation of God impossible. For surely the required motivation would be or include a sincere love for God. If a person genuinely had this motivation, what danger of manipulation could exist? Of course, we humans may not be able to discern with certainty whether our motivation is pure, but traditional theists would not doubt that God can. Moreover, even apart from the point about God's concern with motivation rather than actions, this explanation gives no reason for God to keep humans blind to God's will. How could simply knowing what God wants them to do allow them to manipulate God? Manipulation requires knowledge of how God will respond to various human actions, not just of what God wants humans to do.

A third reason for alleging that human defectiveness makes God's hiddenness appropriate also involves God's goals for humans. It is that humans, who are in fact wretched, must learn that they are. If God were less hidden, it would be more difficult for them to learn this. A justification for divine hiddenness employing this reason was articulated by Thomas Morris, in a work mentioned earlier in this chapter.[6] He points out that dramatic miraculous theophanies would be clear evidence that God exists and cites atheists David Hume and N.R. Hanson, both of whom mention a voice from the clouds – Hanson adds a visual image – as something that would convince them that there is a God (92). Morris says that theists face the challenge of explaining why "God does not act in such a way as to disambiguate the world for all his rational creatures" (87). In response to explanations of divine hiddenness offered by some theists who suggest that divine hiddenness results from our inability to see God because of our sinfulness, he says that while this might explain our inability to see God's handiwork in creation, it does not explain why God does not do dramatic miracles.

To explain this inaction by God, Morris draws on Blaise Pascal's idea that humans are both great and wretched. If God were clearly known without our having proper self-knowledge, including knowledge of our wretchedness, it would promote pride. Thus, God makes Godself known only to people at the proper stage of self-development. The religious obscurity of the world makes us realize that we are not self-sufficient, and promotes humility: "The act of seeking reinforces, entrenches, and develops both humility and the love for the truth" (19). Of course, as Morris admits, some people, rather than seeking, will follow the alternative strategy of retreating into their own resources "and, with Bertrand Russell, build the soul's habitation on a foundation of unyielding despair. But Pascal joins the biblical authors in saying that those who seek will find" (102). Morris adds that Pascal, as a committed Christian and not just a theist, says that Jesus Christ shows us God through his divinity and "our wretchedness in contrast with the standard he presents of human perfection" (104).

Is Morris's explanation adequate? First, as he acknowledges, some will not become seekers. But choosing Bertrand Russell as an example of a non-seeker is surely paradoxical. True, Russell did not seek God – he did not believe there is a God to be sought. However, he did seek the truth. If there had been a dramatic, miraculous theophany, it is likely that he and other non-seekers would have believed there is a God and might have begun to seek God. Moreover, many morally and religiously sensitive non-Christian seekers seem, as far as we can tell, to seek God, and they often do not become Christians as a result of their seeking, thus calling into question either the promise that those who seek will find God or the Christian belief of Pascal and Morris that finding the truth about God includes finding Jesus Christ. (Of course, it remains possible for Christians to say that non-Christians who genuinely seek God will find out about Christ in the next life if they do not find out in this life.)

Moreover, Pascal's citing Jesus Christ is instructive. If seeing a clear case of perfected humanity would enable us to know our own wretchedness, then God could accompany a dramatic theophany with supernaturally communicated information about, or images of, perfected humanity in Jesus Christ. Or perhaps it would be enough to communicate God's standards for human beings along with the theophany; then God could point out privately to each individual ways in which that individual had fallen short of the standards. Or perhaps even that would not be needed; perhaps just the clear manifestation of divine greatness would be enough. This might be what is suggested about Job when God speaks to him out of the whirlwind (Job 38–42). These examples show that a dramatic theophany need not allow humans to be proud or to remain ignorant of their wretchedness. This raises a problem for Morris because he seems to admit that we should expect a dramatic theophany unless one can provide a good reason for there not to be. But the reasons he provides are not adequate.

But perhaps Morris and Pascal's point is not so much the accuracy of our beliefs but our confidence in their accuracy. Perhaps their point is that the obscure indications of God we are given will make us unsure and thus drive us to depend more on God. But the very obscurity of the indications might also leave us unsure whether there is a God and whether this God (if there is one) is dependable. We know as a matter of empirical fact that the obscurity of the indications has provoked some people to become agnostics or atheists, and it has not prevented other people from having great certainty about the accuracy of their beliefs, even to the point of persecuting those who do not agree. Thus, the obscurity seems neither a good way to move humans to depend on God nor a reliable way to prevent humans from being arrogant toward other humans because they have (what they believe to be) true beliefs about God.

On the other hand, if people were brought to a knowledge of God by a dramatic, miraculous theophany, is it really likely that they would be prideful and not properly humble? Dramatic miracles to reveal God should humble us before the love and power of God, who did these things so that we could know God (or know God better or more clearly). It is far more likely to evoke pride if we could acquire accurate beliefs about God on the basis of the limited, ambiguous indications we have now, for we would (seem to) be acquiring this knowledge without any specific divine aid.

Morris does suggest several reasons that he thinks even a complete non-believer might find to be indications (though not conclusive proof) that Christianity is true. Prominent among them is his discussion of Pascal's use of the diagnosis of the human condition and the picture of ideal human existence given by Christian anthropology. But Morris's attempt to show that Christian anthropology has the best account of the human condition and of ideal human existence is significantly weakened by two factors: his failure to discuss alternative accounts (for example, a Buddhist, Hindu, or naturalist account), and the fact that Pascal and Morris are products of a culture heavily influenced by Christian theories and concepts, thus raising the question of how much their perception of the human condition is biased by Christian categories rather than being an unbiased description of the human condition and of ideal human existence.

In addition to reasons for thinking that Christianity is true based on its anthropology, Morris also discusses reasons based on its idea of how humans can be restored to wholeness. However, these reasons are not as strong as Morris seems to think. Many rely on accepting biblical narratives as historically accurate (for example, accounts of miracles and predictive prophecy, of Jesus' teachings, and of Jesus' ideas about his own identity). But biblical scholarship has called into question the historical accuracy of these accounts. While the scholarship is admittedly controversial, its existence does lessen the force of these evidences. Other reasons Morris gives may have explanations other than the religious superiority of Christianity. For example, he cites the fact that Christianity has been accepted by people from a wider variety of cultures than any other religion. But Christianity has been more missionary (and therefore has tried harder) than other religions. Moreover, much of its greatest success among non-Western people (including Native American people) came at times when it was the religion of the Western rulers of those people; perhaps at least part of the reason why many of these people embraced Christianity had to do with its being the religion of powerful and successful Westerners.

By way of review, I have argued that the reasons Morris gives for divine hiddenness are not clearly superior to some possible alternative ways to bring humans to humble themselves and seek God; in particular, dramatic miraculous theophanies accompanied by detailed presentations of how God wants people to live seem at least as likely as the methods Morris defends to accomplish what Morris presents as God's goal. Nor have the methods Morris claims that God is employing met with anything like uniform success. Finally, the reasons he suggests that non-Christians have for the truth of Christianity are too inconclusive to show to non-Christians that Christianity is a more plausible religion than are others. These problems with Morris's justification for divine hiddenness give us good reason to try other proposed justifications.

The Hiddenness of God as Appropriate to Make Room for Faith

We have considered three of the most common reasons for thinking that human defectiveness makes it appropriate for God to allow humans to remain blind to things about God, and none of them seems adequate. So we will turn to claims that what makes it appropriate for God to be hidden is that hiddenness makes possible the achievement of a certain divine goal for humans. The goal may be variously specified. It may be described as making room for faith, or as allowing for an uncoerced choice for God, or as giving humans the freedom to choose to believe or not to believe in God. And it is claimed (or supposed) that if the existence of God and perhaps certain other things about God were clear, the specified goal either could not be achieved or would be more difficult to achieve. Reasons of this sort are perhaps the most common sort of explanation given by traditional Christian theists (especially contemporary ones) for the hiddenness of God. One of the best-known developments of this sort of explanation is that given by John Hick.[7]

Hick understands God's purpose in creating humans to be that they should come "to love and be loved by God";[8] moreover, this human love must be freely given. If the love is to be freely given, a person must have "*cognitive* freedom in relation to his Creator" (*Evil* 313, italics his). This cognitive freedom requires not only that human beings be endowed with the requisite capability, but also that they live in an appropriate environment. For if a created being lived "face to face with infinite plenitude of being, limitlessly dynamic life and power, and unfathomable goodness and love, there seems to be an absurdity in the idea of his seeing rebellion as a possibility" (*Evil* 314). Therefore, humans must be born and live in an environment in which they are not face to face with God; Hick calls this a condition of being at an *epistemic distance* from God. Hick, however, is far from clear about what degree of divine obviousness must be excluded in order to meet this condition. Must the environment be such as (1) to make faith irrational, or (2) to make neither faith nor lack of faith irrational, or (3) to make faith rational, though still not putting humans in a face-to-face relation with God?[9] I think Hick intends the second, though some texts could be construed as support for the first.[10] But by itself the requirement that humans not live face to face with God is not enough to exclude even alternative 3. So one might well wonder whether God should not create an environment such that, even if we are not face to face with God, correct beliefs about God are more rational than incorrect ones. But if that would make faith too easy and there is some virtue in faith's being difficult, then why should not God create an environment such that correct beliefs are irrational, to make faith even harder and increase even more the virtue of having it? These questions indicate that Hick should give some reason why the world should be of one or another of these sorts; mere appeal to the need for epistemic distance, even if correct, is not sufficient.[11]

Hick might charge that this criticism assumes a view of the nature of faith that he does not share: faith as believing (putatively) divinely revealed propositions. In contrast, Hick understands faith to be a way of perceiving (interpreting) the whole world.[12] It involves seeing events not just as natural events but also as the activity of God. Hick offers as an analogy that another human being can be seen both as a physical object in one's natural environment and as a person who makes a moral claim on one. Thus, the issue of the appropriate degree of divine obviousness is a matter not of how clear it is that certain propositions are true, but of how clear it is that a certain way of seeing things is the correct way (or to what extent it naturally arises in us, as belief in the existence of material objects naturally arises in us).

However, my criticism does not presuppose a view of faith that Hick rejects. As the last sentence in the previous paragraph suggests, the criticism could be framed explicitly in terms of the view of faith that he accepts. Hick does admit that there could be degrees of divine obviousness greater than that found in our world but still less than a full disclosure of the divine being (*Faith* 155–6). Moreover, there seems no reason why faith in Hick's sense of a way of perceiving the world could not be combined with faith in the sense of believing some divinely revealed propositions. For the latter could guide and enlighten the former; it could help the believer see more accurately God's activity in the world.[13]

Therefore, even if Hick is correct about the nature of faith, if God indeed has the sort of power that the traditional view attributes to God, then it would seem possible to combine a certain degree of divine obviousness with certain clearly revealed propositions to guide the faithful in the their interpretation of the world. Later in this chapter I will suggest ways this could be done without so overwhelming people as to make a free response impossible. If such a combination were possible, it would seem appropriate, for even the most cursory survey of the religions of the world reveals that the mere patency of the world to a theistic interpretation is no guarantee that all theists will agree on the details of that interpretation. At the very least, Hick owes his readers an explanation of why God did not make religiously important matters about Godself more clear. Of course, those who understand faith as believing divinely revealed propositions upon the authority of their proposer are no better off than Hick; if, as they hold, God did reveal certain propositions, they also should explain why God did not make it more clear which putatively divinely revealed propositions are actually divinely revealed.

Moreover, there are other, and even more serious, problems with Hick's explanation of the hiddenness of God in terms of the need for epistemic distance. That explanation assumes that faith is a voluntary cognition. He says that faith, though a species of cognition, is more subject to voluntary control than are many cognitions. Hick speaks of "man in his freedom" being "willing or unwilling to become aware of God" (*Evil* 313). Presumably Hick would say that faith will be accompanied by at least a tendency to live in a manner that is appropriate in light of what the person with faith believes about God and the world. But with all these qualifications, it remains the case that for Hick faith is primarily a matter of cognition, but a cognition that is voluntary. That is why epistemic distance is so crucial; if there were no such distance, or if the distance were sufficiently less, certain beliefs about God would be inescapable, and faith as a way of seeing the world that is at least partly voluntary would be impossible.

But there are at least two problems with using this understanding of faith to explain the hiddenness of God. One concerns its voluntariness if faith is indeed a species of cognition. Is Hick right in saying that faith is a species of *voluntary* cognition? Hick holds that it is a cognition in the sense of a way of seeing (interpreting) the world. (Others would say it is the believing of certain propositions.) But in either sense, are cognitions typically (or ever) voluntary? I think not. With perceptions of or beliefs about God, as with other perceptions and beliefs, people find themselves seeing the world theistically or not (or believing that God exists or does not). Of course, how we come to see the world (as well as what beliefs we come to hold) does depend on what influences we are exposed to and what experiences we have, but most people's seeing the world theistically or non-theistically (or believing that God exists or does not exist) is not the result of their choosing influences and experiences to produce that way of seeing the world (or that belief about the existence of God).

In some of the analogies he uses to illustrate faith, Hick acknowledges this. For example, he says that we have the freedom to choose whether or not to regard the speech of another as intelligible words or as mere gibberish. But, he adds, this is a formal freedom; we have in fact become habituated to interpreting speech as intelligible words and have lost any real (Hick says "material") freedom in this regard though he says that a child first learning language has it (*Faith* 176–7). However, even if the young child has a real (not just formal) freedom in this regard, her cognitive and moral abilities are too underdeveloped to make possible any responsible use of this freedom. Therefore, when this analogy is applied to people who have been religious believers or nonbelievers all their lives, it would seem that any more than formal freedom they ever had could not have been used responsibly. Even people who change from theism to atheism or vice versa generally do not experience this change as based on their refusal or willingness to see God; rather, as a result of various experiences and reflections, they find their way of seeing the world (or the beliefs they hold) changing.

To be sure, some of those who cease to be believers do so as a result of a rejection of God, though this is often an unwillingness to live in obedience to God rather than (as Hick suggests) an unwillingness to be aware of God. But is the loss of faith always the result of a rejection of God? It hardly seems so; indeed, some people lose faith reluctantly, struggling to maintain it, but failing to do so. Moreover, Hick's view implies that all failure to see the world theistically (or to believe that God exists) is a failure that rests on an unwillingness to do so. That is, Hick's view implies (though I know of nowhere that Hick explicitly draws the conclusion) that there is no "honest unbelief," no unbelief that rests on honest error rather than on an *unwillingness* to recognize God. Many Christians have held such a view, but does Hick? In his more recent work, he certainly rejects this view of non-Christian religions.[14] Moreover, in his *An Interpretation of Religion*, Hick may be implicitly refusing to accept it in relation to all naturalists, for he affirms that some naturalists too can be responding to the Real.[15]

If Hick's account of faith as a species of voluntary cognition is not plausible, this has serious implications for Hick's whole project. For the justification of epistemic distance is that it makes possible a free (voluntary) faith in God. But if the cognitions that Hick calls faith (or its lack) are typically not really free or voluntary, as I have argued, then this justification for epistemic distance fails. This same conclusion follows for others who understand faith in Hick's sense as well as for those who understand it as believing certain propositions. If cognitions are not typically voluntary, then there is no reason for God to be hidden, for a person's not seeing the world theistically (or not believing that God exists) is not a voluntary decision for which that person should be held accountable.[16]

Some might try to defend the voluntariness of faith by citing the phenomenon of religious conversion, for religious conversions typically are voluntary. However, they are not primarily changes in cognition. Rather, they are changes in one's commitments and one's attitudes. One is converted by taking Christ as one's Lord or by deciding to follow the way of the Buddha. The conversion often follows a different way of seeing the world or coming to have new or different beliefs. But these new cognitions do not result from voluntary decisions, though they provide reasons for one to make the new commitments that are the essence of religious conversions.

This point about religious conversions brings us to the second, and more basic, problem with Hick's view of faith: Hick's taking it to be a species of cognition. That is, the fundamental problem with Hick's view of faith is that it equates faith with something like perception that God exists. This account separates (what Hick calls) faith too greatly from what Hick himself takes to be God's goal for human development: that humans love God (*Evil* 317). Hick's position on God's goal is not idiosyncratic. Virtually all Christians (and most other theists) would say that God's goal for humans is not just that humans perceive the world as God's creation and the realm of God's activity (or believe that God exists and believe certain other things about God). Rather, they claim that God's goal is, roughly, that humans will trust in God, be committed to God, love God, want to do God's will, or more likely all of these. I will describe this sort of goal as *having faith in God.* (Henceforth, unless otherwise indicated, *faith* and *having faith* will be used in this sense rather than Hick's.) That this is what Christians and most other theists understand to be God's goal for humans has important implications for the explanation of divine hiddenness currently under consideration.

First, it implies that even if it were obvious to everyone that God exists and even if certain things about God's nature and will and activity were obvious, that would not by itself be equivalent to, or inescapably result in, people's having faith in God. If these things were obvious, that might inevitably result in people's perceiving God or believing the corresponding propositions about God; but it would not (even almost) inescapably result in faith, because believing all these things (or perceiving the world in a theistic way) does not logically imply or even psychologically guarantee that humans will have faith in God, that they will love, trust, commit themselves to, and desire to follow God. The possibility of not having faith in God while holding crucial (presumedly) true beliefs about God has been noted in Christian Scripture.[17] Indeed, sometimes passages in the Bible condemn people for rejecting God precisely because God is clear, not obscure as Hick holds.[18]

How might Hick or other proponents of this sort of explanation reply? I think the most likely reply would be that I have understated how psychologically difficult it would be not to regard these perceptions of (or beliefs about) God as important and not to have faith in God if one had them. In more detail, the reply might go as follows. We are speaking of perceiving (or believing that there is) an omnipotent, omniscient, all-good, and loving God who has the power to make one's life full or miserable. Suppose this were so clear as to make failing to believe it irrational. How could anyone not regard this as important? This being has the power to outweigh all other influences on one's life. And if one were rationally convinced that this being is loving, how could one fail to love and trust this being?

Hick might say that even this understates the situation. For Hick postulates the need for epistemic distance not to prevent these matters from being so obvious to everyone as to make it irrational not to believe them, but to prevent one's enjoying the vision of God in such a way that the divine presence overwhelms all other factors in one's awareness. For a person enjoying the vision of God in this sense there is nothing of which that person is more clearly or more powerfully aware than being in the presence of an almighty being who loves her. While Hick's point about the consequences of someone's enjoying the vision of God has considerable merit, not enjoying the vision of God does not by itself also preclude one's being in an environment in which belief in God is rational for everyone. Even if Hick is right that an uncoerced faith would be impossible for anyone enjoying the vision of God, it does not seem as though an uncoerced faith would be impossible in an environment lacking that vision but nevertheless far more conducive to rational theistic belief than ours is.

But even this weaker claim is challenged by Michael Murray in "Deus Absconditus,"[19] in which he defends a soul-making theodicy. He claims that either a promise of reward or a threat can be so strong as to render ineligible for a person any choices not to act in accordance with it. He develops his argument in relation to a threat, saying that

> there are at least three factors which determine the degree to which a threat-induced desire is compelling: threat strength, threat imminence, and threat-indifference. The degree to which the desire compels me to act in accordance with the threat is directly proportional to the first two and indirectly proportional to the third. (72)

Then he argues that if it were too clear that God exists and would inflict everlasting punishment on unbelievers, for most people the threat strength of everlasting punishment and the threat imminence would be great enough to overwhelm their threat indifference and therefore render ineligible any choice other than to obey God.

However, it seems to me that both Hick and Murray overlook something very important in their arguments. Both claim that if certain things about God were clear, this would make it psychologically very difficult (or even impossible) not to have faith in God (or at least not to obey God). Let us for the moment suppose that it does. Why would this be undesirable? Their answer – typical in such arguments – is that faith (or obedience) would not have been freely adopted. But this simply does not seem true. It seems that such faith (or obedience) would be as free as any response one makes out of a clear perception of the goodness of something. It would not be coerced in the way that an action is coerced if done only at gunpoint. For the latter involves adding a factor otherwise irrelevant to the situation, without which the action would not be done. But merely providing a person with information that is accurate and that introduces no factors irrelevant to the situation does not coerce the person or destroy freedom. (The information about God and the consequences of faith and obedience, on the one hand, and unbelief and disobedience, on the other, is assumed to be accurate.) Indeed, generally we consider that no decision is fully voluntary unless it is based on accurate information about the situation. Thus, the charge that the faith would be worthless or of reduced value because it is not free seems incorrect.

But perhaps this charge has a more legitimate point that might be expressed this way: the "faith" that occurs in such a situation would not be genuine or would be worthless (not because it is not free, but) because it is based on wrong motives. For it would be based on self-interest because there would be no realistic possibility of people's failing to see that obedience to God is in their self-interest. This charge has more plausibility, but even it is open to serious challenge. For it confuses (or equates) seeing that commitment to God is in one's self-interest with being motivated to commit oneself to God out of self-interest. That is, the charge seems to assume that if one has faith in God when one rationally believes that an almighty, all-knowing God loves one, one's motive must be selfish. But why need this be? Of course, some people who hold these beliefs about God might follow God because they think it would be in their self-interest. Theirs would not be genuine faith. But why could not rational belief that God loves them motivate people to love God out of gratitude or some other worthy motive? (Murray's approach makes this more difficult to see because he concentrates on the threat without considering the impact of other things about God that would also be known if the threat were known, such as the promise of everlasting beatitude made possible by God's love.) Some followers of politicians join themselves to these leaders because they believe (perhaps even rationally believe) that the politician's program offers great hope. So do many of those who associate themselves with various causes and give time and money to advance those causes. Both groups include many who do not want anything for themselves (even though the program or causes may benefit them as well). So even if various things about God were so clear to everyone as to make nonbelief irrational, their being clear would not necessarily make it more difficult for God to achieve God's presumed goal of having humans come to a genuinely selfless devotion to God. Their being clear might make that goal more difficult to achieve with some people, but it may be easier with others.

Moreover, even if in some people "faith" is born out of selfish motives, why should one think that these motives cannot and will not change to unselfish ones? When parents begin the process of moral education of their children, they typically use a system of rewards and punishments. Right actions are rewarded, and wrong ones punished. But parents hope – and experience often (though certainly not always) confirms – that children do come to value the moral ideals and rules as intrinsically worthwhile. If they did not, they would never act in a morally correct way without some plausible threat of punishment or promise of reward. But people do sometimes act in a morally appropriate way without any such inducement. If this is sometimes true of people as they grow from children to adults, is it not also possible that it is sometimes true of people who out of selfish motives initially (appear to) come to faith? Indeed, is it not likely that it is sometimes true? Of course, this does not always happen. But defenders of divine hiddenness do not claim that God's following a policy of being hidden evokes unselfish faith in everyone (at least in this life). So it would be difficult for them to criticize the (possibly only) partial success that is likely if God were less hidden on the grounds that it is only a partial success.

I find it odd that traditional Christian theists have not been more concerned about this potential benefit that would seem to occur if God were less hidden. According to a very common traditional interpretation of New Testament accounts, it was their having seen the risen Christ that inspired the first disciples to commit (or recommit) themselves to him. Should their motivation for this post-Easter (re)commitment to Christ be suspect because they supposedly had a very strong basis for their beliefs about Christ, having seen the risen Christ? (The historical accuracy of these accounts is irrelevant. The issue is whether Christians who have interpreted them as attributing this motive to the disciples have, presumably unwittingly, thereby attributed to the disciples an unworthy motive.)

Murray does deal with this issue in relation to Paul. He admits that Paul did not lose morally significant freedom by having been converted through "a powerful theophany," and he admits that if everyone were like Paul, this would "show the theist that divine hiddenness is not required to maintain the integrity of human freedom" (77). In response he claims that Paul had a high degree of threat-indifference and that there is no reason to think that all people, or even most people, are like Paul in this regard. But Murray overlooks the fact that, according to the Scriptures that tell about Paul and that he accepts, all the apostles and 500 believers were granted the same powerful theophany as Paul, a vision of the resurrected Christ. Though admittedly we know nothing more about the 500 than their allegedly having seen the risen Christ, surely it is unlikely that all of them had a much higher degree of threat-indifference than most people. And we do know about the apostles other than Paul that they all abandoned Jesus at the time of his arrest; thus, at that time their threat-indifference just to physical death was not even great enough to allow them to remain loyal to Jesus. If the risen Christ appeared to them just a few days after their arrest, it is unlikely that their threat-indifference would have changed significantly in that short interval. Therefore, these early believers provide a very strong reason to doubt all arguments that claim that powerful theophanies remove the possibility of significant moral freedom.[20]

To review, we have seen four serious problems with Hick's explanation of the hiddenness of God. First, it rests on a view of faith as a species of voluntary cognition, but there are serious grounds for doubting whether faith in Hick's sense of a way of perceiving (or in the sense of believing some propositions) is voluntary. Second, if God were more clearly perceivable (or if it were more rational to believe that God exists), most people would perceive or believe appropriately, but this would not by itself be, or guarantee, the achieving of God's goal for humans. This point is present but somewhat masked in Hick's explanation because he understands faith as a sort of cognition and thus separates what he calls faith from what he admits is God's ultimate goal for people, that they will love (trust, be committed to) God.[21] Third, Hick argues that enjoying the vision of God would preclude an uncoerced faith (and an unselfish love for God?); but even if this is so, Hick does not consider what degree of divine hiddenness would be most appropriate for achieving God's goal or give any reason for thinking that this is the amount characteristic of our world. Fourth, we have seen reasons for thinking that God's goal for people might well be promoted rather than hindered if the reality of God (or the truth of certain beliefs about God) were clearer. It is far from established that if the perception of God or the truth of certain beliefs about God were clear to people, those people would (almost) inescapably come to faith (in my sense) and that, if they did, the faith would (almost) inescapably be worthless because it is not freely chosen or is based on selfish motives. On the contrary, we have seen reasons to think that an unselfish faith could, either initially or in the long run, well be based on beliefs about God that are clearly rationally justified. These four reasons provide strong grounds to doubt the adequacy of the defense of the hiddenness of God based on its alleged appropriateness for achieving God's goal of having people relate to God in unselfish love. As I have indicated, they also apply to those who think of faith as believing certain propositions or doctrines and who explain the hiddenness of God in terms of the alleged need to make possible an uncoerced or free faith.

Moreover, not only are there reasons to doubt that God's being hidden is necessary to achieve God's goals, but there is also at least one reason to believe that it is an inappropriate way to achieve them. Simple fairness would seem to require that God provide greater clarity about God's existence, nature, and will. Most theists claim that humans are expected to make momentous decisions about their lives, decisions that will have a great impact on their destiny; but if certain information about God is not clear to humans, then they have to make these decisions lacking crucial information about the context in which they are to decide, the standards to which they are expected to conform, and the consequences of various choices. How can this be fair? It is as though a person were transported to a foreign country, not told its laws or customs, and then expected to live by them. Analogously, according to Hick, humans are born into a world designed to make it obscure that there is a God and what a proper response to God is, and then expected to respond properly. And according to most theists, our spiritual well-being depends on making a proper response to God. Moreover, even if our ignorance about God is partly or entirely our fault, if God loves us and wishes us to have faith in God, then there are good reasons for God to do what God can to make our situation more clear to us.

Unclarity about the Will of God as a Special Problem

None of the reasons we have considered have been adequate to explain the hiddenness of God, and they seem particularly inadequate in relation to the unclarity of God's will. Certainly divine transcendence does not explain it: that God's nature is incomprehensible provides no reason to think that God's will for human behavior is also incomprehensible (if God has a will regarding such matters). Human sinfulness might make people blind to what God wants, but it seems self-defeating in the extreme for God to allow people to remain ignorant of God's will. If God is omnipotent, presumably God has the power to make God's will for human behavior so clear that all will recognize it. Nor need God's making God's will this clear make it impossible or even very difficult for people to obey out of proper motives.

God could employ any of several means whereby humans could know God's will on various matters and know that it is God's will. For example, God could regularly give the same commandments and instructions to all people in their own language in a publicly heard voice with no detectible source. Or God could "whisper" in each person's ear what God wants done in that person's situation. Or God could furnish selected humans with God's commandments and could certify by dramatic miracles the divine source of certain moral rules and judgments, in a fashion somewhat like that in which, according to the account in Exodus, certain miracles accompanied and certified the giving of the Ten Commandments. Any such technique should be repeated on a regular basis so that people would not have to rely on oral tradition or written records, though even these would presumably be less suspect if there were agreement among them. But the press of new issues would be another reason why people might need continued, suitably certified divine guidance.

If God made clear to everyone what is right and what is wrong, there would be great gain in that most people's uncertainty about what is the right thing do would be eliminated. This uncertainty is a significant cause of disagreement and confusion in the world today. It is not the only cause, perhaps not even the primary cause: out of fear or selfish desires, some people do what they are confident or strongly suspect is wrong. But there are many issues on which many people are just not sure what is right or are honestly (and not willfully) mistaken about what is right: for example, perennial problems such as matters on which different religions give different moral rules and more recent problems such as how to respond to the possibilities opened by medical technology. Many people would do what is right on such matters if they knew what it is. Such people would be greatly helped if God were to make God's will very clear.

But it might be asked why people should think that the publicly heard voice with no detectible source or the "whispers" come from God, or that the dramatic, apparently miraculous events are really miraculous acts of God. Perhaps God could say so. But still, why believe that further claim? I think this objection has more theoretical plausibility than practical reasonability. (Remember Morris's citation of what Hume and Hanson said about such an occurrence.) If these phenomena could not otherwise be explained, and if everyone always saw or heard the same message about a particular situation or issue, I think most people would ascribe it to God. Moreover, presumably the results of following the directions would always be good, and therefore would generally be perceived to be good. This would provide an additional reason to think they came from God. And even if it were not believed that they came from God, the goodness of the results from following the directions would provide an additional reason for people to follow them. (Surely there would be no reason for theists to complain if some people followed these directions because they believed that doing so produced good results rather than because they believed that God commanded them; indeed, such a motive would seem to be the unselfish sort that Hick and others desire.) Note, however, that this goodness would presumably be for people in general, not necessarily for every individual who has to decide whether or not to follow some direction in a particular situation. Loving one's neighbor as oneself can sometimes require self-sacrificing actions. Thus, even if following the divinely given directives produced what were generally perceived as good results, it is unlikely that it would always be selfish motives that would motivate individuals to follow these directions. So there is no reason to think that clarity about God's will for human actions would make it impossible or even very difficult for people to develop correct motives for doing what is right.

One other possibility about the usefulness of greater clarity about God's will should be discussed. Suppose I were wrong in my earlier argument against the alleged appropriateness of the hiddenness of God's existence and nature, and it is appropriate that these be hidden. Even keeping them hidden would not preclude God's giving clear direction to people about right and wrong actions. God could give clear directions in such a way that they would not be clearly God's direction. For example, God could provide each person with a conscience that is always the direct expression of God's will for that person in whatever situation the person is (though without the awareness that it is God's will) rather than being at least largely the result of internalizing elements in a person's culture. In other words, unlike the actual consciences we humans have, the sort of conscience I suggest would be a completely reliable guide to what each person should do, and everyone's judgment about what is the right thing to do would agree. This approach need not be detrimental to the hiddenness of God's existence and nature, for people need not connect such a conscience with God; it could be interpreted as just a brute fact about humans that they have this infallible sense about what is right. Moreover, this sort of clarity and agreement about what is the right thing to do would not take away human freedom or the need of humans to decide whether they will do what is right; as we have noted, sometimes humans do not do what they confidently believe is right. It would, however, eliminate uncertainty and honest mistakes as sources of wrong actions and of the frictions caused by honest disagreement about what is the right thing to do. Moreover, if an infallible conscience of this sort were combined with a genetic predisposition to be kinder and gentler, as was suggested in the previous chapter, there would be much less moral evil and much less conflict among people.

Other Explanations of the Hiddenness of God

In the foregoing I have provided what I believe are strong reasons to doubt the adequacy of any of the explanations of divine hiddenness that we have considered. Though I do not claim to have discussed all possible reasons, I do think I have discussed the reasons most often proposed by traditional theists. Suppose I am right that none of these reasons are adequate. What other sorts of reasons might there be? All of them require modification of some important traditional Christian belief about God.

We might give up the assumption, common among theists, that God cares whether or not people have faith in God and love God. If God does not care, then there is far less reason for information about God to be clear. But if God does not care whether people have faith in God or love God, then either God does not love people or faith in God and love for God are not necessarily important for human fulfillment. I think most Christians (and other theists) would be reluctant to give up the belief that faith in God is important, but not as reluctant as they would be to give up the belief that God loves people.[22] Should Christians (and other theists) give up the belief that faith in God is important for fulfillment of all human beings? Giving up this belief need not imply that such faith is not important in the lives of certain individuals, but it would imply that equally fulfilled human lives might be lived without faith in God. Moreover, even if we give up the idea that faith in God is important for everyone, we still might wonder why God does not employ some means whereby people could know the right thing to do in a situation, even if they do not necessarily think the information comes from God. (For example, God could make each person's conscience an accurate indication of what is right for whatever situation the person is considering.) Thus, I conclude that the strategy of giving up the belief that faith in God is important is not a promising way to explain the hiddenness of God. Giving up the belief that God loves people would explain that hiddenness (God just does not care!), but it is a way that most Christians would be very reluctant to adopt. It is difficult to reconcile with the belief that God is perfectly good. So let us seek other sorts of reasons.

All the proposed explanations we have found inadequate, except those based on the belief that *act* and *will* are not appropriate categories to be applied to God, are reasons why God would not choose to make Godself clearer, though God has the power to do so. The only other sort of reason that I can think of is that God cannot make this information about God any clearer. I mean this not in the sense that God is so transcendent that humans are unable to understand anything about God, nor in the sense that God is of such a nature as to make *act* and *will* inappropriate categories in terms of which to conceive God. Rather, I mean that God's relation to the world is such that God cannot manipulate its details in such a way as to make the information about Godself any more clear. All communication with human beings that would make these matters more clear would require manipulating details of the world: writing in the sky, speaking from the sky, "whispering" in people's ears, performing dramatic miracles, or causing each person's conscience to be an accurate indication of what God wants done in the situation being considered. If God's relation to the world is such that God cannot perform these manipulations, then the hiddenness of God is what we would expect.

Stated this baldly, the proposed explanation is likely to seem *ad hoc*. Moreover, it violates many traditional ideas of God's power. But perhaps neither of these reasons constitutes an adequate justification for rejecting the proposal without further consideration. A discussion of the issues involved in this proposal will be undertaken in Chapter 8.

In the face of the difficulties of solving within the framework of traditional Christian theism the problems of evil discussed in Chapters 2–3, some theists have pronounced them beyond our present powers to solve. But that should be done only after all else has failed. And before we pronounce a problem insoluble, we should be very sure about the truth of the premises that generate it. How justified is confidence in the correctness of the belief about God's power and the other beliefs that generate these problems? We must ask this question because one significant indication that something is wrong with one's premises is that they produce an insoluble problem.

But suppose that it were argued that it is reasonable for us to accept the insolubility of these problems. It might be claimed that God could have decided to be hidden, and as part of that hiddenness to hide the reasons why God is hidden.[23] But is this position consistent with other things its proponents believe about God? Most theists say that God has revealed certain things, including that God loves humans and wants them to have faith in God. I argued above that if these things are true of God, then God should not be hidden. To be sure, I could be wrong. But so could those theists who hold the beliefs that render this problem and the problem of suffering insoluble. Once again I ask: how strong are the reasons for accepting the premises that generate the insoluble problems?

Of course, many traditional theists have not pronounced the problems insoluble and have devoted great efforts to producing a satisfactory theodicy. The adequacy of their attempts is still under discussion. Much less attention has been focused on justifying the hiddenness of God than on justifying suffering. But these problems share some crucial assumptions, not only one having to do with God's power, but also assumptions about God's attitude toward humans and God's purpose for them. Eventually we will have to consider the assumptions that generate the problems. But first we will consider a third problem of evil, and then another kind of defense of traditional theism.

Notes

1 *Making Sense of It All: Pascal and the Meaning of Life* (Grand Rapids, MI: William B. Eerdmans, 1992), p. 89.

2. "The Hiddenness of God," *Religious Studies* 26 (1990): 141–61. Page numbers in parentheses in discussions of McKim refer to this paper.

3. These three, in addition to retribution, are the only purposes for punishment generally given. For example, see the discussion by Stanley I. Benn, "Punishment," *Encyclopedia of Philosophy*, ed. Paul Edwards (New York: Macmillan and the Free Press, 1967), vol. VII, pp. 30–31.

4. As we will see, my claim that it makes faith in and love for God more difficult is controversial. I will defend it in some detail. Here I am making only the prima facie claim that it is more difficult for one to love and trust another person if it is not clear to one that the other person is real and what the other person is like.

5. This explanation is discussed by McKim (146).

6. *Making Sense of It All*, ch. 6. Because Morris stresses that God is hidden in order to accomplish certain goals with respect to humans, his discussion could also be placed in the next section of this chapter. But Morris stresses a human defect (lack of self-knowledge and humility) as a condition God wants to correct. Therefore, I am discussing his proposal in this section. Page numbers in parentheses in the rest of this section refer to this work.

7. Since presenting the theodicy discussed in the text, Hick has developed an interpretation of religion that sees the belief system of each religion as a Kantian-like phenomenal schemata for understanding the noumenal Ultimate Real. This later development raises a question about the extent to which Hick would still advocate the explanation discussed in the text. Nevertheless, it is worth discussing because it articulates very well a type of explanation that is widely held today.

8. *Evil and the God of Love* (New York: Harper and Row, 1966), p. 317. In this section, subsequent references to this work will be indicated by putting in parentheses the word *Evil* followed by page number(s).

9. Of course, there are different ways of understanding faith (I discuss Hick's just below in the text). However, my point that it is not clear what degree of divine obviousness must be excluded to make room for faith is relevant to any understanding of faith held by a person who says that God must be hidden to make faith possible. On the other hand, on the understanding of faith I advocate later in the text, faith would still be possible (and important!) even if the environment met condition 3.

10. Hick speaks of our environment as having an "apparently atheous character," and he says that epistemic distance "makes it virtually inevitable that man will organize his life apart from God" (*Evil* 317, 322). On the other hand, in an earlier work Hick also says that "man is a worshiping animal, with an ingrained propensity to construe his world religiously"; *Faith and Knowledge* (Ithaca, NY: Cornell University Press, 1957), p. 180. In this section, subsequent references to this work will be identified by putting in parentheses the word *Faith* followed by the page number(s).

11. Michael Martin raises this question of Hick and points out some of the difficulties with each alternative in *Atheism: A Philosophical Justification* (Philadelphia, PA: Temple University Press, 1990), pp. 427–30. I suspect that Hick would say that once humans are put in an environment in which they are not face to face with God and in which events normally occur in accordance with natural laws and creaturely choices, it is somewhat a matter of chance how hidden God is. Some cultures may be such as to accentuate the hiddenness of God and others might reduce it, but God's basic intention was to create a world that is neutral with respect to faith. But we still need an explanation why a basically neutral world (or some other) is the most appropriate.

12. This view is expounded and defended in *Faith*, ch. 6. It is also expounded in a more recent work by Hick, *Philosophy of Religion*, 4th edn. (Englewood Cliffs, NJ: Prentice-Hall, 1990), pp. 64–67, though it is not there explicitly identified as the view Hick accepts. Nevertheless, in the absence of an explicit disclaimer by Hick, the similarities between the two expositions, extending sometimes to verbal identities, justifies the claim that this was still Hick's view as late as 1990.

13. Though I agree that Hick has distinguished two different views of the nature of faith, I do not think faith ever exists apart from both a way of seeing the world and the believing of some propositions. But those who agree with Hick will take faith as a way of seeing the world as basic and believing the propositions as derivative; that is, they will say that one believes certain propositions about God because one sees certain events as revelatory of God. Those who disagree with Hick will take believing propositions as basic, and say that it generates a way of seeing the world.

14. For example, *Problems of Religious Pluralism* (New York: St. Martin's Press, 1985), and *An Interpretation of Religion: Human Responses to the Transcendent* (New Haven, CT: Yale University Press, 1989).

15. He says that some people see Buddhism "simply as a way of meditation which can produce inner peace, stability, and detachment … and can … be practiced independently of any religious commitment …. Further, in addition to the attraction of meditation, the Buddhist ideal of un-self-centered consciousness, living in compassion towards all life, has for many an intrinsic value that claims their allegiance." He goes on to say that "for some contemporary post-Christian thinkers this ideal is valid and *salvific* even within a basically naturalistic conception of the universe" (*An Interpretation of Religion*, p. 187, my italics). The thinkers discussed include Feuerbach, Braithwaite, Randall, Phillips, and Cupitt.

16. An objector may respond that not seeing the world theistically is something for which a person should be held responsible even if it is not the result of a voluntary decision. For (the objector may continue) that the person does not see the world theistically is an effect of his sinful disposition, which blinds him to God. To this possible objection I have two replies. First, the objection changes the theory under discussion, for Hick does not claim that God's hiddenness is a result of our sinfulness. Second, I have already discussed this explanation of divine hiddenness earlier in this chapter.

17. The writer of the Epistle of James notes that the demons hold correct beliefs about God – "and shudder" (2:19). Such a point probably also underlies the statement attributed to Jesus that "not everyone who says to me 'Lord, Lord' shall enter the kingdom of heaven, but he who does the will of my Father who is in heaven" (Matt. 7:21).

18. For example, the Psalmist complains that the Ephraimites "did not keep God's covenant. They forgot what he had done, and the miracles that he had showed them" (Ps. 78:10–11). I owe this point and this citation to Robert C. Mesle, *John Hick's Theodicy: A Process Humanist Critique* (New York: St. Martin's Press, 1991), p. 78.

19. *Divine Hiddenness*, ed. Daniel Howard-Snyder and Paul K. Moser (New York: Cambridge

University Press, 2002), pp. 62–82. In discussions of Murray's position, page numbers in parentheses in the text refer to this essay.

20. It might be more cautious to say only that they provide a strong reason for those (like Murray) who regard the New Testament documents as historically reliable on this matter. But even those who do not have this regard for the documents must confront the fact that the New Testament writers evidently did not think that dramatic theophanies remove significant moral freedom.

21. We should note that the issue of how *faith* is defined is not crucial. Provided that the purpose of divine hiddenness is alleged to be to preclude a too-easy perception of God and that God's goal for human is understood roughly as I claim, the same argument can be made in Hick's terminology or mine. Moreover, my criticisms will apply to any defense of the hiddenness of God as an appropriate means to achieve God's goal that understands God's goal to be that people would have faith in God (in my sense) or love and be committed to God.

22. A willingness to give up the claim that faith in God is important in the life of everyone is exemplified in the work of certain recent religious pluralists such as John Hick (in the later phase of his life, in such works as *An Interpretation of Religion* and *Problems of Religious Pluralism*).

23. William P. Alston makes a suggestion of this sort in relation to the problem of suffering in his article "The Inductive Argument from Evil and the Human Cognitive Condition," *The Evidential Argument from Evil*, ed. Daniel Howard-Snyder (Bloomington, IN: Indiana University Press, 1996), p. 123, n. 22.

CHAPTER 4

Miracles as a Problem of Evil

Over the course of two thousand years, Christians have differed in the uses they have made of claims about miracles. Throughout most of the history of Christianity, many Christians used what they believed to be miracles as evidence supporting the divine origin of Christianity and/or its status as the true religion. Miracles were thought to have this evidential value because they were conceived of as events in which something occurred that involved a suspension of some law(s) of nature.[1] That is, in a miracle, God is believed to have caused the occurrence of some process which, apart from the exercise of divine power, would have been impossible in that situation – impossible because that occurrence is not within the natural capacities of the creaturely entities involved. (It is worth noting that there is no term in the Old Testament or in the New that is equivalent to "miracle" in this sense.[2] Thus, our concern in this work is with a concept that originated after biblical times, though one whose development was probably stimulated by reflection on certain biblical narratives. Hereafter, unless otherwise indicated, the term "miracle" will refer to this post-biblical concept.[3]) Because only a supernatural agent (God) could suspend a law of nature, miracles were seen as evidence of divine activity in support of some person, movement, or idea. For example, the plagues in Egypt at the time of the Exodus were seen as evidence that Moses spoke for God; the conclusion of Elijah's contest with the priests of Baal (I Kings 18) was seen as a sign that he spoke for the true God; the miracles worked by Jesus were seen as indications of his special relationship with God. This apologetic use of miracles typically was based on the acceptance of biblical narratives of the events as historically accurate.

However, in the past three centuries the usefulness for Christian apologetics of claims about miracles was strongly challenged by two developments. One was a philosophical attack given classical expression by David Hume. The central point in this attack is the claim that it is always more rational to believe that a miracle did not occur than to believe that it did, because it is more likely that the accounts of the event are in error than that a law of nature has been suspended. The accounts may be in error because of misperceptions and/or misdescriptions by the eyewitnesses, errors in transmission of the accounts, or deliberate lying by some of the people involved as eyewitnesses or transmitters. Moreover, even if the details occurred as narrated, it is possible that our conclusion that there was a suspension of some law(s) of nature rests on our having some mistaken ideas about what the laws of nature relevant to the event are.

This line of criticism is widely (though not universally) judged to raise some serious difficulties for the apologetic use of alleged miracles. I believe that this judgment is correct for all the alleged miracles that I have ever heard of. But I also believe that there could be events about which it would be more rational to believe that they involved temporary suspensions of some laws of nature than it would be to believe any alternative explanation of the events or of the accounts of the events.

I gave examples of such events in the previous chapter, such as a voice with no discoverable source heard by all people throughout the world in their own language giving the same message to everyone.

The second line of criticism that has been raised for the apologetic use of alleged miracles grows out of developments in biblical criticism over the last two centuries. Biblical scholars developed a variety of methods to attempt to reconstruct how the documents that compose the Bible reached the form in which we have them. Often their conclusions gave reasons to doubt the historical accuracy of the accounts. The conclusions of biblical scholars about how the biblical documents reached their final form made specific the general concerns in the Humean line of criticism about the purposes and reliability of the people who were eyewitnesses of the events and those who were transmitters of the accounts of the events.

The combined effect of these two lines of criticism raises several problems for the apologetic use of alleged miracles, not only in the sense of making them unusable in converting nonbelievers who know about these lines of criticism, but even in the more modest enterprise of defending the rationality of the beliefs involved in being a Christian. However, it is not my purpose in this chapter to discuss any further these issues about the apologetic use of miracles. Instead I wish to develop and defend the thesis that there is another problem of evil involved in claims about miracles, both those in the Bible and the sort that some claim occurred in post-biblical times.

Whether a Christian believes that God worked only the miracles (or some of the miracles) thought to be described in the Bible or believes that God continues to work miracles in post-biblical times, I claim that believers in the actual occurrence of miracles typically must imply that God is guilty of a kind of injustice – a quality that seems morally problematic, and thus one that, I assume, believers would not want to attribute to God. My argument does not claim that all miracles, no matter when or in what pattern they occur, must involve injustice on God's part; rather, it is an argument against a certain complex view of their purpose, location, and obviousness, a view that is rather common today among Christians who believe that miracles have occurred. However, because it is difficult to formulate another empirically plausible view of the purpose, location, and obviousness of miracles, problems with the view I discuss pose a challenge for anyone who believes that miracles have actually occurred. Thus, it suggests the conclusion that even theists should not claim that God has actually worked miracles, lest they imply that God is unjust or be driven to claims about the occurrence of miracles that are empirically false or at least implausible.

The claim that the view of miracles to be discussed implies that God is unjust suggests why my argument about miracles in this chapter is another problem of evil. I call this problem with claims about miracles a third problem of evil and distinguish it from the other two because I believe that the claim that God has performed miracles raises a distinct set of issues with which some of today's most popular theodicies seem inadequate to deal. For example, as we have seen, many theodicies offered by traditional theists today treat natural evils as unavoidable results of the operation of a system of laws of nature. Humans suffer natural evils because of the joint operation of these laws and the choices humans make, as when a tornado touches down (because of the operation of certain laws of nature) on the spot where some people have chosen (for reasons that have nothing to do with that tornado) to locate their home, and they are killed. People who advance such theodicies usually are not theological determinists, and they would not say that God intended to cause the death of that person while sparing his neighbor who lives a block away. That one person is killed by the tornado and another person survives is, as I said, the joint effect of the operation of natural laws and human choices. But those who claim that God has *miraculously* saved someone's life must claim that God intended to save precisely that person's life, and by not miraculously intervening did not intend to save the life of the person who died. Thus, the claim that God has worked a miracle implies that God has singled out certain persons for some benefit that many others do not receive; this is central to my claim that it implies that God is unjust. The balance of this chapter is largely an articulation and defense of this claim.

Obvious and Inferred Miracles

No event would be categorized as a miracle unless it is unexpected and thought to have some good purpose; it would not be categorized as a suspension of some law of nature unless it is unexpected, and it would not be attributed to divine agency unless its purpose is believed to be good.[4] Among events that are categorized as miracles, I find it helpful to distinguish two types, which I will term *obvious miracles* and *inferred miracles*. When people who categorize an event as a miracle (think they) know enough about the processes involved in the event and the relevant accepted laws of nature to determine that the former could not happen unless the latter were suspended, the event (if it actually is a miracle) is what I will term an *obvious miracle*. For example, anyone who accepts the principle of inertia and who understands the account in Joshua (10:12–14) of the sun's standing still in response to Joshua's command to involve the earth's instantaneously ceasing to rotate on its axis could determine that the latter could not happen unless the former was suspended. But if there is not enough detailed information known about the processes involved in the event and the relevant laws of nature to determine that the event must have involved a suspension of some law of nature, the event (if it actually is a miracle) is what I will term an *inferred miracle*. In inferred miracles the categorizer infers that the event involved a suspension of some law of nature because the outcome is both unusual in comparison to the outcome of many apparently similar situations and better than the usual outcome, such as a person's recovering from an illness from which few recover or walking away with virtually no injuries from a crash at 60 miles per hour. In other words the difference is this: in an obvious miracle there is a logical inconsistency between statements describing the event and statements describing some accepted laws of nature; in an inferred miracle one lacks a sufficiently detailed set of statements about the event or about relevant accepted laws of nature to yield a logical inconsistency, but one infers that there would be an inconsistency if true statements of both types were sufficiently detailed.

Justifying the claim that the latter are miracles involves a problem not faced by analogous claims about the former. In obvious miracles, there is a direct inconsistency between the belief that some event occurred in the world and the acceptance of some law of nature, but in inferred miracles that there is such an inconsistency is inferred on the basis of the unlikeliness of the outcome, as in the recovery or the survival mentioned in the previous paragraph.[5] In such events no human knows both the relevant laws of nature and the relevant antecedent conditions of the event well enough to say that the event violates any law of nature. But both events are sufficiently unusual and unexpected (statistically unlikely) and sufficiently in line with what believers think a loving and merciful God might do that some believers call them miracles. And some who call them that might mean the term not just in the sense of a wonderful and surprising event, but in the strong sense of the temporary suspension of a law of nature accomplished by the power of God because of the goodness of God.

Just as part of the reason for thinking that an event is an inferred miracle typically depends on comparing it with similar events, so does the reason for my charge that attributing this sort of miracle to God implies that God is unjust. The basis for my objection to this sort of miracle is the total absence of any pattern in the occurrence of the alleged miracles. For example, of all the people with what doctors believe to be terminal cancer, some "miraculously" (that is, unexpectedly) recover; most do not. Those who recover are not confined to believers, nor even to believers and those who will eventually become believers. Nor are those who recover confined to people for whom prayers were offered; nor do all people with this medical diagnosis for whom prayers are offered recover. Nor is there any other discernible pattern among those who recover, and certainly not any discernible pattern related to what believers think to be important to God. Moreover, the problem is not merely the lack of any discernible overall pattern. More specifically, there may be two cases that are similar in all ways that seem relevant including all the ways that Christians believe are important to God, such as the moral and spiritual qualities of the people involved, their degree of need, and the prayers made by and for them; yet in one case there will be a recovery (that some deem a miracle), and in the other case no recovery. Quite likely it is true that believers are more likely to call an event such as a recovery a miracle if it occurs following prayer for this result. But there would be reason to think that there was some miraculous divine action only if such events happened more frequently after prayer than in situations in which there was no prayer. Otherwise there is no reason to think that there was a special divine action in these events rather than just the operation of the same unknown natural processes that resulted in the unexpected good outcomes in the non-prayed-for cases. That it does not happen significantly more frequently is the basis for my claim that there is no discernible pattern.

Assuming that it is unjust to treat equals unequally, this lack of any discernible pattern and the fact of different outcomes in similar cases suggest the injustice of what God is alleged to have done. We should note that these two factors also suggest another possibility: what are taken to be miracles are not; instead they are the result of the operation of natural factors as yet not known or understood. Unexpected events, outcomes that occur only rarely in situations of a certain sort, occur also in contexts in which no one even suspects that a miracle might have occurred, for the outcome is inimical or irrelevant to human concerns. A person may die in a sort of situation in which death is very unusual. Or some animal or plant of no importance to any human may survive (or die) in a sort of situation in which most animals or plants of that type die (or survive). Such events are thought to be the result of "chance" or of unknown natural factors. If unusual events with such outcomes sometimes happen (presumably) without any miraculous divine intervention, why should one think that unusual outcomes that are beneficial to human concerns involve a miracle? It seems more reasonable to conclude that, like events in which the outcome is inimical or irrelevant to human concerns, these events are "chance" outcomes or outcomes due to unknown natural factors. However, if at least some of the inferred miracles that are alleged to occur are genuine miracles, then the patterns in which they occur raise problems about the justice of God. Let us see in more detail why this is so, and what might be said in reply to my charge of injustice.

However, before we pursue these issues, there is one other problem with alleged inferred miracles that I wish to point out. People who believe that such miracles occur are speaking of events that are not clearly impossible in light of accepted laws of nature; rather, their reasons for regarding them as miracles are the events' unusualness and conformity to what they take to be divine purposes. If these are believers' only reasons, then they should categorize as miracles all events with these features. Not doing so would be arbitrary and lack any apparent justification. The only way for a person to avoid this arbitrariness about which events are miracles and which are not, other than to deny that any are miracles, is to say that all events with these features are miracles – for example, all events in which a patient recovers after doctors had said that the situation is hopeless. Believers do not say this.

Miracles as Involving Injustice by God

However, even if believers eliminate this arbitrariness by identifying as miracles all the events that meet their precise criteria (whatever those be), the resulting view would still imply that God is guilty of injustice. So too would a view that identifies as miracles all events that involve an apparent inconsistency between what is believed to have occurred and accepted laws of nature. In what sense do these views imply that God is unjust? They do so in the sense that they imply that God arbitrarily (for no reason) confers a benefit on one person that God does not confer on others whose lives and circumstances are relevantly similar – in merit, need, or some other way(s). I say this because either there are some features of the lives and circumstances of miracle recipients that are the reason why God confers the benefit in the miracle, or there are not. If there are, then it is arbitrary for God to confer this benefit on some people with these features and not on others with the same features. If there are no such features, then it is unjust because God is arbitrarily (on this alternative, there is no reason for) bestowing a benefit on one person that God does not bestow on another.

To this charge of injustice, it might be replied that even if God does confer benefits on some people and not on others, this would not be unjust because God is not under any obligation to give humans something. I think this reason is questionable. Though God was under no obligation to create us, God's own nature might preclude God's treating us in certain ways once we had been created; for example, it would seem to deeply violate any concept of divine goodness if God were to create us or any sentient creatures with the intention that they should experience nothing but great suffering for their entire existence. Moreover, Christians assert that God loves humans; and if two similar people are in similar situations, it is not loving to treat them differently.

It might be replied that it is not unjust to give a gift to one person I love and not to another whom I love equally. Perhaps not, provided what is given is not something needed. But even in this case, how will one child feel if a parent gives a gift to a sibling and not to the first child even though there is no reason in the situation for the distinction – for example, it was not either's birthday, neither had suffered any hurt? However, when what is given is needed, such as restoration to health or even the knowledge of God, and when it lies within the resources of the giver to give what is needed to both people, then it does seem unjust and unloving to give it to only one.

Nor is it plausible to say that those who do not receive a miraculous benefit receive some equivalent non-miraculous benefit. One person "miraculously" recovers from cancer; a similar person dies in agony from cancer. It is hard to conceive of other gifts (at least in this life) that would be as great as recovery, especially since often we know that the victim of cancer died soon and without anything good happening to him that we know of. Moreover, even if sometimes there were an equivalent non-miraculous benefit conferred, to avoid God's being unjust an equivalent non-miraculous benefit would have to occur always, in relation to people who do not miraculously survive accidents, illnesses, and other threats to their well-being. That we could very often fail to observe comparable non-miraculous gifts for these people seems implausible in the extreme.

According to the argument thus far, it is unjust for God to perform miracles for some people and not for others, because in so doing God confers upon some people benefits that others with similar characteristics do not obtain. We have two remaining possible responses to this argument to be considered: God has reasons for performing miracles for some people and not others, reasons adequate to undermine the charge of injustice; and there are no benefits given to some that are not given to others. To assess these responses, we need to consider with greater specificity the goods that God allegedly confers in miracles.

In the Christian tradition two kinds of goods have been mentioned. One has to do with enhancing the recipient's knowledge of God or faith in God; the other has to do with various temporal goods, such as life, health, offspring, and other goods that are needed or desired. I will term a miracle that provides the first sort of good an *epistemic miracle*, and one that provides the second sort of good a *practical miracle*. Of course, a miracle could provide both sorts of goods; for example, a healing miracle performed by Jesus would be a practical miracle and could also highlight Jesus' role as a revealer of God and thus be an epistemic miracle.

Most Christian theologians and philosophers have stressed the epistemic function of miracles. They have held that miracles are intended to certify or to confirm that some event (or some associated message[6]) is revelation.[7] In order to do this, an event must be an obvious miracle, not just an inferred miracle, because it is not clear that an inferred miracle is really a miracle. It is worth pointing out that it is difficult to see how one can claim that some miracles were done with an epistemic purpose and also claim that God must remain hidden to allow room for faith, as we discussed in the previous chapter. That is, traditional theists cannot consistently make both claims. If God performs clear, dramatic miracles to evoke and/or confirm certain beliefs about God, then it cannot be crucial that God be hidden to allow room for faith; if it were crucial, then these miracles would have a purpose that conflicts with the purpose of allowing room for faith. Traditional theists can insist on the importance of God's hiddenness to allow room for faith, or they can say that God performs epistemic miracles, but they cannot consistently say both.

Theologians and philosophers have been most concerned with the epistemic benefits of miracles, but popular piety has also been concerned with practical miracles. Believers tell stories of healings (those at Lourdes are famous examples) and of other sorts of non-epistemic benefits conferred through miracles. I know of no other alleged purposes for miracles. Moreover, the two purposes I have discussed encompass the primary purposes that believers think God has in actions toward humans: to bring them to a knowledge of and faith in God (the epistemic purpose) and to graciously save them from harms and restore them to wholeness. Therefore, in the remainder of the discussion I will assume that all alleged miracles have an immediate purpose that is epistemic or practical or both.

Epistemic Miracles

According to the view of miracles being discussed, epistemic miracles are concentrated in, or perhaps even confined to, periods of time that might be called revelatory periods. In Christianity such periods were, for example, the times of the Exodus, of the Old Testament prophets, and of Jesus and the beginnings of the Church. In times other than these, epistemic miracles are believed to occur either not at all or rarely.

Before examining this view in detail, it is important to recognize that there are strong reasons for a believer in the actual occurrence of miracles with an epistemic purpose to hold a view like this of their temporal location (that is, that they occurred in the past during revelatory periods). For most Christians and all non-theists would say that they had never observed any miracles. Of course, those who do not believe that there exists a God who can work miracles would certainly say they had never observed any; but such people typically do not even admit that they have observed any events that seem impossible to explain in light of accepted laws of nature, which we might call *candidate events*. (I am overlooking events observed by scientists that occasion questions about whether the accepted laws of nature are adequate, but that no one is tempted to term miracles – for example, the observation of traces on photographic plates that led to the discovery of radioactivity.) Therefore, today either miracles do not occur at all, or they occur in such a way that most people do not believe that they or even candidate events occur. Thus, claiming that miracles with this purpose are confined to (or at least concentrated in) revelatory periods is an understandable strategy in light of the absence of such miracles today.

Moreover, even if there are some people today who claim to be eyewitnesses to what I term obvious miracles, that would not constitute a serious problem for my argument. My objection to the claim that epistemic miracles occur is that God's performing epistemic miracles for some people and not others would involve injustice on God's part. So even if God does perform obvious epistemic miracles for some people today, the large number of people for whom no obvious miracles (or candidate events) are performed would still constitute an adequate ground for my objection.

My criticism of this understanding of the purpose and location of epistemic miracles is that it implies that the eyewitnesses of the miracles had a decided benefit many other people do not have. For they would have experienced an event designed to enhance the development of faith in them but others would not have. If it would have been unreasonable to expect them to believe that certain events are revelatory without the confirmation provided by an obvious miracle, it is unreasonable to expect other people to believe that the events are revelatory unless they see miracles confirming the revelatory status of those events or have grounds as strong as the eyewitnesses had to believe that the miraculous events occurred as described. In order for others to have equally strong grounds, either they would have to see events that are as clearly miraculous and that confirm a message endorsing the earlier events or they would have to have extremely well-documented eyewitness accounts of the events that the eyewitnesses saw. (The documentation would have to be extremely strong because the events are contrary to laws of nature. Even those who believe that miracles occur usually agree that stronger evidence is needed to justify belief in their occurrence than would be needed for non-miraculous events.) Alternatively, they could observe miraculous events that made no reference to the earlier events but that conveyed to them a content or message equivalent to that of the earlier events. This would not confirm the revelatory status of the earlier events, but it would be a way of treating them no worse than the eyewitnesses of the earlier events. For God to fail to provide other people with some such grounds is for God to treat those people unjustly: God gave the eyewitnesses an epistemic advantage denied to other (potential) believers.

To the claim that performing epistemic miracles for some people and not for others is unjust, it might be objected that not every giving of an epistemic advantage entails injustice. I may tell a secret to one person and not to another without being unjust to the other. This is true in some cases, but not when the secret concerns a matter about which the people have an equal, very great need for the information and there are no grounds for me to treat the first differently from the second, particularly if I claim to love them both. And Christians typically hold that what was revealed in (or confirmed by) epistemic miracles is very important for a person's knowledge of God and faith relation to God, which are matters of the greatest import for everyone. But, an objector might continue, even if both people do desperately need the information, telling something to one person and not to another need not entail injustice if I know that the second person will soon come to believe or at least hear what I told the first without my telling her. This is also true, but we are speaking of matters many people never hear about. Moreover, the objector's suggestion overlooks something crucial: the difference under discussion is not just between those who are told something and those who are not; it is between those who are told something accompanied by a miracle and those who, if they hear it at all, do not receive an accompanying miracle or equivalently clear divine confirmation. Perhaps an important reason why many hear without believing is that they do not have the clear confirmation given by an epistemic miracle; in any event, if the religious message to some people is accompanied by obvious miracles and to others it is not, the latter have been placed at a disadvantage. The fact that some people do come to faith without epistemic miracles is irrelevant to the question of whether it is just for God to perform obvious epistemic miracles that some people can experience and not do so for others. Thus, none of the objections considered in this paragraph provides a way to save God from the charge of injustice in giving certain people an epistemic advantage.

Sometimes it is said that though later potential believers lack the advantage of experiencing epistemic miracles, they have a different, compensating advantage: they have seen the spread of the Church. (As we saw in the previous chapter, the widespread acceptance of Christianity is cited by Morris and Pascal as evidence that Christianity is true.) The spread of the Church is alleged to be confirmation of the truth of its proclamation. But it would provide no confirmation for potential believers at times and places at which the Church is not known to have spread, such during the second century and in those mission fields where the potential believers are not acquainted with facts about the growth of the Church. Thus, in relation to these potential believers even if not in relation to us, the growth of the Church would not provide an alternative to miracles as grounds to consider the Christian proclamation true.

Moreover, sociologists and psychologists can provide a wide variety of other reasons for the growth of various religious groups including the Christian community. These reasons involve such things as the power of deeply held beliefs to influence one's own behavior and the beliefs of others, tribal and national loyalties, financial considerations, and the example of esteemed others. I do not know of any way to show that such reasons do (nor that they do not) completely explain the growth of the Christian community. But such reasons do provide grounds to doubt the claim that the growth of the Church provides rational confirmation of the truth of its proclamation, and they probably make it not irrational to believe that the growth of the Church can be explained without assuming the truth of its doctrines. Thus, even for those who know about it, the growth of the Church is not a confirmation of the truth of Christianity equivalent to that provided by obvious miracles.

But perhaps it is wrong to construe the purpose of miracles as being the provision of rational grounds to believe that a revelation occurred; it might be claimed that the intended force of miracles is emotional or psychological rather than rational.[8] That is, perhaps (contrary to most Christian claims) miracles occurred not in order to rationally certify the revelation, but in order to provide a powerful, though ultimately non-rational, inducement to accept something as revelation. This alternative, however, fares no better than the previous one. If God could not expect many (any?) eyewitnesses of a prophet or Jesus to accept the revelation without the motivation provided by a miracle, then why should God expect anyone today to do so without similar motivation? Again, the suggestion that the success of the Christian community provides an alternative motivation fails for the same reasons as it failed earlier in relation to the thesis that miracles are intended to provide rational confirmation for the revelation.

We should not be surprised that the problems with saying that miracles are intended to provide rational grounds for accepting a revelation also occur when it is said that miracles are intended to provide a psychological, but non-rational, inducement to accept the revelation. For those problems have to do not with the adequacy of miracles as rational grounds (or as emotional inducement), but with what I claim is the injustice of God's providing some people and not other people with these grounds or causes. Thus, the problems would hold no matter how miracles are said to promote acceptance of the revelation.

I conclude that if miracles are intended to play any role in rationally grounding faith or in inducing one to have faith, then potential believers who observe the miracles are in a favored position in relation to other potential believers. Therefore, I hold that God has treated some people unjustly unless for all people (1) God causes events whose status as miracles is equally clear, or (2) God gives grounds for believing that the miracles occurred that are as strong as those possessed by the original eyewitnesses. I take it that there is universal agreement that condition 1 is not met; I also take it that later believers do not have grounds to believe that miracles have occurred that are as strong as those of the eyewitnesses. While there is disagreement about how strong the evidence provided by the Bible is, no one would contend that it is as strong as that which the eyewitnesses had.

Perhaps it will be objected that no evidence about the occurrence of an event could be as strong as that provided by eyewitness observation, so God could not possibly provide later potential believers with evidence as strong as that provided to eyewitnesses. But this will not save God from the charge of injustice, for if it is so, then God should have continued to perform obvious miracles. If God did not do so, at least God could have made the documentary evidence regarding the occurrence of the event strong enough that obvious historiographical objections would be precluded. For example, God could have caused there to be eyewitness accounts written immediately after the alleged events, perhaps even accounts by hostile witnesses, such as Pharaoh for the events in Moses' time and the Jewish leaders for events in Jesus' time. If God caused miracles for the sake of potential believers at the time of the revelations, then God could and should have done more for later potential believers. If God did not do more, then God seems guilty of injustice.

This concludes my discussion of the theory that God performs epistemic miracles for only certain people. I have argued that this theory puts the eyewitnesses of the miracles in a greatly favored position. My argument is not a challenge to claims that accomplishing some divine purpose requires supernatural intervention, such as the claim that the Atonement requires the Incarnation. Even if these claims are true, the divine interventions need not be manifested in or accompanied by an obvious miracle. For example, God could have become incarnate or resurrected Christ without doing anything that would be perceived as miraculous – no one had to see the risen Christ. How humans could know or make justified claims about such divine actions apart from some obvious miracle is another question. My point is simply that God could have done what is alleged to be necessary, say, to satisfy divine justice or to resurrect Christ without an obvious miracle. But if God is alleged to have embedded the divine intervention in, or accompanied it with, an obvious miracle, then my argument would apply to this aspect of God's action.

Note too that I have not argued that it is unjust for God to make certain events revelatory even though only certain people can directly experience those events. Rather, my argument is that (1) accompanying these events with obvious, often dramatic miracles (or having such miracles as constituents of revelatory events) for the purpose of rationally certifying them or inducing faith puts the eyewitnesses in a specially favored position, (2) putting people in such a position is unjust to others unless God performs equally clear miracles for later potential believers or gives them something of equal evidential or motivational value, and (3) God has done neither.

But can I avoid implying that God is unjust if I admit that particular events experienced by only certain people are revelatory? Whether or not I can avoid it depends on God's role in the revelatory events. So that they do not fall under the strictures of my argument about miracles, we will have to assume that the revelatory events neither are themselves miracles nor are confirmed by miracles. Then their occurrence is the result of natural processes, yet somehow they also manifest God. Why? If our theory is that God's being manifested depends on an additional divine activity of some sort in relation to this event that God does not exercise in relation to other qualitatively similar events, then this understanding would seem to imply that God is unjust. On the other hand, suppose our theory is that whenever events in which God did nothing qualitatively different from what God does in relation to other events have certain properties, God is manifest in them. (In Chapter 8 I will describe one way this might occur.) This theory would not involve God's being unjust, for it would not involve God's doing anything to treat some people differently from others who are qualitatively similar.

But it might be objected that even this latter theory suggests a kind of injustice, for not everyone has heard about these revelatory events, so some people are specially privileged. But the fact that some people have not heard about these revelatory events would show that God is unjust only if the fact that some people had heard and others had not heard depended on some divine initiative in which God treats qualitatively similar people differently, and there is no reason to think that there has been such an initiative. That some people have access to these revelatory events and others do not is the result of the normal operation of creaturely processes. Nevertheless, it might be objected, some people have access to saving divine revelation, and others do not. This situation may not be the result of injustice in the sense defined in this chapter, but it still does not seem right in some important sense. I sympathize with the sentiment underlying this objection. But it seems not right only if others do not have access to some saving divine revelation, not necessarily the one recognized by Christians. Whether or not they have is disputed, and we cannot pursue the issue here. But enough has been said to distinguish my thesis about miracles from the issue raised by the claim that revelation is given in historical events.

Practical Miracles

Practical miracles is my term for miracles that are intended to confer some benefit not directly related to the knowledge of God or faith in God. The benefit could be such things as healing, preserving lives, or meeting other human needs and desires.

Since these actions need not have any epistemic purpose, their being miracles need not be obvious to anyone. However, as with epistemic miracles, the claim that God performs such miracles implies that God is unjust, for God is conferring benefits on some people that God does not confer on other similar people in similar circumstances. I want to consider two possible lines of response to this problem with claiming that God performs practical miracles.

The first response is that there is no injustice because there are no benefits given in miracles to one person that are not given to others. Taken at face value, this claim seems just plain false. As we noted earlier, for everyone on whom it is claimed that God bestowed benefits through a miracle, there are apparently similar people in similar situations on whom no similar benefit is bestowed, either in a miracle or in the ordinary course of events. Not everyone who is terminally ill unexpectedly recovers, not everyone who is hungry receives food (or the means to obtain food), and not everyone in a life-threatening situation survives.

So perhaps it will be claimed not that similar benefits are given, but that appropriate benefits are given. One terminally ill person is miraculously healed; another very similar person is not healed because God knows that she would suffer even more or she would become wicked if she were healed. Thus, God is doing for each what is most beneficial for each. Because this response makes claims about humanly unknowable hypotheticals, I do not think there is any way to conclusively disprove it, but certain considerations make it extremely implausible. With regard to the claim that the person would suffer even more if she were healed, I reply that we know of too many cases in which human lives are shattered by some natural or moral evil to think it likely that the most loving thing for God to do in most situations of this sort is to let the creaturely world run its course in these cases without divine intervention.[9] For example, a baby suffers from some disease that leaves it permanently in a vegetative state, or suffers from some abuse that leaves it severely brain-damaged and physically crippled. Such tragedies may well leave the baby without the capacity ever to develop a genuinely human spirituality. And it surely is not true that in all such cases the child develops in some way that is more wonderful than any of the ways the child would likely have developed if it had not suffered from the disease or abuse; nor is it always (or even nearly always) the case that humans around the abused child respond in loving ways and grow spiritually to a degree unlikely without the tragedy. Sometimes such things happen, but far from always. (Even if they did, if this were the reason why God did not miraculously heal the child, the victimization objection could be raised.)

The appearance of injustice is only strengthened if God sometimes intervenes miraculously in response to prayer, as some people believe. The problem again is that it appears that God sometimes does so and sometimes does not do so in situations that are apparently similar. That these are situations involving a request by one whom God loves only compounds the problem, for it is not loving to refuse the reasonable requests of someone whom one loves. But what if the requests are not reasonable? Then God should not have granted the requests in other similar situations. If the cases are similar, it is hard to see that one request is reasonable and another is not.

At this point the second line of response might be advanced: it might be claimed that cases that appear similar to us might not be similar. Two people might utter the same words in a prayer, but one mean them and the other not. And two outcomes might not appear similar to us but might be similar in their significance in the lives of those in whom they occur. I freely grant that we may sometimes be in error in our judgments about similarities. The question is whether it is likely that we are wrong about similarities in every case in which it appears that similar prayers are responded to in very dissimilar ways. Moreover, recovering and not recovering from an illness appear so dissimilar that the lives and personalities of the people involved would have to be very different for these outcomes to be similar. So I find it implausible to think that we are often wrong, and extremely implausible to think that we are always wrong, in our judgments about similarities on these matters.

Suppose, however, it is suggested not that we are usually wrong in our judgments of similarities that we can discern, but that there is some other underlying consistency that we do not discern but that some day (say, in heaven) we will understand. We have no evidence that there is such an underlying consistency, though I know of no way to give a conclusive proof that there is not. But there is a moral argument against this suggestion, too. For it would seriously handicap believers if God were to leave them ignorant of the principles of God's actions in matters that so deeply affect both them and others in the world in which they are to conform to God's will. If there is some unknown characteristic of people or unknown kind of situation because of which God will do something miraculous, then for believers not to know this makes it impossible for them to act appropriately (to acquire the characteristic or to bring about the situation). Thus God should inform people if there are unknown important conditions on how God treats them. It might be replied that God does not inform us of the reason why God intervenes miraculously to help some people and not others because the reason is too complex for us to understand. We will consider this possibility in the final section of this chapter.

Miracles and Religious Ambiguity

There is one other line of defense that might be offered by those who claim that God has performed some miracles, either epistemic or practical. A person might argue that only in what John Hick has termed a "religiously ambiguous" context can people choose freely whether or not to serve God. In such a context suffering must be more or less randomly distributed; in a world in which certain human qualities are regularly connected with miraculous divine interventions, many people would be motivated to turn to God by desire for those benefits rather than by genuine love for God. Because people's freely turning to God out of love is an overriding value, providing the context needed to make this possible is also of great value. Since the existence of a regular connection between certain creaturely qualities and miraculous divine actions would be inconsistent with that value, God should not provide it. Therefore, either miracles must occur in what seems to be a random fashion, or they should not occur at all.

In the previous chapter, I argued that there are no good reasons for the sort of religious ambiguity that this response presupposes. But even if, for the sake of argument, we grant the claim about the sort of context required for a free human response to God, why should God perform any miracles? Many people do come to faith apart from miracles, and many people (at least seem to) go through life without any direct benefit from practical miracles. Why should God perform miracles for anyone? We have looked at the reasons that have been proposed and found them inadequate. To suggest that God might have good reasons that we do not know is an appeal to our possible ignorance; it can never be decisively refuted, but several points in this chapter make it implausible. First, if the context of religious ambiguity is to be maintained, any miracle God performs cannot be an obvious one. If defenders of miracles appeal to religious ambiguity as necessary to achieving a good of overriding value, they would be guilty of a serious inconsistency if they affirm that God performs obvious miracles for anyone. What about inferred miracles? These are not obvious miracles, so they would not necessarily destroy the religious ambiguity of the context. But why should God miraculously intervene? If two people are in qualitatively similar situations, there would be no relevant difference in their situations on the basis of which God might decide to miraculously benefit one rather than the other.

It might be objected that my line of argument in the previous paragraph assumes that people's possessing certain qualities is a sufficient condition for God to help them. Instead, it might be claimed that people's possessing certain qualities provides a reason for God to help some people, but God does not help all with such qualities (perhaps to help preserve religious ambiguity). But then the decision about whom to help among those who possess that quality is arbitrary. For either there are sufficient reasons, or the decision about whom to help among the group in question is arbitrary. It is true that humans decide to help some and not to help others who are equally needy, yet we do not usually call such decisions arbitrary. But humans must make a choice because their resources are limited; if they had the resources, presumably they would help everyone. God does not face this limitation. God's reason for limiting those whom God helps is supposedly the maintenance of a religiously ambiguous context. If that is so important, then why should God miraculously help anyone?

Perhaps it will be replied that God arbitrarily chooses some people to help in order to provide a revelatory foretaste of the future overcoming of the evils that afflict people. But this suggestion attributes to God the motive not of helping the particular people aided but of using the help to reveal (something about) God. However, we have already seen that on the assumption of the importance of religious ambiguity, this revelation cannot involve obvious miracles, so it must be possible to discern God even in events that do not involve obvious miracles. So God's helping people by non-obvious miracles seems unnecessary; it involves arbitrarily choosing people to receive a miraculous benefit that is not necessary for any known purpose of God. They certainly are not needed as an evidential basis for faith, for people come to faith without this basis. And if they are said to be necessary for certain people to come to faith, then if God performs a miracle for them in order to bring them to faith, God is being unjust unless God performs a miracle for everyone whom a miracle would bring to faith. The claim that God performs a miracle for every such person implies that all persons who do not become people of faith would not become people of faith even if God performed a miracle for them. This seems to me highly implausible, despite the statement attributed to Abraham in the parable of the rich man and Lazarus (Lk. 16:31).

Conclusion

The discussion in this chapter reveals serious problems with the claim that God has performed miracles in something like the fashion many traditional Christian theists believe that God has. Most people never claim to experience any obvious miracle or candidate event. Practical miracles, if they occur, seem to benefit some people arbitrarily. The injustice in the pattern of both types of alleged miracles and the lack of any obvious miracles for which there is good evidence widely available constitute at least prima facie reasons to conclude that no miracles occur. Given these problems, what reasons are there to think that any miracles have occurred?

It might be suggested that it has been revealed that miracles occurred. But what reason do we have to accept something as a revealed truth? Traditionally miracles have been supposed to provide this basis. Thus, we seem to be caught in a vicious circle: we need clear miracles to confirm the revelation, but the suggestion we are now considering is that we need the revelation to identify the miracles. Even if traditional theists are right about miracles and revelation, the vicious circle prevents either from providing good support for the other.

But even if all the proposed supports for the belief that God performs miracles are inadequate, the defender of miracles always has this as a fall-back position: God chooses people to receive miraculous benefits for reasons known to God and not to us humans, or God chooses people arbitrarily because doing so makes possible the achieving of some divine goals unknown to us. This response is an instance of what I term the ignorance defense. Like all instances of this defense, it gives no reason to think that various claims about God are true; it argues merely that our inability to solve some difficulties in relation to these claims is not a sufficient reason to doubt them. The adequacy of this defense in relation to all the problems of evil is the topic of the next chapter.

Notes

1. In ancient and medieval times, because of differences in the way the order of nature was understood, people would have expressed this point in terms of exceeding the natural powers of the creatures involved in the event. But however the point is expressed, the idea is conveyed that something occurred that is impossible given the way the universe and the creatures that comprise it normally operate.
2. The nearest terms in the New Testament are "sign," "wonder," and "mighty deed" (in Greek, *semeia*, *teras*, and *dynamis*, respectively). Each of these terms refers to an event, often unexpected and/or wonderful, in which God is (believed to be) manifested without implying that the event necessarily involves a suspension of laws of nature as we understand them today (or something that exceeds the powers of the creatures involved). However, some of the events to which they refer, if certain details happened

as they are described, have aspects that involve such suspensions. The information about New Testament concepts is taken from Bernard W. Anderson, "Signs and Wonders," *Interpreter's Dictionary of the Bible*, ed. George Buttrick et al. (New York: Abingdon Press, 1962), vol. IV, pp. 348–51.

3. The requirement that a miracle must involve a temporary suspension of some law of nature, which is typical in philosophical discussions of the concept, is central to the problem I am discussing in this chapter: a miracle in this sense implies a type of divine activity qualitatively different from the sort of divine activity present in most events. I will argue that such activity, in the sort of patterns in which miracles are claimed to occur, would constitute a kind of injustice by God. My criticism would not apply if *miracle* is understood to be simply an event in which God is manifest (or more weakly, God is taken to be manifest) but in which God does not suspend any laws of nature.

4. Of course, the attribution of any of these properties is relative to the beliefs of the attributer. If an event did involve a suspension of some law of nature, an observer ignorant of the law and of the sorts of processes that occur in accordance with it would not recognize that the event involves a suspension of a law of nature and might not find the event unexpected. Likewise, an observer who does not see the purpose of the event as good would not attribute it to God. This is presumably why the Pharisees in the New Testament are represented as saying of certain wondrous deeds allegedly done by Jesus that they were done by the power of Beelzebub.

5. Of course, no such inference need be made if one means by 'miracle' simply an unexpected event that a person interprets as manifesting God, but that need not involve any suspension of a law of nature. Not even an atheist need deny that miracles in this sense occur.

6. I will not continue to mention this alternative explicitly, but I intend it to apply in the following discussion.

7. Various important Christian authors have claimed that God causes miracles for this purpose. For example, Thomas Aquinas says that God does miracles "for the profit of mankind" in two ways: "one for the confirmation of the truth preached, another to demonstrate the holiness of someone whom God wishes to propose to men as an example of virtuous living" (*Summa Theologiae* [New York: McGraw-Hill, 1964–], 2a2ae, q. 178, art. 2). John Calvin says that miracles are done in order to confirm the divine authority of certain people and the divinity of Christ (*Institutes of the Christian Religion*, ed. John T. McNeill, trans. Ford Lewis Battles [Philadelphia: The Westminster Press, 1960], I, viii, 5). He also says that they are sometimes done to strengthen the faith of some people (ibid., IV, xiv, 18). According to Richard Swinburne, one very important reason for accepting an alleged prophet as genuine and the prophet's message as a revelation from God is that the giving of the message is accompanied by miracles and that the prophet accurately predicts events whose occurrence requires a miracle (*Faith and Reason* [New York: Oxford University Press, 1983], pp. 185, 189f. Though Swinburne does not think that these are the only reasons for accepting the prophet and the message, he does think they are very important in the overall case for such acceptance. (The other reasons are given on pp. 183f.). But only the ways that involve miracles could give one reason to think that the prophet has knowledge of matters beyond ordinary human ken.

8. I know of no one who has proposed this theory, but it seems to me to be a possible line of response that I want to evaluate. Moreover, a defense for this theory might be constructed by reflecting on the fact that some people label as miracles events of the sort I termed inferred miracles. It seems that in deciding what events to label with this term, the psychological impact of the event on the observer and the observer's feelings about the event play an important role.

9. It is important to note that I am discussing a view that claims that God does sometimes intervene to perform practical miracles. The comments that follow in the text would not apply to a view that says that God absolutely never works practical miracles, for then there would be no injustice to anyone arising from an unjust distribution of practical miracles. But there would also be no true claims that God works practical miracles.

CHAPTER 5

The Ignorance Defense

In Chapters 2–4 we discussed ways in which (I claim) the world is not as we should expect it to be if traditional Christian theism is true, and we evaluated explanations that have been or might be offered by traditional Christian theists to explain this discrepancy. In this chapter I want to discuss another way in which some traditional Christian theists have tried to deal with this discrepancy: by arguing that because humans lack knowledge and wisdom that God has, we should not expect to be able to understand why God permits (or perhaps even in some cases causes) many of the apparently evil events that occur. Because this sort of response to the problem of evil is built on our lack of knowledge, I term it the *ignorance defense*. Though this argument has been developed primarily in relation to the first problem of evil (suffering and human wickedness), there seems no reason in principle why it could not be deployed in relation to the other problems of evil as well. Therefore, I will assess it in relation to all three problems, though most of the presentations of the argument will focus on suffering and human wickedness.

Rowe's Argument

Though this line of response to the problem of evil is quite old,[1] the last twenty or so years have seen a large increase in the attention directed toward it in the literature of the philosophy of religion. One important impetus for this increased attention is an article by William Rowe entitled "The Problem of Evil and Some Varieties of Atheism," first published in 1979.[2] In that paper Rowe presents the following argument:

1. There exist instances of intense suffering which an omnipotent, omniscient being could have prevented without thereby losing some greater good or permitting some evil equally bad or worse.
2. An omniscient, wholly good being would prevent the occurrence of any intense suffering it could, unless it could not do so without thereby losing some greater good or permitting some evil equally bad or worse.

---

3. There does not exist an omnipotent, omniscient, wholly good being.(127–8)

Rowe's article generated considerable discussion in the form of criticism, defense, and refinement of the argument. Though some of the discussion might be interpreted as a response to the second premise of the argument,[3] our concern in this chapter will be with issues that grew out of responses to the first premise.

In his discussion of premise 1, Rowe concedes that he does not *know* it to be true, nor can he conclusively prove it is true. But he claims that it is rational to believe that premise 1 is true, and he presents arguments in support of the rationality of that belief. To do so, he introduces, as an example, a fawn in a forest fire caused by lightning: the "fawn is trapped, horribly burned, and lies in terrible agony for several days before death relieves its suffering. So far as we can see, the fawn's suffering is pointless" (129–30). An omnipotent, omniscient, all-good being could have prevented or alleviated the fawn's suffering, and it does not appear that such action would have prevented any greater good or necessitated any evil at least equally as great. Our inability to see any greater good or any equally great evil does not prove that there is none, but it makes it rational for us to believe it. Moreover, this fawn's suffering is only one instance of a vast number of cases of apparently pointless suffering that afflict humans and animals. Even if there is some apparently pointless suffering that, despite appearances, is not truly pointless, it is surely rational to believe that at least some of the apparently pointless suffering is truly pointless. In a footnote, Rowe points out that even much of the suffering that is "related to greater goods (or the absence of equal or greater evils) does not, in many cases, seem so intimately related as to require its permission by an omnipotent being bent on securing those goods (the absence of those evils)" (132, n. 5). He gives no examples, but I presume that the suffering involved in surgical procedures to cure or alleviate diseases and injuries would serve as examples.

In the years since Rowe's paper appeared, little attention has been given to the second premise, but many articles have appeared discussing premise 1. These articles, however, do not attempt to show that premise 1 is false. Instead, they argue that Rowe's argument gives us no good reason to accept his conclusion because we have no good reason to accept his first premise. Theists who make this argument can rely on other grounds for their belief that traditional theism is true. If these other grounds are adequate, all they need to do in relation to Rowe's argument is to show that it does not provide good grounds to undermine their belief that traditional theism is true. In this chapter, we will discuss and evaluate some of the most important ways in which theists have attempted to show that we have no good reason to accept Rowe's first premise.

Wykstra's Ignorance Defense

One important line of criticism of Rowe's first premise is exemplified in some articles by Stephen J. Wykstra focusing on the issue of when one is entitled to make a claim about the way things epistemically appear to one. Wykstra first raised this criticism in an article entitled "The Humean Obstacle to Evidential Arguments from Suffering: On Avoiding the Evils of 'Appearance.'"[4] He defends what he proposes as a necessary (not sufficient) condition "for one's being entitled, on the basis of some cognized situation s, to claim, 'it appears that p'" (152). This condition, which he calls "'the Condition of Reasonable Epistemic Access', or – for short – CORNEA," he states as follows:

> On the basis of cognized situation s, human H is entitled to claim 'It appears that p' only if it is reasonable for H to believe that, given her cognitive faculties and the use she has made of them, if p were not the case, s would likely be different in some way discernible by her. (152)

Applying CORNEA to Rowe's fawn example, he asks this question: if there were an outweighing good that justifies God's allowing the fawn to suffer, "how likely is it that this should be apparent to us" (155)? To answer it, he points out that God's knowledge and wisdom are much greater than ours. "How much greater? A modest proposal is that his wisdom is to ours, roughly as an adult human's is to a one-month old human's" (155).

However, Wykstra's comparison may be both too weak and too strong. It may be the former because it probably understates the gap in content between God's knowledge and wisdom, on the one hand, and our human knowledge and wisdom, on the other. But in another sense it is also too strong. Adult humans have reached a level of mental functioning that makes them capable of rational thought and speech. They can understand and use the concepts of justifying goods and of goods beyond their ken. They can be told of such goods and, if given adequate grounds, come to justifiedly believe that they exist even if they cannot conceive them concretely. For this reason, a more apt analogy for this aspect of the comparison of human and divine knowledge might be a four-year-old child who has some early-stage cancer and is told by his parents that part of his body is sick though he does not yet feel bad, and that doctors will put him to sleep and fix the sick part. Therefore, he will be sore and have to stay in bed for a while, but this will fix the sick part of his body, and he will be well. Such a child would not be able to conceive of cancer and of the consequences of not treating it, but he can be told and understand that the suffering he will have to undergo is necessary to making him better. Loving parents would not put their child through this sort of surgery without at least this sort of an explanation and without also giving the child extra parental love and support while the child is suffering. If the child is confident of the parent's love and wisdom, this explanation would comfort and reassure him, and the extra parental love and support would help him bear the suffering. But millions of people suffer without feeling any (to say nothing of extra) divine love and support,[5] and none of us have been given for the suffering an explanation that is clearly from God. Surely we adult humans are capable of at least hearing and understanding some explanation of why God permits us to suffer, but we have not been given it in any clear way. That is, we do not have an explanation that tells us this and is clearly from, or certified by, God.

Some theists have suggested various explanations for suffering, but all we have are their suggestions, all predicated on the assumption that traditional theism is correct and that they have drawn at least possibly correct inferences from it about suffering. How strong the grounds are for the assumption that traditional theism is correct we will explore in Chapters 6–7. But we certainly do not have any message that is *clearly* from God on this matter, nor have any Christian traditional theists claimed that God revealed why God permits suffering. At this point we will simply note that even if there are justifying reasons beyond our ken, there seems to be no reason to think that God could not have told us that there are in such a way as to give us good grounds to believe it, and most people suffer without feeling any special divine comfort.

Rowe and Wykstra: Another Round

Among the various responses Rowe's paper evoked, he singled out Wykstra's as especially important and worthy of a reply.[6] In his reply, Rowe focuses on this question: does the greatness of God's knowledge and wisdom in comparison to ours justify the belief that we should often expect to be unable to discern the goods that justify God's allowing evil? He argues that the answer is negative.

Rowe claims that the reasonable assumption that God (if God exists) grasps goods beyond our ken prior to their occurrence gives us "no reason to suppose either that the greater goods in virtue of which he permits most sufferings are goods that come into existence far in the future of the sufferings we are aware of, or that once they do obtain we continue to be ignorant of them and their relation to the sufferings" (164–5). Rowe does concede that if the goods are in the distant future, then we should expect that much of the suffering in the world would appear to us to be pointless. However, he argues that the claim that many of the justifying goods are in the far future is not implicit in what I termed traditional theism itself, but is an additional claim, which would therefore need independent justification (166–7).

This reply by Rowe did not go unanswered, and it will be instructive to pursue this exchange one step further. In a response to Rowe, Wykstra says[7] that the claim that many of the justifying goods are in the far future is reasonable for us to believe on grounds "which we know independently of H [traditional theism]" (140). He points out "that humans cannot see, by unaided powers, what life will be like N years from now" (142–3). If the God-purposed goods that justify suffering are farther than that in the future, it would not be surprising that we would not see them when the suffering occurs. He adds that because moral freedom is difficult to understand, it may be difficult for us to see what its exercise "requires in the way of God's permitting moral evils" (149, n. 20).

How plausible is Wykstra's main suggestion that the goods are beyond our ken because they are too far in the future? Wykstra does not indicate whether he thinks that for each evil there is some justifying good or he thinks that there are kinds of goods for various kinds of evil, but no one-to-one correlation between particular evils and particular goods. We shall consider first the possibility that he means a one-to-one correlation.[8]

Wykstra makes the undeniable suggestion that by our own powers we cannot see what human life will be like N years from now. If we are talking about life today, I have no doubt that he is correct, even if N is some small number (say 30). Did anyone, thirty years ago, see the role that computers would play in human life (at least in the developed world), or the collapse of the Soviet Union and its consequences, to name only two important matters? Perhaps some far-sighted people foresaw the outlines of one or both of these events, but others did not, and the predictions of the far-sighted ones were no more than speculative guesses. Presumably Wykstra would argue that if thirty years ago God had permitted some evil for the sake of some good that lay more than thirty years in the future, we would not have been able to see any justifying good when the evil occurred. But for God to do this, God must be able to know what human life will be like that far in the future. How likely is this?

I suspect that Wykstra assumes that God can see what human life will be like at any time in the future, for he draws an analogy between God and very intelligent parents, who can grasp goods in the far future for their child. However, as we saw in Chapter 2, not all traditional theists agree that God knows all the details of the future actions of free agents. If God does not know exactly what will happen in the future, how much better knowledge of the future than humans have is it reasonable to think that God has? On the assumptions of this form of theism, God does have a complete knowledge of the mind and character of every human being and of the ways human beings interact, as well as complete knowledge of the laws and operations of the non-human natural world. However, I do not think that even knowing these things perfectly will help much in knowing what human life will be like in the future. Consider the things that God does not, indeed can not, know on this theory. God does not know who will be born and exactly when any person will die. For who is born depends on the sexual activity of humans, and these are free choices. And exactly when a person will die depends on when there occur causes sufficient for that person's death, and these often depend on the free actions of people. Of course, God will presumably have a better idea of the probabilities of various events in the next few minutes than humans do, but this does not provide a reliable basis for predictions about conditions several years in the future because those predictions would involve multiplying many probabilities, each of which is less than one. For example, try to imagine what the Computer Age would be like if both Bill Gates and Steve Jobs had been killed in freak auto accidents before they launched Microsoft and Apple, respectively. Though we would certainly be in the Computer Age, I suspect that there would be great differences from the way it is today. I have pointed out that, according to the type of theism we are considering, God could not foreknow that these men would not die early in their careers, so God could not foreknow that the Computer Age would be as it is.

If not even God knows what human life will be like some years in the future, then it would seem that God might not be justified in permitting a particular evil (whose present occurrence is certain) for the sake of a particular future good (whose occurrence is at most only probable to some degree). The uncertainty about the future even for God complicates considerably the attempt to claim that we do not see the justifying goods because they are too far in the future. We have seen that one reason it complicates the attempt is that not even God can be certain that the justifying good will occur. It complicates for another reason as well: if the future is uncertain even for God, then not even God can be certain that the good will not occur even if the evil is not permitted, for some other conditions might occur that bring it about. These two complications assume that the justifying good is one that creaturely factors can and must bring about. If the good were one that God could bring about just by willing it, then the earlier evil would be unnecessary. If the good were one that only God could bring about, then the earlier evil would be useless in bringing about the good.

The foregoing criticism assumes that Wykstra is interested in providing reasons why we would not see future goods that justify God's permitting evil events if the goods are thought to be correlated one-to-one with particular evil events. But perhaps Wykstra is thinking of providing reasons why we would not see justifying goods if certain *kinds* of goods were thought to justify certain *kinds* of evils, without there being a one-to-one correlation. For example, it might be thought that there are certain goods that justify God's permitting people to die, though there are not any particular goods for the sake of which God permits this particular person to die at this particular time. When and how a person dies would presumably be the result of the workings of nature in accordance with natural laws ordained by God and the free actions of whatever creatures have free will.

One immediate problem with this suggestion is that various kinds of evil have been with human beings for millennia. So if there are kinds of goods that lie in the future of these kinds of evils and if humans have not seen them because they are in the future, they must still be in the future. Indeed, given that evils of the kinds in question have been occurring for millennia but the goods are still in the future, the most plausible location for them in Christian belief is at the end of the world (or after death). But if these goods are that far in the future, how likely is it that they will occur? If their occurrence depends on some human activity, there seems to be no way God could be sure they would occur if (as we are assuming) God does not foreknow the free actions of human beings. And if God does not know they will occur, then the uncertainty about achieving them calls into question their suitability as a justification for God's permitting various sorts of evils. Moreover, even if somehow the kinds of goods that would obtain in the future justify the kinds of evils that now occur, one could still wonder whether they justify God's permitting every evil of this type, no matter how great or how severe. For example, perhaps in order to give humans meaningful free will, God has to permit them to do evil to one another. But does this entail that God must permit any human to do any evil to other(s), no matter how great the evil? It does not seem so. If I may adapt Wykstra's parent analogy, good parents will often allow their children to fight among themselves so that they can learn how to settle differences on their own. But good parents also will intervene if they see that one of the children is going to use a gun to resolve differences with the other children. In using this analogy, I do not intend to suggest that God should intervene at the same point (to prevent all murders), but I do want to suggest that a justification for permitting evils of certain types does not necessarily justify God's permitting the worst evils of those types. And as I suggested in Chapter 2, a survey of history seems to show that on many occasions humans have perpetrated evils about as great as were technologically and psychologically possible.

It seems that the only way God could be certain that the (to us unknown) goods would actually obtain at the end of the world is that God intends to bring them about regardless of what particular evils occur or do not occur. (For example, if God were to send Christ back at the end of the world – as many Christians expect – then this would be something God has decided to do, regardless of what particular evils occur or do not occur.) But this will not help anyone wishing to employ a Wykstra-like argument. For if the justifying goods are something God has decided to bring about regardless of what particular evils occur or do not occur, then there is no reason to affirm and good reason to deny that God's permitting the evils is necessary for the goods to obtain.

The foregoing evaluation of Wykstra's argument assumes that we humans do not see the justifying goods because they are in the future. But as we saw, Wykstra acknowledges that there might be other reasons why we do not see the justifying goods. We might not see the goods as goods, or we might not see their connection with the evils. How plausible are these suggestions? Certainly there are goods God knows of that we do not. But since the goods that would justify God's permitting evils among human beings are goods for which God's permitting the evils is a necessary condition, permitting the evils must be logically or causally necessary for the goods. It would seem, therefore, that the goods must be goods for humans or other inhabitants of earth at the time of or in the future of the evils. How likely is it that there are such goods that we are ignorant of?

In light of the magnitude of some evils that have occurred (and presumably God has permitted), the goods must be very great indeed. Might we be ignorant of them? It does not seem impossible. The goods might be something that the culture does not recognize as goods. For example, in a slave-owning culture, God might permit some evil necessary to bring about the ending of slavery. People in the dominant class in the culture would not see this result as a good, so they might be perplexed that God would permit an evil that seemed to produce this result. However, any plausible examples of this sort involve goods that are implicit in some more general good that is recognized by the community, so later generations are likely to recognize the good once it has been achieved. Thus, the goods are unlikely to remain unrecognized.

The goods mentioned in the previous paragraph are goods that are implicit in some goods recognized by the community. Could God know of and act to bring about goods for humans that are not even implicit in the goods for humans that (believers think) God has made known? One problem with this suggestion is that most Christians, including traditional Christian theists, believe that God has made known to humans values and types of behavior that God favors and others that God opposes. If there are other important things in either category that serve as goods to be achieved (or evils to be avoided) for the sake of which God permits various evils, then one wonders why God did not make these known along with the things God allegedly did make known. Not telling humans about these values and behaviors would seem not to serve any useful purpose and would seem to make it more difficult for humans to do what God wishes.

The other possibility is that though we are aware of the goods, we do not see their connection with the evils, so it does not seem to us that there any goods that justify God's permitting the evils. This suggestion faces the problem that the connection can not be very obscure, or not even God could foreknow that permitting the evil would produce this good. For obscure connections involving humans tend to depend heavily on the free actions of humans, and we are assuming that God does not foreknow the free actions of creatures.

Obviously, many of my objections to Wykstra's argument would be undercut if we changed the assumption about God's foreknowledge of the free actions of creatures. If God has middle knowledge, then God could foreknow that permitting some particular evil would result in some particular good that would not obtain without this or some even greater evil.[9] However, we can take note of other problems with Wykstra's argument that obtain regardless of what assumption one makes about divine foreknowledge of the free actions of creatures. His argument gives us no reason why God should not tell us what the goods made possible by the evils are, or at least clearly reassure us that there are such goods. Nor does it give us any reason why God should be hidden in the ways discussed in Chapter 3, and in particular why God's will for human behavior is not clear on many matters. Nor does it give us any reason why God performs miracles in the seemingly arbitrary pattern discussed in Chapter 4.[10]

In response to these objections, people who wish to defend a Wykstra-like position could try ratcheting up the argument. That is, they could admit that leaving us ignorant on these matters is another evil, but they could say that we have no reason to think that we should be able to discern the goods for whose sake God permits this evil any more than we have reason to think we should be able to discern the goods for whose sake God permits other evils. I admit that this is a possible position. Of course, this Wykstra-like move requires the assumption that God has foreknowledge of the future actions of free creatures (in order to avoid the objections I raised earlier assuming that God does not); I regard this assumption as implausible, but I would not claim that it has been shown to be false.

I have two other questions to raise about Wykstra-like arguments. One will be easier to raise after the discussion of some issues in the next section, so we will defer it till then. The other is this: what reasons do their advocates have for the beliefs about God (including the assumption of divine foreknowledge) that motivate them to adopt this position? In particular, what reasons do they have for the assumption that God is omnipotent? I ask this because it is this assumption that underlies the conviction that whatever evils occur are ones that God at least permits. In Chapters 6 and 7 we will consider reasons that have been or might be given for this assumption. Before we do this, we will examine another form that the ignorance defense has taken.

Alston's Ignorance Defense

The responses to Rowe's sort of argument that we have been looking at are built on the overall contrast between the extent of God's knowledge and wisdom, and the extent of human knowledge and wisdom. Another line of response is exemplified in an article by William P. Alston entitled "The Inductive Argument from Evil and the Human Cognitive Condition."[11] He points out that arguments such as Rowe's depend on an implicit negative existential claim: there is no good reason for God to permit this suffering. Alston considers specific reasons for permitting suffering suggested by Christianity, and argues that often we are in no position to judge whether the sufferer meets those conditions. Thus, Alston intends his article to be based on far more specific, and therefore limited, claims about the extent of human ignorance than is Wykstra's.

Alston's article is set up as a response to arguments such as Rowe's, and he discusses Rowe's argument itself. He, like Rowe, suggests that Rowe's first premise would be justified by establishing one or more instantiations of it and using existential generalization. Letting E designate such an instantiation, Alston formulates the general form of any particular instantiation of Rowe's first premise and calls it 1A, which he states as follows:

1A. E is such that an omnipotent, omniscient being could have prevented it without thereby losing some greater good or permitting some evil equally bad or worse. (p. 98)

An evil that meets this condition Alston terms a *gratuitous evil*. His purpose in this article is therefore to argue that because we are ignorant about certain fairly specific matters, we can never be justified in believing that a particular evil is gratuitous. Before setting forth his argument, Alston also makes some comments, one of which merits mention here because of its relevance to concerns in this book. It concerns what he calls *general policy* theodicies. "Consider the idea that God's general policy of, e.g., usually letting nature take its course and not interfering, even when much suffering will ensue, is justified by the overall benefits of the policy" (101). Though intervening in any one case of suffering would not subvert the policy, "it would seem that general policy considerations of the sort mentioned could justify God in refraining from intervening in this case. For if it couldn't, it couldn't justify His nonintervention in any case, and so He would be inhibited from carrying out the general policy" (101). Therefore, he proposes that Rowe's argument be understood to recognize the good of maintaining a general policy. As he puts it: "we can say that E is permitted in order to realize the good of maintaining a beneficial general policy except where there are overriding reasons to make an exception, and the reasons in this case are not overriding" (101). I think that Alston is correct about the legitimacy of general policy considerations, but it also seems to me that there are at least two possible problems for most Christian theists in employing them in the present context. One is the problem of whether the general policy is itself justified. However, it is probably appropriate to reply, as Alston does, that this is a question to which we humans lack the knowledge and wisdom to give a justified answer. The other problem is that many Christians, including many – perhaps most – traditional Christian theists, believe that God has intervened at various times. This is a problem because, as we discussed in Chapter 4, many of the interventions seem designed to alleviate evils or achieve goods of far smaller magnitude than many of the sufferings that occur (and therefore presumably are permitted by God). As we saw in that chapter, the seeming oddness of this pattern either raises questions about God's goodness and wisdom (if God really did intervene as claimed and did not intervene in more serious matters) or suggests that the alleged interventions did not really occur (and thus raises the question of whether God ever intervenes in a miraculous way).

Alston points out that Christians have suggested many reasons why God might permit instances of suffering, and it might well be that there are different reasons for different instances of suffering. Someone wanting to justify a premise such as Rowe's first premise would have to show that it is reasonable to think that none apply. Alston discusses the following possible reasons that have been suggested by Christians: (1) it is punishment, (2) it contributes to soul-making, (3) it humbles us and turns us toward God, (4) it deepens our relation to God, (5) it might have good consequences for onlookers or for sufferers themselves, such as bringing them to repentance, (6) it is a consequence of allowing the exercise of free will, and (7) it is a consequence of a stable natural order. For concreteness, he often refers to one of three cases of suffering: the fawn described by Rowe (call it Bambi), an instance of the rape, beating, and murder of a five-year-old girl by her mother's boyfriend (call her Sue), and "an adult sufferer from a painful and lengthy disease (fill in the details as you like)" (call him Sam).[12] However, even after discussing all these reasons, Alston does not claim that he has shown that "no one could be justified in supposing that God could have no sufficient reason for permitting suffering in the Bambi and Sue cases" (119). So he concludes by pointing out that even if there were some instances of suffering such as these for which we were justified in asserting that none of the reasons considered, either individually or in combination, would justify God in permitting the suffering, we still could not justifiedly claim that some other good of which we were ignorant or some unknown connection with a known good would not justify God in permitting the evil. We are just too limited in the sort of knowledge and abilities we do have to be justified in making such a claim.

At this point Alston is employing a version of the ignorance defense that is more similar to Wykstra's than what Alston said earlier. For he is appealing to unknown goods and/or unknown connections between suffering and known or unknown goods rather than to our inability to determine whether certain situations provide appropriate conditions for God to permit suffering (for example, is Sam's spiritual state such as to merit punishment?) and/or whether certain goods justify God in permitting some instance of suffering (for example, does soul-building justify permitting this suffering?). The mention of connections between suffering and goods also suggests, as Alston points out, that there are conditions for the realization of various goods, and we may be ignorant of these as well as of the goods and connections between the two.[13]

Alston makes an interesting case for the significance of certain particular human cognitive limitations in relation to our ability to make justifiable assertions about whether there is some good or some condition of realization of some good that would justify God's permitting some instance of suffering. I am inclined to think that he is right about each of the reasons he suggests if we consider each instance of suffering individually. That is, if we just look at each instance of suffering, for the reasons he suggests we cannot be confident that many of the possible justifications he suggests do not apply. Thus, on the grounds he has staked out, Alston is right.

However, suppose we shift our perspective and look not at each instance of suffering individually, but instead look at the totality of instances. Then we must realize that those who employ the ignorance defense cannot consistently say that for all they know, any of Alston's suggested reasons might apply to any instance of suffering. For some of Alston's suggestions are inconsistent with other suggestions when they are applied to the totality of instances of suffering. To be specific, it is not possible to use the free will suggestion and the lawful order of nature suggestion unless they are applied to (almost) all instances of suffering when they could possibly apply. Each of these must be adopted as general policies or their alleged value vanishes. If humans are to have free will in order to have the opportunity to develop their characters, then they must have it on at least most occasions when it would be possible to exercise it, and if nature is to operate in accordance with natural laws, then it must do so at least almost all the time. Nature cannot – a logical "cannot" – just occasionally operate in an orderly way, nor would there be much point in allowing humans an occasional exercise of free will (because it is the repeated exercise of free will that is allegedly needed to build and display character). Thus, as Alston himself recognizes, if God uses these two reasons at all, then God must use them in almost all instances when they could apply – that is, God must follow a general policy of respecting them. And if God does follow a general policy of respecting them, then these together might well provide a sufficient reason why God permits at least almost all the instances of suffering that occur. (We assumed this in the theodicy we were using in Chapter 2 as the most plausible theodicy for a traditional Christian theist.)

It is important to note, however, that even if God follows some general policy of permitting evils brought about by the orderly operation of nature or by free creaturely actions, that does not entail that God does so because God values either the orderly operation of nature or free creaturely actions for their own sake (though God may so value them). God may follow these general policies because of some further goods that God knows will be brought about by following them.[14] For example, God may follow the policy of permitting whatever evils occur from the orderly operation of nature because God knows that following this policy will best promote human dependence on God. But that does not entail that in every instance of suffering brought about by the orderly operation of nature, God knows that the occurrence of that evil will promote human dependence on God better than not permitting that particular occurrence would do. In other words, if God follows these general policies, it is possible that types of suffering are permitted in order to achieve types of goods, but that not every particular token of suffering is permitted in order to achieve particular tokens of goods. For example, even if God follows the general policy of allowing free human actions to cause suffering in order to move humans to repent, it might be that God did not permit *Sue* to suffer in order that *these particular* onlookers might be moved to repent; that she would suffer as she did was not foreknown when God designed the system, nor did God decide not to intervene in this instance in order that *these* onlookers might see *Sue* suffer and be moved to repent.

Thus, traditional Christian theists attempting to apply Alston's argument to the range of suffering we know about do not have as many options as Alston seems to give them when he considers each instance of suffering individually. For they cannot consistently invoke the two general policy considerations and make much use of the other suggestions in relation to specific instances of suffering. Either they must use general policy considerations in at least almost all the instances where they could possibly apply or they must never use them. Of course, they might claim that their ignorance is such that they have no good way to choose whether (1) to use the general policy considerations at least most of the time, or (2) never to use them, and use instead reasons that depend on the specific details of the situation (call these specific case reasons). That is, they might claim that they are ignorant of whether God permits most of the evils God permits because God is adhering to certain general policies or because for each of the evils God has some specific case reason.

However, I would disagree with this claim. I do not believe that our ignorance is such that we have no good basis for deciding whether general policy considerations or specific case reasons are the more plausible way of understanding why God permits most instances of evil. Though in relation to an instance of suffering considered individually our ignorance may render us incapable of having a justified confidence that some specific case reasons do not apply (as even Alston acknowledges), we often lack any positive reason for thinking any do apply. However, we have good reason to think that (almost) all instances of suffering that we know of can very plausibly be seen as consequences of nature operating in an orderly fashion and/or of choices by creatures with free will. That all instances of suffering are the result of these two sorts of factors is widely believed by people in our culture, including many Christians, for reasons that are not dependent on religious considerations. And it is assumed by many theodicists who do not use the ignorance defense but rather take God's following these general policies to be the problem to which they must respond. Therefore, in relation to at least almost all instances of suffering and perhaps all instances, we have good reason to think that if there is a God who permits suffering, the immediate reason (though not necessarily the ultimate reason) why God does so is that God follows certain general policies. Our knowledge of the way suffering occurs in the world makes this conclusion far more likely than the conclusion that there is some specific case reason why God permits each instance of suffering.

Nor is it possible for both general policies and specific case reasons to apply to most cases of suffering. To see why, suppose that Sam contracts some painful disease through the ordinary operation of the laws of nature or that Sue suffers as a result of a misuse of free will by some human being; suppose also that neither instance of suffering is such as to justify divine intervention. Then any other reason for God's permitting these particular instances suffering would be superfluous and depend on luck. It would be superfluous because there is already (we are supposing) a sufficient reason for God to permit the suffering. Of course, there could be two or more reasons, each of which would be sufficient alone. However, the applicability of a second reason would depend on luck. Let us see why.

That Sam or Sue is even born depends on chance matters not wholly within God's control if human beings have a free will with whose operation God does not generally interfere. That Sam contracts a particular disease usually would depend on a complex of natural factors and Sam's free choices. Though presumably God ordained the laws of nature, God does not control and cannot predict (if God does not have middle knowledge) exactly what will result as humans make free choices in their natural environment. (And even if God has middle knowledge, it might not be possible for God always to use each instance of suffering for some particular purpose.[15]) Thus, not even God could foreknow that Sam would contract this disease. Therefore, God could not plan to use Sam's suffering from this disease to achieve one of the other goods mentioned by Alston, such as punishing Sam or enhancing his spiritual life. Nor could God be sure that Sue would suffer as she did if her going downstairs when she did and the acts of her mother's boyfriend were acts of free will. If she had encountered her mother's boyfriend when he was less drunk or after he had passed out, she might not have suffered as she did. Or if she had decided not to go downstairs at all and thus never have encountered him, she might not have suffered as she did. Thus, not even God could foreknow that she would suffer in this way. Therefore, God could not plan to use Sue's suffering to achieve one of the specific case goods mentioned by Alston, such as bringing the onlookers to repentance. That either of these people suffered as they did is thus a matter of (bad) luck; to claim that God permitted it to achieve any of these other goods overlooks the (assumed) fact that God had a presumably sufficient reason to permit it: following general policies God had adopted regarding natural laws and human free will. If there are other good consequences in any particular case, this is a matter of luck, since not even God could plan for these consequences to occur.

Thus, the suggestion that God follows a general policy of respecting the lawful order of nature and human free will render otiose any of Alston's other suggestions except as providing possible reasons why God designed a system like the one we have. It would also render otiose any other unknown goods or unknown connections between known or unknown goods and known or unknown conditions necessary for their realization used as specific case reasons. This very important result also applies to Wykstra-like arguments that appeal more generally to the great differences between divine and human knowledge and wisdom. For if one says that God permits suffering because of a general policy of respecting human free will and the lawful operation of nature, then appeals to other goods and/or conditions of realization – known or unknown – are otiose unless one also attributes middle knowledge to God (as perhaps Wykstra does; it is not discussed in his article).

This result is instructive because the way Rowe sets up his argument and the way Wykstra responds to it suggest that both are asking whether some particular good justifies God's permitting particular instances of suffering such as Bambi's and (in later discussions) Sue's. That is, their model is a person deciding whether to permit some specific thing to occur in order to achieve some particular good, such as a person deciding whether to permit surgery to correct some condition. But if, as I have argued, God permits most instances of suffering because God has adopted general policies of permitting the orderly operation of nature and the exercise of creaturely free choice, then there is no particular good envisaged for the sake of which God permits Bambi or Sue or any other particular creature to suffer. Of course, if these presumed policies admit of a few exceptions (as most traditional Christian theists are likely to insist), then the details of each particular case of suffering do enter into God's decision, in that they do not provide an adequate reason for God to make that particular case of suffering an exception to following the general policies. Nevertheless, if the exceptions to following the general policies (logically) must be relatively few, then the details of particular cases and possible particular future goods to be achieved by God's permitting some particular instance of suffering cannot be the primary reason why God permits most instances of suffering.

The foregoing seem to me to be the most important problems with Alston's version of the ignorance defense. He argues that to justify acceptance of Rowe's first premise, the critic must show that none of a variety of possible goods known to Christians and no unknown good and no condition for the realization of goods can justify God's permitting any instance of suffering; this is a task that Alston argues is beyond human abilities. In response, I argued that by far the most plausible version of this approach claims that if God exists and permits evils, God does so in (almost) every instance because God is following the general policies of allowing natural laws and human free actions to operate without interference. If these general policies are followed, then in (almost) all instances of suffering other alleged goods and conditions for their realization, *whether known or unknown*, are irrelevant to justifying God's permitting various instances of suffering; at most they can serve as possible reasons for God to have adopted the general policies. If some do provide such reasons for God to have adopted the general policies, then the relation between suffering permitted and goods envisioned must be on the level of types, not tokens. For if (as we are assuming) God lacks middle knowledge or any other providentially useful sort of foreknowledge, then not even God could know that every instance of suffering resulting from the orderly operation of nature or from human free actions results in a particular token of one of the goods whose achievement is the reason why God adopted the general policy of not intervening.

Thus, on the issue of justifying God's permitting *some particular instance of suffering*, appeals to our ignorance, either our general ignorance compared to God that Wykstra employs or the more specific sorts of ignorance with which Alston begins, are (almost) always irrelevant. However, they are relevant on the issue of our incapacity to evaluate whether God's adopting these general policies is justified. As Alston points out, we are in no position to make a justified evaluation of these presumed policies. We lack knowledge of the data and we lack the capacity to process the data necessary to give a justified evaluation of the policy. Thus, for all we know, God is justified in adopting such a policy (if there is a God who decided to adopt it); but also, for all we know, God is not justified.

This last point is important, for it represents perhaps the most significant difference between the defense we are now discussing and the theodicy considered in Chapter 2, particularly as developed by Hasker.[16] The two are very similar in content. Both assert that God permits suffering because of a divine commitment to the policies of generally respecting the lawful operation of nature and creaturely free will. But they differ in that advocates of the theodicy discussed in Chapter 2 argue that this divine commitment is made for reasons we humans can see to be morally appropriate, but advocates of the defense currently being discussed argue that we humans are not competent to evaluate whether or not such a divine commitment is morally justified. Thus, they must reject the arguments both of the theists who want to use this as a theodicy and of their opponents who claim that these divine commitments are not morally justified. However, the theodicists' case rests on the judgment that God's purpose of enabling humans to develop morally and spiritually not only is a good one, but also is worth the gratuitous evil and victimization that God must permit; advocates of a defense contend that we humans are incompetent to make that judgment. Therefore, advocates of a defense must reject the arguments of the theists who want to use this as a theodicy as well as those of their opponents who claim that these divine commitments are not morally justified. Theirs is an easier case to make than that of their theodicist compatriots. For the latter try to show that we have reason to think that such commitments are morally appropriate, whereas the former try to show only that we have no good reason to think that they are not appropriate. But being in this position of having an easier case to make comes at a cost. That cost is placing a heavier burden on justifying the beliefs about God that generate the problems of evil. For defenses do not attempt to enhance the plausibility of traditional theism; they seek only to show that a particular argument does not lessen (or does not significantly lessen) its plausibility. But then whatever plausibility it has, it must derive entirely from other considerations. In contrast, if a theodicy is plausible, then it contributes to the plausibility of traditional theism.

So at this point we can ask what justification there is for thinking that there is a God who is omnipotent, omniscient, and all-good, and who adopted such a policy. That all (or almost all) instances of suffering are caused by nature operating lawfully and/or the actions of free creatures is something most people (in our culture, at any rate) believe on non-theological grounds. Thus, believing that the world operates this way is consistent with believing that there is such a God who has adopted this policy, but it gives no reason to think that there actually is such a God. Of course, if there is such a God and if nature is generally orderly and creaturely free will usually operates without supernatural interference, then it is plausible to think that God has adopted the policy of respecting these factors. But what justification is there for thinking that there is such a God?

This question becomes all the more urgent when one realizes that if there is a God who (almost) always permits whatever suffering these factors would cause, it is perplexing that God has not plainly told us, so that we do not have to rely on human speculations and arguments on so important a matter. Surely an omniscient God would know that we humans would be very troubled about why God permits so much suffering. This seems to be a particularly difficult question for those theists who believe that God has told us (revealed to us) certain things. Why would God reveal those other things to us and not help us with this issue? Of course, one can make the response that I suggested for Wykstra and that Alston actually gives: God's not telling us why is just another source of suffering (another sort of evil) whose reason we do not understand. One can make this response, but I cannot help wondering when the mixture of things God allegedly revealed to us and things God did not reveal will seem so strange to even traditional Christian theists that they will question whether God has really told us what they allege.

The Other Problems of Evil

We have examined some versions of the ignorance defense in relation to the first problem of evil. One can also use it in relation to the problems of evil discussed in Chapters 3 and 4. In relation to the problem of divine hiddenness, one can say that God has adopted a general policy of being hidden except in certain special circumstances, and that we are not competent to evaluate the wisdom or the moral appropriateness of this policy. In Chapter 3 I argued that none of the reasons for divine hiddenness considered there seems adequate to justify the policy, but an advocate of the ignorance defense could still claim that we are not competent to evaluate this policy. The defender might add that attempts to show that the policy is wise or morally appropriate are as misguided as attempts to show that it is not; both tasks are beyond human competence. This response used in relation to the problem of divine hiddenness comes at the same cost as it did when made in relation to the problem of suffering. That cost is placing an even heavier burden on attempts to justify the belief that there is an omnipotent, omniscient, all-good God who has adopted the general policy of being hidden. Of course, if there is such a God and God is hidden, then it is plausible to think that God has adopted such a policy,[17] but what justification is there for thinking there is such a God?

Moreover, God's being hidden and God's not telling us why God permits the evil that occurs do not seem required as aspects of God's presumed general policies of respecting creaturely free choice and the operation of laws of nature. Divine action to remove uncertainty about these issues would presumably require supernatural intervention, but not so often as to threaten either of these general policies. Thus, those who wish to use the ignorance defense in relation to these two issues have to make the further claim that for all we know, God has some reason for not removing human uncertainty on these issues, and there is no reason to think that we humans are competent to discern or assess that reason. Earlier we saw that some theodicies by traditional Christian theists involve the claim that greater clarity regarding God's existence and will would provide a psychological hindrance to free human choices to ignore or reject God; in response, I argued that these alleged difficulties need not occur, and that there are good grounds to think that God's allowing such lack of clarity about God's existence and will is morally questionable, since it makes informed decision-making by humans about their situation in relation to God very difficult, if not impossible. But even if my earlier arguments against these theodicies are successful, proponents of the ignorance defense could claim that for all we know, God has other reasons we do not discern, reasons sufficiently strong to outweigh the moral difficulties inherent in the fact that God's presumed choice not to remove our uncertainties forces us to make uninformed decisions about whether and how we will relate to God and live our lives.

In Chapter 4 I argued that the pattern of alleged miracles is in tension with the purposes for miracles that believers have alleged and/or with the justice of God that believers affirm. The pattern is inconsistent with a purpose of certifying revelation; and the pattern of helping some people and not helping others who seemingly need or merit help at least as much as the beneficiaries of alleged miracles is in tension with the justice of God. But traditional Christian theists can employ a version of the ignorance defense and claim that for all we know, God might have reasons for performing miracles on the occasions believers allege, and not on other occasions when we might expect them. They might also claim that we should not draw any negative conclusions from our inability to explain why God chose these occasions to perform miracles and did not do so on apparently similar occasions, for there is no reason to think that we are competent to discern the divine reasons. I think they would be correct in making these claims. But the appeal to human ignorance in relation to this problem also comes at a cost. In this case the cost is justifying the claim that there is an omnipotent, omniscient, all-good God who has intervened to perform these miracles. Here the primary question is not whether there is such a God, but whether such miracles have been performed. For if miracles have been performed, then there is at least a supernatural being who can suspend the laws of nature. But how can we justify the claim that miracles have been performed? Typically, Christians have tried to justify such a claim by appeal to alleged revelation or by appeal to the Bible as a reliable record of certain events or by appeal to some contemporary experience of miracles. In Chapter 4 we discussed problems with alleged contemporary miracles. This still leaves for discussion both alleged revelation and appeal to the Bible as a reliable record of certain events often considered to be miracles. These topics will be taken up in the next chapter.

Conclusion

In summary, proponents of the ignorance defense might claim that God follows the general policies of allowing suffering to occur in accordance with the operation of natural laws and with creaturely free choice, and that for all we know, God has adequate reasons for adopting and following these policies. Proponents can also claim that God has reasons for not telling us clearly that and why God has adopted these policies and for not making more clear the divine existence, nature, and will. They can also make this claim in relation to the apparent anomalies in the pattern of miracles God has allegedly performed. But none of these claims give us any reason to think that there is a God of the sort that traditional Christian theists affirm nor that the other claims that they make about this God are true. Proponents of the ignorance defense generally admit this, for (they say) they are merely showing that certain arguments against traditional theism do not succeed because the arguments presume that humans know more than humans do. However, the more stress proponents place on human ignorance, the more they place in question their own positive claims about God. On what basis can they claim to know the things about God that generate the problems of evil; in other words, on what basis can they claim to know (or justifiedly believe) the claims involved in traditional theism and (if used) other religious claims (for example, the claims about the Christian understanding of sin mentioned by Alston, and the claims about an afterlife as a context in which "for all we know" there will be compensations for inequities in this life)?

Thus, the results of this chapter place heavy responsibility on the traditional theist to justify certain claims, especially the claim that there is an omnipotent, omniscient, and all-good God, but also the claim that miracles have been performed in the pattern alleged by many Christians. The need to justify these claims, especially the claim that traditional theism is true, provides the motivation for the next two chapters. The justification could be alleged revelation, or something discoverable by human beings apart from revelation. Therefore, Chapter 6 discusses alleged revelation as a ground for Christian religious claims. The discussion is fairly general, so it applies to a wide range of religious claims about God, including those involved in traditional theism. Chapter 7 looks at grounds other than revelation used to attempt to justify one of the claims involved in traditional theism: that God is omnipotent. Though in principle claims about all three alleged characteristics of God require justification, this is the part of traditional theism that I regard as the most questionable and the one on which I have therefore chosen to focus my attention when I ask about grounds other than revelation for the claims involved in traditional theism.

Notes

1. Even in biblical times, believers who were grieving or perplexed about evil events were told that God's ways were higher than their ways, that God's ways were beyond human understanding.
2. The article was first printed in the *American Philosophical Quarterly* 16 (1979): 335–41. It has been reprinted many times, including in *The Problem of Evil*, ed. Marilyn McCord Adams and Robert Merrihew Adams (Oxford: Oxford University Press, 1990), pp. 126–37.

In the discussion of Rowe's article, page numbers in parentheses in this section refer to the reprint in Adams and Adams.

3. For example, the work by William Hasker discussed in Chapter 2 might be seen as a response to the second premise, for there Hasker tries to give reasons why God properly might not prevent all the suffering God could.

4. Wykstra's article was first published in the *International Journal for Philosophy of Religion* 16/2 (1984): 73–93. Like Rowe's article, it has often been reprinted. In this section I will be citing from a reprint in *The Problem of Evil*, ed. Adams and Adams, pp. 138–60. Page numbers in parentheses refer to this source.

5. In a later article, Rowe notes the absence of divine comfort, and uses it, in conjunction with a comparison of what a loving parent would do, to conclude that the goods justifying God's permitting evils must not be beyond our ken. For if they were, God would provide the extra comfort; "The Evidential Argument from Evil: A Second Look," *The Evidential Argument from Evil*, ed. Daniel Howard-Snyder (Bloomington, IN: Indiana University Press, 1996), p. 276. In the text, rather than drawing Rowe's conclusion, I prefer to leave the absence of extra comfort and the absence of an explanation that is clearly from God as problems for the traditional theist.

6. Rowe's reply is entitled "Evil and the Theistic Hypothesis: A Response to Wykstra," first published in the *International Journal for Philosophy of Religion* 16/2 (1984): 95–100. I will be citing from a reprinted version in *The Problem of Evil*, ed. Adams and Adams, pp. 161–7. Page numbers in parentheses refer to this source.

7. "Rowe's Noseeum Arguments from Evil," *The Evidential Argument from Evil*, ed. Daniel Howard-Snyder, pp. 126–50. Page numbers in parentheses refer to this work.

8. Though I speak of a one-to-one correlation, I would not want to deny that there might be several goods associated with some one evil. As long as the existence of the goods in this collection is the justification for God's permitting some particular evil, then I would call the correlation one-to-one.

9. Another possibility, suggested by Richard Creel in *Divine Impassibility: An Essay in Philosophical Theology* (New York: Cambridge University Press, 1986, ch. 3), is that God foreknows all possibilities and can plan appropriate responses to whatever possibilities actually occur. This would enable God to be sure of being able to bring about the desired good even if certain very great evils occurred. However, this suggestion does not show that God is justified in permitting all the evils that occur, for the suggestion implies that there are many different ways to achieve the goods God intends. It seems very unlikely that all these different ways involve great evils.

10. Wykstra acknowledges something like this in a note to the article we are discussing. He says that his "reply would not be apt if someone were to argue that if God exists, he would give us faculties ample to grasp all goods served by current sufferings, out of regard for our potential bewilderment" (149, n. 18). I have not argued that God should give us such faculties; I have simply argued that God should inform us. Of course, giving us such faculties could be seen as a way of informing us (or as a way of obviating the need to inform us).

11. The article originally appeared in *Philosophical Perspectives 5: Philosophy of Religion, 1991*, ed. James E. Tomberlin (Atascadero, CA: Ridgeview Publishing, 1991), pp. 29–67. It was reprinted in *The Evidential Argument from Evil*, ed. Daniel Howard-Snyder, pp. 97–125. Page numbers in parentheses in this section refer to the version reprinted in the latter source. Alston has a later paper in which he reflects on this paper and on some other discussions of the problem of evil: "Some (Temporarily) Final Thoughts on Evidential Arguments from Evil," *The Evidential Argument from Evil*, ed. Daniel Howard-Snyder, pp. 311–32. But at most, one of the points he makes in the later paper is relevant to the issues

I raise about this paper. I will mention it later when appropriate. Alston has expressed reservations about this paper, so he should not be thought now to accept everything found in it. Nevertheless, I wish to discuss it because it is an excellent presentation of a view that might well be held by some advocates of the ignorance defense.

12. Sue was introduced into discussions of the problem of suffering (though without being given a name) in an article by Bruce Russell, "The Persistent Problem of Evil," *Faith and Philosophy* 6/2 (April 1989): 121–39, which we discussed in Chapter 2. This particular evil actually occurred.

13. In the later paper mentioned in note 11 above, Alston stresses the significance of human ignorance about the conditions of realization as well as about the goods and the connections between the suffering and the goods. This stress in the later paper is the point I referred to in note 11 when I said that at most one point in Alston's later paper is relevant to my discussion in this chapter.

14. The suggestion being explored in this paragraph assumes that God had a relatively wide range of possibilities for designing a universe with a lawful order of nature and creatures with free will, so that out of that range God could select a universe in which suffering would have the possible consequences Alston discusses. But as Alston himself acknowledges, perhaps God could not create a lawful universe with free creatures that did not include something like the sorts of suffering our universe includes. In that case, though God could be aware of the possible benefits of suffering, it might be misleading to say even that they were intended.

15. My argument for this claim is similar to Plantinga's for the possibility of transworld depravity. It is possible that any world God could actualize in which nature operates lawfully and there are free creatures would be a world that would contain instantiations of Rowe's first premise. I don't know that this is so; I just claim that it is possibly true for all I or any other human know.

16. The distinction between a theodicy and a defense in relation to the problem of evil is that a theodicy attempts to offer some reason(s) for God's permitting evil that we humans can understand might well justify the permission of the evil, whereas a defense seeks only to show that the occurrence of evil is not an adequate reason to reject theism. The ignorance defense is one kind of defense (rather than theodicy), for it attempts to show that we humans are incompetent to judge whether the evils of the world are an adequate reason to doubt that God exists.

17. It is plausible because, as we saw in Chapter 3, even if other alleged reasons for God being hidden also are relevant, still God could do things that would make God less hidden (unless that hiddenness is the consequence of a divine transcendence that not even God can overcome, but most Christians deny this); that God is not less hidden is therefore plausibly seen as the result of a divine policy of being hidden, or at least of a policy of not doing more to overcome other factors that allegedly contribute to God's being hidden, such as human blindness to God that results from human sinfulness.

CHAPTER 6

Identifying, Interpreting, and Certifying Revelation

All of the claims and arguments of traditional theists discussed in Chapters 2–5 begin with the assumption that God has the three characteristics that constitute traditional theism.[1] If their grounds for this assumption are strong enough, then even if certain responses to the problems of evil do not seem adequate, traditional theists could conclude that either the responses are adequate, or that there is some other justification for God's permitting the evils we discussed. But why should one assume that traditional theists are correct in their assumption that God has these three characteristics? If this assumption creates problems to which the responses seem inadequate or at best, for all we know, true (but also, for all we know, false), then one obvious question is how strong are the grounds for the assumptions that generate the problems. Perhaps the strongest possible ground would be divinely certified clear revelation that this assumption is true. Whether we have good reason to think that there is such revelation will be our topic in this chapter. But there are also other possible grounds for the assumption. These other grounds will be discussed in the next chapter.

Philosophers usually base their arguments most directly on considerations other than alleged revelation. However, I wish to discuss alleged revelation first because I think that beliefs about revelation often play a significant role in the belief systems of traditional theists.[2] In this chapter, I want to argue that the alleged Christian revelation cannot provide strong grounds for conclusions about the nature of God and God's will.[3] One claim about God's nature is one of the beliefs of traditional theism that generates the problems of evil: the claim that God is omnipotent. This is the part of traditional theism I am most interested in challenging in this work.

Certain biblical passages have been seen as teaching that God is omnipotent. Perhaps in some of them their authors were expressing a belief of this proposition. Though I think perhaps questions might be raised about the proper interpretation of some of these passages, I will not challenge the claim that some authors were expressing this belief. For the fact (if it is a fact) that certain biblical authors expressed this idea in certain passages has normative significance for our idea of God only if what those authors said in those passages expresses something that God is revealing through the passages or has revealed to the authors so that they could communicate it to others. Unless God did something like this, their belief is just some human opinion, to be assessed as we would assess that same belief put forth by anyone else. I want to argue that the phenomena of the Bible make it very unlikely that God is revealing any particular proposition through the Bible, or that God has revealed any to biblical authors so that they could communicate it to others. My argument for this claim applies to all propositions purportedly revealed in or through the Bible. Thus, my argument in this chapter is for the general claim, not for that claim in reference to any particular passages or to any particular allegedly revealed proposition, including the proposition that God is omnipotent. Of course, if my argument succeeds, then it applies in particular to propositions about God's power.

My argument that it is unlikely that God is revealing any particular propositions through the Bible or its human authors is based on the following claim, which I term claim N: there is no proposition, doctrine, or truth that is both clear and clearly divinely revealed because every alleged revelation has at least the first and often the second of the following two characteristics: (1) it is not clear that the alleged revelation is actually a revelation, and (2) it is not clear exactly what is allegedly revealed. I am not claiming that there have never been any revelations, but only that all the alleged revelations have at least the first and often both of these two characteristics. Their having them prevents any alleged revelation from providing good grounds for drawing conclusions about the nature and will of God. It also constitutes another problem for traditional theists, for it raises the question of why any revelation (if there is any) has at least the first and often both of these two characteristics. Certainly the God affirmed by traditional theists has the power to give revelations that are clearly revelations (as argued in Chapter 3) and whose content or message is also clear.

To defend claim N, I will look at some understandings of what constitutes a revelation and how one should identify and interpret it. I will argue none of them gives us good grounds to doubt claim N. Of course, I cannot consider every such attempt, but I believe that my discussion will be sufficiently general to suggest that other articulations of these topics also will not be able to give us good grounds to doubt claim N. Toward the end of the chapter I will also suggest a way of understanding alleged revelations that seems to me consistent with the phenomena of alleged revelations in the Bible.

Possible Models of Revelation

In his book *Revelation and Religious Belief,* George Mavrodes distinguishes three models of ways in which revelation might be thought to occur: the communication model, the manifestation model, and the causation model.[4] The communication model is perhaps the most familiar to Christians. In this model, "one thinks of God as speaking with men and women, as saying something to them; and these human recipients, for their part, are represented as the hearers of the word of God" (111).

In the manifestation model,

> we are likely to think of something like an *encounter* with the divine reality. The language we use to express our conviction about a revelation in this mode is likely to be drawn from the terminology of perception and similar modes of experience. It is in thinking of God's revelation in this mode that people find themselves talking about *seeing* God, about *feeling* the divine power, about being *flooded* by the love of God, and so on. (37, italics his)

What is revealed in this model is God. God reveals a specific thing about Godself by manifesting it – that is, by "making the corresponding fact accessible to human experience" (87). Mavrodes gives as an analogy a man revealing that he is bald by removing his hat. We might also think of a person revealing his love or cruelty by some action he does.

In the causation model, God causes us to have certain beliefs. Mavrodes suggests a variety of ways God might do this. God might cause the belief to be innate, but to rise to consciousness only under certain circumstances; for example, God might cause someone to have an innate belief that an omnipotent, omniscient, all-good being created the universe (we shall use U to designate the proposition involved in this belief) and cause the person to be such that the person becomes conscious of the belief when she contemplates the heavens. Or God could cause a person to have an innate belief-forming "mechanism" such that the person comes to hold belief U when she experiences certain conditions. Or God could simply directly cause the person to have the belief U, perhaps when the person is having certain other experiences. Or there may be other ways. But the phenomenological similarity in all these cases is that the person simply finds herself believing U. She may realize that she came to believe U under certain circumstances, but she need not regard these circumstances as providing evidence for U. Such a belief would be, in Alvin Plantinga's terminology, a basic belief, perhaps a properly basic belief. Moreover, the person need not believe that God caused her to believe U. (Let us use the letter C to denote the belief that God caused one to hold some other belief such as U.) One could well believe U without additionally believing C.

In this chapter, we are concerned with whether we have adequate grounds for thinking that any propositions are both so clear and so clearly revealed by God as to carry divine authority. On the causation model, there might well be propositions revealed by God – that is, beliefs of propositions that God caused us to hold – but the question is whether we have good grounds for thinking that any particular belief we hold is one God caused (or causes) us to hold. We may think this about some belief we hold, and we may even be prima facie justified in doing so. If everyone – or nearly everyone – held the same beliefs about God and held them in this way, then we might have good grounds for thinking that God really had caused these beliefs in people. But a problem arises when we discover that some others hold in this way beliefs about God that are inconsistent with the ones we hold. This discovery does not by itself prove that our beliefs are false, nor does it entail that we should abandon the beliefs. For it seems that no matter what we believe about God, someone holds a belief inconsistent with it, so there is no way of retreating to some non-controversial belief. However, the disagreement may give us reason to ask whether there are any other grounds or considerations that show either (1) that God caused the belief, or (2) that in some other way the belief carries divine authority. We have no direct access to such belief-forming mechanisms, so we cannot examine the mechanism to see whether God caused the belief. We need some other way to determine whether or not God did so and/or whether the belief carries divine authority.

Suppose that God caused one to believe C in addition to the original belief U. Would that help? It would not, because the belief C would be a belief that one simply finds oneself holding. Since others believe C in relation to beliefs inconsistent with U, that one believes C in relation to another belief U is not conclusive grounds to believe that either U or C carries divine authority (provided we are correct in assuming that God does not cause inconsistent beliefs about God). Unfortunately, any other beliefs revealed by divine causation would suffer the same defect, so they could not provide grounds for showing options 1 or 2 in the previous paragraph. In each case, the crucial belief would be experienced as something that one simply finds oneself believing in certain circumstances. This might be a sufficient basis for some people to hold the belief, and perhaps they would be prima facie justified in doing so. However, as I argued in relation to belief U, because there are people who on the same basis hold beliefs inconsistent with one's own, that one finds oneself believing C would not be adequate grounds to conclude that C or U was caused by God and therefore carries divine authority.

On the manifestation model, the revelation may be public – that is, such as to be perceived by more than one person at a time. As Mavrodes suggests, revelation in this model can reveal facts, which can be the basis on which one might come to believe a proposition about what is revealed. His example was a man revealing that he is bald by removing his hat. However, when we consider this model in relation to some purported divine revelation, we find at least two possible problems with concluding that some proposition has been revealed by God. First, one could doubt that it is really God who is revealed. If the event were some obvious miracle, that would give good grounds for believing that it is indeed God who is revealed. But if one has no good grounds for believing that an obvious miracle has occurred (as I argued in Chapter 4), one might well wonder whether it is really God who is revealed. Second, one could doubt whether one had formulated a correct proposition from the purported manifestation.

For a concrete example, consider the Holocaust. Consider some of the things that might be said to be revealed there. God is not revealed in the Holocaust. The Holocaust reveals that God is not concerned. God is revealed as identifying with and suffering with the victims. God is revealed as long-suffering and patient with human sin, even horrendous human sin. Of course, since the last two propositions are not inconsistent, perhaps more than one of them is revealed. But on what grounds should we decide that one or more of them are something God revealed rather than just possible beliefs that might arise in us as we consider the Holocaust or conclusions we might draw from the Holocaust? Even in relation to events in the life of Jesus, one can wonder. If Jesus never ate some particular food, would that reveal that God does not like or approve of that food? If Jesus never gave female followers high positions, would that reveal that God does not want female priests and bishops? Would it even reveal that Jesus intended that no women should exercise leadership among his followers? Does Jesus' changing water into wine manifest a divine approval of wine and/or divine preference for wine over water? The absence of a clear spoken word on these matters inevitably creates uncertainty. Of course, some of Jesus' followers may formulate propositions about these matters, but can we be sure that their formulations are correct? In order for these or other formulations to carry divine authority, we need some clear divine indication that God is truly revealed in the events and that the formulations correctly express something God revealed by manifesting it.

These reflections may lead us to look at the third model, the communication model. This is the model of God speaking to people; thus, it might seem the most promising model for revelation of divine truths. At least in this model, what is allegedly revealed is already verbally formulated; however, as I will point out, there remain significant problems in interpreting even verbal formulations that comprise alleged revelations. Moreover, there remains the issue of whether something purportedly spoken by God has in fact been spoken by God or at least carries a divine imprimatur. Inconsistencies between claims about what God has spoken show that not all these claims can be true. Thus, again we need some reason other than the fact that someone alleges that God has communicated some truth if we are to have strong grounds to believe that God communicated the truth.

The upshot of these reflections on the models of revelation articulated by Mavrodes is that though, if there is a God, God may reveal Godself in accordance with any of the models, we do not have any good grounds to think that God has done so, given problems in interpreting alleged revelations, conflicting beliefs about what God has revealed, and the absence of any clear indication that any one of them is actually revealed by God. I think the Christian tradition is right in thinking that only an obvious miracle could give strong grounds to believe that something is a divine revelation, but as we saw in Chapter 4, we have no good reason to believe that obvious miracles have occurred.

This negative conclusion based on reflections on Mavrodes' three models is strengthened when we look at what many Christians consider a central element in God's revelation: the Bible. Throughout the history of Christianity, the Bible has played a central role as a norm for ecclesiastical pronouncements, for doctrinal formulations and debates, and for moral guidance, along with providing a basis for preaching and a resource for devotional activity. If we ask why it has been accorded such authority, a common answer is that God so inspired the writers that the Bible has some characteristic that makes it absolutely unique among Christian writings. This unique characteristic is not simply that of being the earliest written witness to certain events that Christians regard as central, though the Bible contains this, for being the earliest written witness would not require any unique divine inspiration. Rather, this alleged characteristic is that the Bible is or contains revelation.

Because the Bible is composed of words, it seems to exemplify the communication model. It certainly does not exemplify the causation model.[5] Of course, the human authors of the writings that compose the Bible might have been directly caused by God to have the ideas that they express in these writings, but we do not have any good grounds to believe that. As for the manifestation model, the Bible might well (and does!) contain accounts of purported divine manifestations, but we do not have good grounds to believe that these are in fact divine manifestations, and that, if they are, we have correctly understood what God is manifesting. We saw above why purported manifestations of God raise this problem. Therefore, it is vital that the manifestation be accompanied by a verbal commentary if we are to have justified confidence that we are correct about what is manifested.[6] Therefore, the most promising approach to the Bible would seem to be to take it as (primarily, at least) an instance of the communication model. Yet even on the communication model (to say nothing of the other models), the phenomena that the Bible presents do seem to be problematic characteristics of a book intended to provide a revelation of divine truths. Let us see why.

Revelation and Some Problematic Phenomena of the Bible

All the phenomena I will cite seem to me to raise the question whether any statements in the Bible are clear formulations of propositions that are clearly revealed by God. Though Christians are aware of the phenomena I will mention, most fail to give sufficient weight to the implications of these phenomena for determining what, if anything, is revealed in or through the Bible.

First, there are seeming errors and inconsistencies. An example of the former is that Jesus is reported as saying that the mustard seed is the smallest seed in the world (Matt. 13:31–2 and Mk. 4:31); however, it is not the smallest seed.[7] An example of the latter is the disagreement between Matthew (10:9–10) and Luke (9:3), on the one hand, and Mark (6:8), on the other, about whether Jesus commanded the disciples to take a staff or not to take one.[8] These seeming errors and inconsistencies do not serve any positive purpose. Some are easily correctable: Jesus and the Gospel writers could have said that a mustard seed is a very small seed, and they could have agreed on whether or not the disciples should carry a staff. Others are more deeply embedded in the text and have created greater perplexity among some believers: for example, God's reported command, often repeated, that all Canaanites (no exception made, even for children) be killed during the conquest of Palestine.[9] This command seems impossible to reconcile with the justice of God, whether that is understood in terms of our intuitions about justice or as God's justice is portrayed in other biblical passages. But if God did not command it, why did God not cause an accurate record to be made, as God could have done, according to traditional Christians? The significance of these seeming errors and inconsistencies depends on how one understands the relation between statements in the Bible and propositions that God wishes to reveal. The errors and inconsistencies raise serious – in my opinion, insurmountable – problems with the simplest possible view of the relation between statements in the Bible and propositions that God wishes to reveal – that is, the view that all such statements are propositions God wishes to reveal. They indicate that the relation cannot be one of identity. Perhaps only some statements in Bible are propositions God wishes to reveal to us, or perhaps the relation between statements in the Bible and propositions God wishes to reveal to us is more complex and nuanced. But in either case we need a clear description of the appropriate hermeneutic, yet the Bible does not give us one, and in the history of Christianity many different ones have been proposed and used. The remaining phenomena discussed below show some of the problems of interpretation that the hermeneutic must resolve.

Second, there are no clear overall presentations of what most traditional Christians take to be central Christian doctrines (or of any alternative set of doctrines). For example, there is no biblical passage regarding the Trinity or the Incarnation that has the clarity of the Nicene or Chalcedonian creeds. Instead the Bible contains passages that may be the expression of (some aspect of) one of these doctrines, but also may express something different. It may be alleged that these doctrines can be derived from the Bible, but the derivation – even if legitimate – is complex, and mistakes can easily be made. If not, there would not have been the controversies there have been over these matters, such as the decades-long struggle over Arianism. Nor would there now be groups, such as Jehovah's Witnesses, that claim to base their doctrines on the Bible, but deny these doctrines. If God wished to reveal these matters and wished people to believe them, why did God not cause them to be revealed at least as clearly as later believers put matters in the creeds?

Third, there is a similar lack of clarity about other important matters, which may even be central to Christian faith and life, though how central they are is itself disputed. For example, what is the proper mode of baptism, or does the mode matter? What is the proper mode of Church organization? Should there be an authoritative Church hierarchy, and if so, what degree of authority should the Church hierarchy have? Should one person be head of the visible Church, and if so, what powers does that person have? Should women be ordained as clergy? Are Christians permitted to divorce and, if they are, on what grounds?

Fourth, there is a failure to distinguish clearly which matters and ways of putting things apply only temporarily and which are of permanent validity. For example, Paul gives injunctions (I Cor. 11:3–16) about hair length that he supports by appeal to the basic nature of human beings rather than to features of his recipients' culture, but few Christians think these injunctions are binding on Christians today. On the other hand, many Christians feel that the Ten Commandments still apply to them, though they were given as rules for the Hebrew people in their covenant relation to God.

Fifth, biblical writers sometimes express themselves in terms of the way things appear rather than in terms of the way they really are: Joshua commanded the sun to stand still rather than the earth to stop spinning (Josh. 10:12–14).[10] The admission that the Bible exhibits this phenomenon opens the door for great latitude in biblical interpretation; though it has typically been appealed to mostly in relation to scientific matters, in principle there appears no reason why it might not also be appealed to in relation to more central religious matters. And indeed it has. For example, some theologians have claimed that God does not really feel anger; when the Bible says that God is angry, it means only that God behaved in a manner like that in which a human who is angry would behave. (Theologians who believed that God is pure act said that there is no passivity in God and therefore that God has no passions, including anger.) Could this principle also be applied to a passage that speaks of Jesus as the Son of God? If not, why not? Since the Bible does not indicate when a writer is describing things in terms of their appearance, the reader, the leaders of the Church, or the Church as a whole must determine it.

Finally, biblical writers used metaphor, analogy, and other literary devices, but typically they did not indicate when they were using them. While this is sometimes clear, such as the parables of Jesus, other texts are disputed and important. For example, how literally should the words of institution of the communion meal be taken: "Take, eat; *this is my body*" (Matt. 26:26, my italics)?

Let me repeat that (virtually) all Christians admit that the Bible has these features. My point is that it is strange to attribute to God the intention to reveal to humans very important matters that otherwise they could not discover, yet to claim that this revelation is communicated in a document with the six features noted. If a document has these features, the sort of difficulties and disagreements about interpretation that have plagued the Church seem unavoidable. Yet if God intended to reveal something, especially something of great importance and something impossible for humans to discover, why is it not clear what God wanted to reveal and that God is the one who revealed it? What is the point of an unclear revelation? It will hardly do to reply that it is not our place to question how God chooses to do something. This response would be appropriate only if we were certain that God had the intention to reveal truths in or through the Bible (and that God has the power to carry out that intention[11]). The tensions between that alleged intention and the features of the Bible noted above are reasons to doubt that God had that intention (or the power to carry it out).

But before concluding that traditional theists cannot give a plausible account of how the Bible is or contains revelation that God intended to give even though they also acknowledge that it has these six features (or something like them), we should examine some attempts to do just that. We will look at two, each by an important contemporary Christian traditional theist. They represent two different ways to address the issue.

Swinburne's Approach

Richard Swinburne's proposal is spelled out most completely in his book *Revelation*.[12] I think Swinburne would agree that the Bible exhibits the six phenomena mentioned in the previous section, though some of them he describes differently. In particular, he employs the distinction between what is presupposed and what is stated. For example, if a writer belonging to a culture that believed that the earth is stationary and rests on some sort of foundation wrote that God had established the earth on its foundation, he would be presupposing the cosmology and stating only that God keeps the world secure. This seems to me to be a way to make a point similar to the fifth point in the section above, and it bears on some of the worries underlying the fourth point. However, it does not solve the problem created by the distinction noted in the fifth point, for it replaces that distinction with the distinction between presupposing and stating, and it may often be difficult to know where to draw the line between them. The historical reconstruction required may be extensive, and in some cases may yield only highly disputed results. This is particularly true when the culture in question is not that of a whole nation, but that of a small group whose beliefs themselves are in question, such as members in the first-century church. Some of these members were Jews (some from Palestine and some from elsewhere in the Roman Empire), and others were Gentiles from various countries. What is the relevant culture for this diverse group?

Swinburne also claims that the Bible has another feature that increases the difficulties for anyone who would use it as a way to come to know divinely revealed truths. He says that the Bible contains passages whose most natural interpretation is inconsistent with other passages and with central Christian doctrines (192).[13] He resolves such inconsistencies by saying that the passages should be given a less natural interpretation in order to make them consistent with Christian orthodoxy.[14] He also suggests that passages that seem to express a sub-Christian morality be interpreted in some non-literal fashion, such as allegorically or typologically. What is the justification for taking passages in something other than their most natural sense and for interpreting other passages in a non-literal way? Swinburne has two main answers to this question. One is that every passage must be interpreted in its context. And the context of every part of the Bible is the whole Bible. Thus, every part of the Bible must be interpreted in a way consistent with the message of the whole Bible. But if we are to use this principle, we need to know how to derive the overall meaning of the Bible from the meanings of its parts. Swinburne recognizes that "the Bible does not belong to an obvious genre which provides rules for how overall meaning is a function of meaning of individual books" (177). He proposes that the creeds provide the needed guide. This brings us to the second of his main answers: the Church is the authorized interpreter of the message of the Bible.[15] Thus Swinburne's acuity concerning the problems of interpreting documents and his recognition of problematic phenomena of the Bible lead him to claim that the Church is the divinely intended and providentially guided interpreter of the Bible and of Christian truth in general.

This doctrine about the Church enables him to deal with the problems raised by the features of the Bible I noted and by other features noted by him. Are central Christian doctrines not clearly taught? The Church will clarify central Christian doctrines. Are there seeming errors? The Church will tell us they are unimportant. Are there seeming inconsistencies within the Bible or passages expressing sub-Christian morality? The Church will tell us how to reinterpret passages so as to eliminate these problems. Are there hermeneutical problems created by unidentified metaphors, analogies, allegories, and other literary devices?[16] The Church will reliably guide us in resolving these hermeneutical problems. The role he gives to the Church also enables him to solve other problems with using the Bible. Among them is the difficulty of historically reconstructing with any confidence exactly what Jesus taught (105–6; 191). He says that "if … Jesus founded a Church and God gave his signature to the teaching of Jesus by raising him from the dead, then the Church becomes authoritative on what Jesus taught. He said what it said he said, and that was to be understood in the way it said it was" (191) Similarly, it is the authority of the Church that justifies our accepting the canon of the Bible as we have it.

At least two questions arise if one is to give the Church this authority. How can we justify giving the Church this authority? And how should we identify that contemporary group which is the Church? Much of his justification for giving the Church this authority is an *a priori* argument to show that such a body is needed if God gives humans a revelation of a sort they need. But reasons for thinking that such a body would be needed are not reasons for thinking that we have one.

The second question is which body is the Church? It will be the interpreter of an original revelation from God. We must identify the person or group that correctly interprets that revelation today. Obviously, we cannot identify the Church by using the condition that it correctly interprets the revelation, for we would already have to know what the correct interpretation is if we were to use this condition as a criterion to identify the group that correctly interprets it. So Swinburne proposes as criteria continuity of aim and continuity of organization with the group comprised of the original followers of Jesus. He adds that continuity of aim is assured primarily through continuity of doctrine, and he claims that there has been continuity on central matters – the items in the great creeds – until the twentieth century. Those who deny "a major part" of past doctrine implicitly deny that "its being taught by the Church is substantial evidence of its truth, and to deny that is to deny that we have any more access to the original revelation than historical inquiry can provide" (124).[17] And he thinks that historical inquiry cannot provide all that we need. This is an important admission. If so astute a thinker as Swinburne concludes that historical inquiry by itself does not give us adequate access to original revelation, then it seems very likely that at least it is not obvious that historical inquiry is adequate. This provides additional support for my claim that we have no good reason to identify any particular propositions as divinely revealed truths.

Having laid out the criteria for answering the question of which body is to be identified with the Church, Swinburne concludes: "At this point I pass my baton to the historian to show which present-day body preserves best in its doctrine and organization continuity with the Church of the apostles" (142). He admits that this investigation might show that one body is closest or that none is, and he acknowledges that political forces have often played a role in determining what doctrine is promulgated. But he says that God's preserving the Church from error guarantees only that divine influence will "prevent the Church being saddled permanently with false interpretations" (143). Even if Swinburne is right about this guarantee – and one wonders how he knows there is this guarantee – it is not much use in helping us determine what are the correct interpretations. For it provides no help in determining how long, short of permanently, the Church will not be saddled with a false interpretation. This is not a merely speculative question, as a consideration of the history of Christianity reveals. For example, if the Protestant Reformers were right, the historic church (and therefore the Church?) had been saddled with false interpretations for at least a thousand years. If John Hick and others are right, then taking the Incarnation as a literal truth is an error with which the historic church (and therefore the Church?) had been saddled for over 1500 years.[18] Of course, it might be that both the Protestant Reformers and Hick (and others) were wrong. But can we conclude from the fact that the majority of Christian teaching has held a certain position for 1000 or 1500 years that the position is correct? If not, then the guarantee Swinburne offers is of no practical help in settling what is a false interpretation.

But even if we overlook problems with these assurances, it is clear that Swinburne gives the historian a crucial role in determining which body constitutes the true Church. The historian also plays a crucial role in identifying the original revelation, for we need "historical evidence of a miracle brought about by God to authenticate the message" (110). The crucial miracle for Swinburne is the Resurrection. Does historical investigation provide us with the necessary evidence? Swinburne mentions some matters often cited by defenders of an orthodox view and then concludes: "Again I do not propose to assess the historical evidence in detail – that is not my expertise; my point is that if the background evidence is fairly strong, as I have suggested that it is, we do not need too much in the way of historical evidence to make it on balance probable that the Resurrection took place" (112).

I do not wish to assess Swinburne's argument in detail. Instead, I wish to draw attention to some features of his argument and his differences with various opposing views in order to draw some conclusions about revelation and the Bible. Swinburne's work shows his typical erudition and thoroughness, yet his case for Christianity as embodying original revelation and the true Church (the divinely authorized interpreter of original revelation) is by his own admission incomplete. For his case rests crucially on two historical claims, and history is – as he himself admits – not his area of expertise. Thus if Swinburne is right, a full case for Christianity demands more expertise than he commands, and I suggest more expertise than it is reasonable to expect any one person to command.[19] For no historian *qua* historian would have sufficient expertise either; expertise in the philosophy of religion is also needed to carry out such tasks as determining the criteria for genuine revelation and for the Church. And even if there were people who could combine both areas of expertise, they would be few in number. On the other hand, if Swinburne is wrong and a full case for Christianity is much simpler than he believes and the difficulties in interpreting original revelation are much less than he claims, showing that this is so would require sophistication and effort about equal to his. Thus, the task of determining where we should look for divinely revealed truth and its correct interpretation is likely to be beyond the competence of all, or at least almost all, humans. But if God revealed some matters that God wishes humans to know, why did God make (or allow) it to be so difficult – I am tempted to say "impossible" – to discover whether some alleged revelation is God's and how to interpret it?[20]

The problems raised by the uncertainties in identifying revealed truths inevitable in Swinburne's very complicated approach are all the more glaring when it seems implicit in traditional theism that these uncertainties are easily avoidable. God could make important truths known directly to each person or communicate them to some spokespeople whom God certifies. In either case, God could perform obvious, dramatic miracles to show that these truths really have a divine certification behind them.

Swinburne is not unaware of this problem, though he does not think it is as great a problem as I have portrayed it. He thinks that it is good that revelation "not be too evident, even to those who have discovered it," for "they can manifest their commitment to the goals which it offers by pursuing them even when it is not certain that those goals are there to be had" (74–5). But this is a dubious position even if discovering and interpreting genuine revelation is only a moderately difficult task rather than the (virtually) impossible task I think it to be on Swinburne's account. For most humans do not have the time or ability of a Richard Swinburne; to explore these matters in the requisite depth is inconsistent with their other legitimate commitments (such as making a living and raising a family) and beyond their abilities even if they had the time. And if I am right about the degree of difficulty, not even Richard Swinburne has the time to do the whole job.

Swinburne might reply that a human need not do this alone; humans can cooperate, and he thinks it is good that they do (74). But in practice, cooperation requires that I trust someone else's conclusions on some matters that I cannot investigate myself. And on religious matters (and on historical matters crucial to religion), whose views to accept on trust is controversial; there is not a clear consensus of experts. Moreover, Swinburne oversimplifies the situation when he says that believers are showing their commitment by pursuing goals "even when it is not certain that those goals are there to be had." For the uncertainty is not just whether the goals are there to be had; it also concerns whether these are the right goals to pursue, how to pursue them, and whether this tradition is the correct one on which to spend time puzzling these matters out. Given that resolving these uncertainties involves great intellectual abilities and time, Swinburne's way is beyond the capacities of almost everyone, and thus not a fair test of commitment. It would be far better to measure commitment by willingness to pursue clearly correct goals in ways that demand great effort. Why should it be judged good that the ways are not clear (rather than just difficult to follow)?

For all these reasons, I judge that Swinburne's attempt to provide a way to justify claims about revelation and to identify and interpret revealed truths is not adequate. He describes great difficulties in identifying revelation, and gives no adequate reason why there should be such difficulties. If there are particular statements whose theological accuracy is very important, one wonders why God did not clearly identify them as divinely revealed or as carrying a divine certification. If God had wished to make known such propositions, it is surely plausible to think that God would have identified and certified them clearly. One can, of course, draw from the Bible, or on the basis of the Bible, various propositions about God and God's will that one believes are true, but one must realize that these propositions are simply human conclusions about revelation, to be tested like all human propositions.

Plantinga's Approach

Swinburne's approach assumes something like Mavrodes's communication model of revelation and is evidentialist: that is, it uses what is written in the Bible as evidence for propositions about God (and other religious propositions). I have argued that it fails to give us good grounds to accept any propositions as divinely revealed or divinely certified. The failure of this very sophisticated evidentialist approach suggests that it might be well to examine a non-evidentialist approach to the Bible as a medium of revelation. In recent years, such an approach has been articulated in considerable detail by Alvin Plantinga as part of a larger project of developing and defending a non-evidentialist approach to show that religious, in particular Christian, beliefs can be justified, rational, and warranted even if they are not based on other beliefs or propositions used as evidence.[21] In this section we will examine his approach to using the Bible as a medium of revelation; we will also see that it assumes something like Mavrodes's causation model of revelation.

In Plantinga's model, reading or hearing about what Plantinga terms "the great things of the gospel"[22] provides an occasion on which God may graciously choose to cause humans to believe one or more of these great things. The result of this divine activity is that one finds oneself confidently believing that thing (205–6). In this model, the role of the Bible is not to provide evidence for the truth of the beliefs. Indeed, Plantinga is highly critical of the project of using the Bible as evidence for Christian beliefs. He thinks that, considered as a source of evidence for the truth of Christian beliefs, it is not adequate; moreover, he thinks that the degree of conviction produced by beliefs derived in this way falls far short of the full trust and confidence in Christian belief produced by the Holy Spirit (270–79). Not only is the Bible not evidence for the truth of Christian belief, it is also not the cause of that belief. What one reads in the Bible (or hears as messages are spoken) is only the occasion for the Holy Spirit to cause various beliefs; the Holy Spirit is the cause (180, 249–50).

Strictly speaking, this account applies only to God's causing belief in the great things of the gospel, not to causing belief in the inspiration and authority of the entire Bible. Plantinga's project in *Warranted Christian Belief* is to discuss how Christian belief can be warranted, not how belief in the authority of the Bible can be warranted, but he does give brief attention to that topic (375–80). He discusses a few ways in which a Christian might be warranted in believing that the Bible is inspired and authoritative; all of them require the activity of the Holy Spirit. Just as he argues that historical considerations are not adequate to warrant Christian belief in the great things of the gospel, so he also argues that historical considerations are not adequate to warrant belief in the authority and inspiration of the Bible. Such warrant requires that the Holy Spirit cause the Christian to believe some crucial warranting proposition, for example that various books in the Bible are from God or that "the Holy Spirit has guided and preserved the Christian church, making sure that its teachings on important matters are, in fact, true," from which the Christian can infer that "those books of the Bible endorsed by all or nearly all traditional Christian communities" are from God (380). But because the warrant that beliefs acquire in either of these ways depends on the activity of the Holy Spirit, my criticisms of the adequacy of relying on this alleged activity for warrant for belief in the great things of the gospel will also apply to relying on it for warrant for belief in other things allegedly taught in the Bible.

So let us return to Plantinga's discussion of how a Christian normally has warrant for belief in the great things of the gospel. It is noteworthy that his theory gives us no reason why the particular words of the Bible are important. It seems that, in principle, God could have planned to cause belief in the great things of the gospel when a person reads or hears a particular, apparently random, string of letters and numbers.[23] Provided that God planned to use such an occasion to cause true beliefs about those great things and designed humans accordingly, then people whom God causes to believe those things on such an occasion would be warranted in doing so. But though, on Plantinga's theory, God need not have used any words, including those in the Bible, as an occasion for causing people to believe the great things of the gospel, Plantinga does say that God has decided to use what is written in the Bible.

So we can ask more specifically about the relation between what is in the Bible and what the Holy Spirit causes people to believe. Plantinga's general formula is clear enough: the Holy Spirit causes us to believe what God is teaching us in the Bible. But what is the relation between the material in the Bible and what God is teaching us in the Bible? On this crucial matter, Plantinga is uncharacteristically brief and unhelpful. He admits that it "isn't always easy to tell what the Lord *is* teaching us in a given passage" (381, italics his). One reason is that the Bible contains many different kinds of literary material, not just assertions.[24] But "even if we stick to straightforward assertions, there are a thousand questions of interpretation" (381). Some of the unclear matters "are important to the way the church conducts its day-to-day business" (382). Plantinga notes that these problems of interpretation have caused some of the finest minds in the history of Christianity to produce volumes and volumes of commentaries on the Bible. In this effort at determining what the

Lord is teaching, Plantinga says three principles have been paramount: since the Lord is the primary author of Scripture, what it teaches is true; for the same reason, it is appropriate to use a teaching in one passage that is clear to aid in interpreting one in another passage that is not clear, even if the latter has a different human author; and "the fact that the principal author of the Bible is God himself means that one can't always determine the meaning of a given passage by discovering what the human author had in mind" (383–5). In a footnote, Plantinga adds "a further complication: we can't simply assume that there is some one thing, the same for everyone, that the Lord intends to teach in a given passage; perhaps what he intends to teach me or my relevant sociological group is not the same as what he intended to teach a fifth-century Christian" (385, n. 12).

Unfortunately, the three principles are of little help in determining what the Lord is teaching in a passage. Only the second of the three offers positive help, and it requires that what the Lord is teaching in some passages be clear, so that they can be used in relation to the unclear passages. But how should we identify the allegedly clear passages and determine what the Lord is teaching in them? Plantinga provides no help answering this question. It might seem as though we cannot simply use what the human author is teaching. Even if it is clear what the human author is teaching, the third principle warns us that we cannot simply assume that that is what the Lord is teaching. So again I ask: how can we determine what the Lord is teaching? Is it simply that when I read the passage, I get the feeling that some proposition is true, that it is right? One might think so from what Plantinga says: "What is said simply seems right; it seems compelling; one finds oneself saying, 'Yes, that's right, that's the truth of the matter; this is indeed the word of the Lord'" (250). However, in that way lies a veritable interpretative Babel. As Plantinga himself notes with regret, Christians have fought "enormously destructive battles" over (what he at least believes to be) unclear matters (382–3). But Plantinga's principles provide no help in preventing or resolving such conflicts. Upon reading the same or different passages in the Bible, two people may find themselves confidently believing inconsistent propositions. As history shows, this is not just a theoretical possibility; the violence among Christians that Plantinga deplores often arose because some people, reading the Bible, came to believe and to feel certain about propositions that are inconsistent with propositions other people came to believe and to feel certain about when they read the Bible. If two believers adhere to Plantinga's principles, what can they do? The convictions of either one could be warranted, and Plantinga's defense of his model gives each ways to defend herself against various challenges to her being warranted in her belief. But it gives each no way to determine whether she is in fact warranted, no way to determine whether her belief was in fact caused by the Holy Spirit.

They might be able to determine whose belief was caused by the Holy Spirit if the conviction produced by the Holy Spirit were (claimed to be) qualitatively unique. But Plantinga does not claim this.[25] Nor would appeal to what the human writers are teaching be decisive, for one of Plantinga's principles informs us that we cannot assume that what the Lord is teaching is the same as what the human author is teaching. It might be suggested that Plantinga could change his position and say that the Lord is teaching what the human author is teaching or (in non-didactic passages) otherwise expressing. This is at least roughly what the commentators

Plantinga approves of assumed. But this would involve a return to evidentialism, for the biblical passages would be treated as evidence. And thus it would reintroduce the problems Swinburne encountered.

The problem raised by Plantinga's model is not just that others cannot tell who is right. If the two believers have respect for each other and admit their own fallibility as human beings, then each must admit that she might be the one who is in error. Each has no way to check whether her conviction is in fact caused by the Holy Spirit and whether what she is convinced of is in fact true. Provided there are no conclusive defeaters for either conviction, Plantinga's model gives each one no principled way to decide whether to (continue to) have confidence in what she believes.

This raises the question of why a good God, who wanted to communicate various truths to people, would set up a system that leaves earnest believers in such irresolvable conflicts about what the truth is that God wants to communicate. Plantinga would have to admit that God has the power so to communicate with the human authors that they would have and express the beliefs that God wants to communicate. Why didn't God? Is it plausible to attribute to God a method of communicating with humans that would inevitably result in the sort of confusion that has in fact occurred throughout the history of Christianity? Surely God would know that the confusion would result. Then why would God use the method involved in Plantinga's model? Even if God planned that the Holy Spirit would enable believers to see and embrace certain truths as they read the Bible or hear it proclaimed, that is no reason not to make the Bible as clear and consistent as possible. I say this because even if the Holy Spirit does produce the sort of certainty described in Plantinga's model, Plantinga himself admits that non-divine influences can produce an experientially indistinguishable feeling of certainty in people. If we humans can see that this is so, surely an omniscient God would know it in advance of deciding how to communicate with humans. And if God knew this in advance, it seems strange that God would not see to it that there are some intersubjectively available factors by which people with feelings of certainty about inconsistent propositions can determine what God really is teaching. Therefore, the alleged activity of the Holy Spirit is no reason not to make clear in the Bible both the great things of the gospel and the other matters that Plantinga notes. The inexplicable unclarities in the Bible on these matters provide many serious anomalies for Plantinga's claim that God inspired the biblical writers in a unique way so that material in the Bible could provide the occasion on which God would cause Christians to believe things God wishes them to believe and so that it would provide a guide for what Christians should believe on other matters by discerning what is taught in the Bible, a book they trust because the Holy Spirit has caused them to believe that it comes from God.

Plantinga does claim that the Bible is "*perspicuous*: the main lines of its teaching – creation, sin, incarnation, atonement, resurrection, eternal life – can be understood and grasped and properly accepted by anyone of normal intelligence and ordinary training" (374, italics his). But Plantinga does not specify whether someone can see that these are the main lines of its teaching and understand them without the work of the Holy Spirit. I wonder whether everyone of normal intelligence and "ordinary training" (whatever that is) who reads the Bible without having been told what to look for – Is that ordinary training? – would come to the same idea of what the main lines of its teaching are. At this point it would be appropriate to call to mind Swinburne's claim that one needs guidance to know how to read such a disparate body of literature.[26]

If these anomalies and other considerations of the sort I have suggested lead one to wonder whether one's initial belief is really caused by God, and if one realizes that the certainty one feels could come from sources other than the Holy Spirit, then one will seek grounds, *evidential as well as non-evidential*, for thinking that one's current beliefs and various relevant alternatives are true and/or evidence that one's current beliefs were caused by the Holy Spirit or in some other reliable way.

Our discussion of Plantinga leaves us with this conclusion: those who are aware of the diversity of beliefs among Christians should not rest content with an unsupported feeling of confidence in various Christian beliefs, even if that feeling of confidence is supplemented with considerations that show that there are no conclusive defeaters for the Christian beliefs about which they feel confident. Plantinga would have to agree that if God wished people to believe certain propositions, God would have been able to cause them to be stated clearly (for example, in the Bible) and to be certified as divinely revealed. Instead, what we have in the Bible is a collection of writings of various sorts in relation to which, as even Plantinga admits, it is difficult to know what the Lord is teaching. (As disagreements among commentators show, it is also often difficult to know what the human authors are trying to communicate.) Yet Plantinga claims that God has chosen a method of creating belief that involves causing people to believe and feel confident about propositions that occur to them as they read or encounter material from the Bible, though the propositions that they come to believe may not even be what the human author is teaching and though what the human author is teaching may not be clear. Given that, as Plantinga admits, the confidence produced by allegedly divine causation of beliefs can be indistinguishable from the confidence produced by various non-divine causes, it is anomalous to think that God would employ a belief-creating method that leaves even earnest seekers after God who have conflicting beliefs about which each feels certain with no way to determine which of the conflicting beliefs express the truth about God.

Our discussion of Plantinga leaves us with the same conclusion as we drew at the end of the previous section: we can never justifiedly claim with anything near certainty that various propositions of which our belief is occasioned by reading, or is inferred from, the Bible are revealed by God or carry divine certification. If God wished to reveal such propositions, traditional theists would have to agree that God could have caused them to be stated clearly and certified them as divinely revealed; if God actually did wish to reveal them, it is plausible to think that God would have caused this to be done (again assuming, as traditional theists would, that God could do so), especially given the problems occasioned by the Bible as it is. As we have seen, the Bible does not contain anything of this sort. Therefore, I conclude that propositions taught or otherwise expressed are more plausibly thought to be simply human beliefs about God and God's relations to humans, to be tested like all human beliefs, rather than thought to be revealed truths to be held on to unless conclusively defeated.

In light of the fact that in the Bible there are no clear propositions that are clearly divinely certified truths, one other very important conclusion seems justified: *there is no good reason to suppose that the biblical writers themselves were the recipients of supernaturally communicated revealed truths of significance to humans in general.* If God had supernaturally communicated various truths of this sort to the writers, there is every reason to expect that God would cause those truths to be clearly set forth in the Bible and clearly divinely certified. Otherwise, the supernatural communication would benefit only the writers themselves.

Another View of the Bible and Revelation

In this chapter we have been discussing the possibility that the Bible is a vehicle for conveying particular revealed truths. I have argued that the phenomena of the Bible do not seem appropriate if the Bible is to be the medium for conveying propositions that we have good grounds for regarding as divinely revealed. The negative results of the discussion of various approaches in this chapter suggest that the only truly good grounds for regarding some propositions as divinely revealed would be obvious miracles supporting their having that status. This was the most common position throughout most of the history of Christian thought, and it was reaffirmed by Swinburne. However, as I argued in Chapter 4, we today have no good grounds to believe that any obvious miracles have occurred. Yet if there are particular truths God wants to reveal to people, then one might expect them to be clearly stated and certified by an obvious miracle.[27] After all, what is the point of *revealing* something *unclearly*? Neither human free will on the part of the authors nor sinful human ignorance on the part of the readers/interpreters is adequate to explain this unclarity. Given only a level of desire to obey God's will common among ordinary Christians today, God could have appeared in a dramatic vision to the writer and dictated the words God wanted him to write. And even we sinful, ignorant humans can usually reach a far greater – though not always complete – agreement regarding what a particular theologian taught about a particular doctrine than we can about what the Bible teaches on that doctrine.

Nor would it be apt to reply to this point by saying that I am trying to define *a priori* what kind of revelation God should give us. For I am not working *a priori*. I am responding to a popular *human* theory about the Bible: that it contains or is a medium for revealed truths. This human theory claims that in the Bible God has given us revealed truths, or that the Bible is a medium or provides an occasion for conveying revealed truths. The advocates of this theory should explain why these alleged truths are not stated clearly and clearly divinely certified. My objection is not that God has not given us an appropriate sort of revelation, but rather that God has not given us the sort of revelation one would expect if the theory in question were correct. Thus, my objection is a reason to question the theory, not an attempt to hold God accountable to some *a priori* standards for revelation.

If we reject theories that claim that the Bible consists of or contains revealed truths or that the Bible is God's sole (or supremely normative) medium of revelation, what is an alternative? If there is revelation, how might it be understood in a way more consonant with the phenomena of the Bible? Perhaps there are many ways this might be done, but the way that seems to me to be most likely is the following.

God is manifested in various events, and in some events God's character is more clearly revealed than it is in other events just as humans' characters are more clearly revealed in some of the things they do than in others – for example, what they do in responding to some situation involving threats to the welfare of others rather than what they do in eating a meal or taking a walk. Some humans come to believe that God is manifest in some events, and they formulate beliefs about God and the manifestation in relation to the tradition and culture of which they are a part, by using the concepts they have. They also give expression to those beliefs in other ways, such as the histories they write, the stories they tell, and the poetry they write. As they do this, God may also be inspiring them to more adequate formulations, but this inspiration is preconscious and only one factor contributing to the final expressions of their beliefs. In light of this suggestion, we can understand why the Bible does not contain any clear formulations of propositions that are clearly identified as divinely revealed. We can also understand why the Bible contains inconsistencies even about the "great things of the gospel," why it is not clear on many matters important to the life of believers and of the Church, and why it consists of so many diverse types of literature. Thus this suggestion is far more congruent with the phenomena of the Bible than are any of the views we have examined in this chapter. Of course, the congruence between this suggestion and the phenomena of the Bible is no conclusive proof that the suggestion is correct, and the suggestion gives no reason why God does not do more to reveal clearly truths about God's nature and will. In Chapter 8 I will describe an understanding of God and God's relation to the world that supplies a reason.

I regard it as another advantage of the suggestion that it could also be used by religious pluralists to understand how different religious traditions that affirm inconsistent beliefs and practices could all express to perhaps a roughly equal extent beliefs and practices that grew from equally clear and important revelations (manifestations) of God. Though it has not been part of my purpose in this work to argue for religious pluralism, I do find it a far more plausible position than any form of religious exclusivism. And if some sort of religious pluralism is true, then if there is any revelation at all, there are many revelations. If there are many revelations, each generates its own tradition. And since, so far as I know, all the major religious traditions that claim a revelation[28] share the historical and hermeneutical difficulties Swinburne pointed out in connection with Christianity, I find it more plausible to think that God intends that each generation try to respond to what it takes to be divine manifestations freshly and creatively in light of its total tradition and of the knowledge current in its day than to think, as Swinburne does, that there is some essential unchanging core of truth in one tradition that it is crucial – or at least very valuable – for all people to know. Again, if there were such a core, why has it not been clearly identified and divinely certified?

On my view, then, why should Christians accept the authority of their Scriptures, the Bible? They should because they have experienced (what they take to be) salvation in a tradition for which the Bible is the original written source. However, the fact that they have experienced salvation in this tradition does not by itself entail any particular conclusions about what element(s) in that tradition, and in particular what beliefs about God, enabled them to do so, nor any conclusions about what specific feature(s) of the Bible enabled it to play its foundational role. Nor does it offer any guarantee that their beliefs are any closer to complete truth about God's nature and will than are the beliefs of adherents of other religions who experience (what they take to be) salvation in those religions; the beliefs might be simply beliefs that guide them to satisfactory relations with God (or Ultimate Reality) in their particular historical and cultural setting. That the beliefs fulfill this role seems to me to be an adequate reason for God to cause them to feel confidence about the beliefs if God does contribute to their feeling of confidence.

If, as I argued, there are no propositions for which we have clear, divine certification that they are revealed, then we have to work out (or accept) religious beliefs in whatever ways seem most likely to lead to true beliefs. Christians will no doubt continue to use the Bible as one important source of ideas about God and the Christian life. But they will also continue to struggle with difficulties in interpreting and applying what they read. Is this passage meant literally or in some non-literal way? Was the writer simply giving voice to beliefs in his culture, or was he expressing an important true idea about God? Does our changed cultural situation make an appropriate standard of conduct for us different from that of a biblical writer? Thoughtful Christians cannot avoid asking questions such as these as they attempt to determine what they should believe about God and the Christian life. My arguments in this chapter simply underscore the claim that in doing so they should not think that they can start from some clear, divinely certified revealed truths to which they must adhere. The belief that there are revealed truths that carry divine certification is of no use to us unless we can reliably identify them, and I have argued that we cannot. There may be justified beliefs about God and the Christian life, but they will be justified in one or more of the variety of ways we justify other beliefs, not by their falling into a unique category: divinely certified revealed truths.

Conclusion

The view proposed in the previous section implies that on many issues there almost certainly is a variety of positions that may legitimately be called Christian, for each of them may be a legitimate response today to God as manifested and understood in the Christian tradition(s). The variety of positions that Swinburne acknowledges in the Bible even on matters he considers central revealed doctrines suggests that there was a variety even in biblical times. Swinburne advocates reinterpreting passages whose most natural interpretation implies an unorthodox position. I propose admitting that there is a variety of Christian views on the matter and regarding as a mistake the attempt to define one position as essential to Christianity. This is not to say that inconsistent propositions can all be true, but rather that one can respond to God in a fundamentally Christian way by believing any one of different sets of somewhat inconsistent propositions. Most Christians already accept this, at least to some extent, in that they accept as Christians people who differ from them on some doctrinal matters. Adherents of each position may well believe that their position is better than that of other Christians, but they accept as Christians at least some who hold differing positions. If, as I hold, the Bible itself reflects such differences in New

Testament times, then those who accord God a significant role in overseeing the writing of the Bible should explain why God permitted this in the Bible if it is not acceptable to God.

Those dissatisfied with this pluralism within Christianity as well as among various religions should ask whether any other view adequately responds to the phenomena of the Bible and to disputes about its interpretation throughout Christian history. Given the absence of clear and clearly divinely certified revealed truths, and given the problems finding such revealed truths in or through the Bible, it seems that even Christians should conclude that it is very dubious that God gave us any. Therefore, we cannot simply appeal to statements in the Bible or to what is allegedly revealed or taught in the Bible as the basis for our beliefs about God. This was the main conclusion I wished to establish in this chapter. Moreover, as I said early in this chapter, the fact that there are no clear and clearly divinely certified revealed truths constitutes still another problem for traditional Christian theists if they want to claim also that God wished to reveal certain things to humans. For surely an omnipotent, omniscient, all-good God would be able to reveal clearly truths that God wanted humans to know and to clearly certify them as divinely revealed. That there are no such truths gives us good reason to doubt either that God has all the characteristics that traditional theists claim or that God wished to reveal any truths to human beings. For reasons to be discussed in Chapter 8, I suggest that we take it as reason to doubt at least that God is omnipotent in the sense widely believed throughout Christian history. Our conclusions about the Bible show that we cannot simply appeal to statements in the Bible or to what is allegedly revealed or taught in the Bible as a basis for affirming divine omnipotence in this sense. Of course, appeal to allegedly revealed truths has not been the only ground on which this belief has been affirmed. In the next chapter, we will consider other grounds that have been suggested for the belief that God is omnipotent.

Notes

1. To be precise, those who propose theodicies or defenses could be concerned merely with whether the theodicy or defense constitutes a good philosophical argument, without being committed to the truth of the assumptions that generate the problem. However, this is rarely, if ever, actually true of those who propose theodicies or defenses. In any case, I am concerned with what it is most plausible to believe about God, not with the more narrow question of how plausible certain replies to certain objections to traditional theism are.

2. Sometimes indications that they play this role are contained in unsupported claims that something is revealed. For example, after giving a very well-argued defense of what he terms "naive universalism," Daniel Howard-Snyder adds that he believes that "the plain sense of Holy Scripture and the teaching of the Church precludes naive universalism. In short, nothing I've said is even remotely relevant to the view that I hold, namely that God has pretty much informed us that universalism, in both its naive and sophisticated forms is false" ("In Defense of Naive Universalism," *Faith and Philosophy*, 20/3 [July 2003]: 362). Peter van Inwagen, after defending modal skepticism about a number of modal propositions far removed from common human experiences, says that he believes them to be true because he believes, on the basis of revelation, the truth of corresponding indicative propositions ("Reflections on the Chapters by Draper, Russell, and Gale," *The*

Evidential Argument from Evil, ed. Daniel Howard-Snyder [Bloomington, IN: Indiana University Press, 1996], p. 238). In pointing out the reliance on revelation affirmed by both these writers, I am not criticizing them; I am simply illustrating that for some (I would say many) traditional Christian theists, beliefs about what has been revealed are important in their total doxastic structures.

3. I believe that this is also true of alleged revelations in other religions, and some of my argument about the Christian revelation, such as claim N just below in the text, will have obvious applications to other alleged revelations. However, I will not attempt to defend my belief in relation to other alleged revelations.

4. Philadelphia, PA: Temple University Press, 1988. In this section, page numbers in parentheses refer to this work.

5. Alvin Plantinga does present an ingenious attempt to use something like the causation model in relation to the Bible. We will examine his attempt later in this chapter.

6. Moreover, today's readers of the Bible who would try to draw their own inferences from the manifestations face the preliminary problem of whether the accounts of these manifestations are accurate in at least all the important details; our knowledge of how the documents that compose the Bible came to be written in their current form is enough to make this a serious problem.

7. Of course, one could say that the statement is an accurate report of what Jesus said, but Jesus was in error. However, those who regard the Bible as a medium for communicating divinely revealed propositions are very unlikely to admit that Jesus made a mistake, for they typically believe that Jesus was the incarnation of God and therefore unable to err. And if Jesus could be wrong about this, what else might he be wrong about?

8. These are two of the examples discussed by Stephen T. Davis in *The Debate about the Bible: Inerrancy versus Infallibility* (Philadelphia, PA: The Westminster Press, 1977), pp. 96–107. The command to kill all the Canaanites, discussed below in the text, is another.

9. Deut. 2:31–5; 3:1–8; 7:2; and Josh. 6:15–21; 8:25–6; 11:12.

10. Many Christians not only accept that the Bible exhibits this phenomenon, but employ it as a way to resolve some difficulties about what is said in certain passages, such as the one in Joshua. A classic example of this occurred when some leaders of the Roman Catholic Church were contending with Galileo about the geocentric theory of the universe; one of their arguments for the geocentric theory was that Joshua commanded the sun to stand still rather than the earth to stop rotating. But when acceptance of the heliocentric theory was virtually universal, the passage in Joshua was reinterpreted as referring to the way things appear, not to the way they are. Here it was science that led Christians to the "correct" interpretation of the passage; they had not found it by studying the passage itself. This passage, like so many others, contains no indication of whether it is speaking of the way things are, or of the way they appear.

11. As we will see, this qualification is important, but it would not be doubted by traditional Christians, and it is their view that we are currently discussing.

12. *Revelation: From Metaphor to Analogy* (Oxford: Clarendon Press, 1992). Page and chapter numbers in parentheses in this section refer to this work.

13. I agree that the Bible has such passages; indeed, I suspect that I believe that the Bible has more of them than Swinburne does. However, I did not include this alleged feature along with the other six above because the claim that the Bible contains this feature is far more controversial than the claim that it contains the other six.

14. Swinburne's proposal here indicates the importance of according the Church (the reason for capitalizing this word is explained in the next note) great authority, as Swinburne does. For the inconsistency could also be eliminated by reinterpreting the passages consistent

with Christian orthodoxy or – as I shall propose later – by saying that both represent possible Christian positions.

15. Swinburne capitalizes "Church" throughout his book, implying that he is referring to the body that is the divinely authorized interpreter of original revelation, rather than to any and every organization that calls itself a Christian church. This usage becomes especially clear in passages such as the following: "The teaching of a body wildly out of line with the teaching of all earlier Christian bodies with which it can claim any continuity of organization cannot be the Church" (124). In the remainder of this section, I will (try to) follow Swinburne's usage, using "church" to refer to any organized body that calls itself a Christian church, and "Church" to refer to any body that is the divinely authorized interpreter of original revelation (some body that is part or all of the true Church). On some occasions I will insert the (admittedly redundant) term "true" before "Church," to emphasize to the reader what this capitalized term refers to.

16. Swinburne has a very helpful discussion of analogy, metaphor, literary genre, and the sense in which different sorts of literature can have a truth-value (ch. 2–4).

17. There is a problem here, somewhat hidden by Swinburne's terminology. Of course, the fact that a doctrine is taught by the true Church is substantial evidence for its truth. But all we have direct access to is the fact that a doctrine is taught by some church, which may not be (part of) the Church. To assume that because some doctrine was taught by some church, even for centuries, it is a teaching of the Church begs important questions.

18. John Hick, ed., *The Myth of God Incarnate* (Philadelphia, PA: The Westminster Press, 1977).

19. In a subsequent work, Swinburne has attempted to do some of the work of the historian in defense of the rationality of believing that Jesus was resurrected in a sense that includes "the coming-to-life again of a body dead for thirty-six hours" (*The Resurrection of God Incarnate* [Oxford: Clarendon Press, 2003], pp. 1–2). However, for all its erudition, this work does nothing to mitigate the problems already noted with his approach. The argument involves work in natural theology as well as historical reconstruction, because Swinburne argues that showing that God exists and would be likely to give a revelation involving an incarnation and an atonement makes the Christian revelation more probable, and thus reduces the amount of historical evidence needed to justify the belief that Christ was raised in a miraculous way. Therefore, this work does nothing to reduce the concern that Swinburne's approach requires more time and intellectual abilities than most humans possess. And even if Swinburne is right in arguing that considerations from natural theology reduce the amount of historical evidence needed, that does not explain why God did not make sure this very important information was far better documented. Even if better documentation were not strictly required for someone with Swinburne's time and abilities, that is no reason not to give better documentation. Most people would need it, and even a Swinburne need not find useless things that would strengthen his case.

20. After writing this discussion of Swinburne's approach, I was pleased to see that Alvin Plantinga also reaches the conclusion that it is not possible to use biblical materials and ordinary methods of historical investigation, as Swinburne tries to do, to show that believing what both regard as central Christian claims can be rationally justified. Plantinga's argument can be found in *Warranted Christian Belief* (New York: Oxford University Press, 2000), pp. 272–80.

21. Warrant is a central concept in Plantinga's epistemology. He defines it as "that further quality or quantity (perhaps it comes in degrees) whatever precisely it may be, enough of which distinguishes knowledge from mere true belief" (*Warranted Christian Belief*, p. 153). Page numbers in parentheses in this section on Plantinga refer to this work.

22. At various points in his work, Plantinga summarizes these "great things" in verbally different but essentially similar ways. One description is this: "that Jesus Christ is the second person of the trinity, that he became incarnate, suffered, died, and rose from the dead, and that by atoning for our sin he made it possible for us human beings to achieve a right relationship with God" (286).

23. Elsewhere, Plantinga suggests that there need not be anything verbal (written or spoken) in an occasion when there arises warranted true beliefs about God. For example, he suggests that God might have designed us so that, as one contemplates the heavens, there arises (or tends to arise, unless hindered by sin) the warranted true belief that God created them (171–9).

24. As we saw earlier, Swinburne's recognition of this fact led him to propose that the creeds be used as the key to understanding what he believes to be the central message of the Bible. But his approach requires confidence that the creeds are suitable for this purpose. He tries to provide evidence that they are, but Plantinga's whole approach is non-evidentialist. Plantinga might claim that the Holy Spirit convinces believers of the truth of the creeds, but that would not show that the creeds should be used to discern the central message of the Bible.

25. Plantinga writes that "the existence of the experiences that go with the operation of the *sensus divinitatis* (or IIHS – internal instigation of the Holy Spirit) are compatible with there being no omnipotent, omniscient, wholly good creator of the universe" (334). If they are compatible with there being no God, then they can be caused by non-divine factors.

26. *Revelation*, p. 177.

27. This same question seems to me to be applicable to Nicholas Wolterstorff's thoughtful and carefully argued *Divine Discourse: Philosophical Reflections on the Claim that God Speaks* (New York: Cambridge University Press, 1995). Because his concern in the book is divine discourse rather than revelation, I have not discussed it in the text. But because his topic is related to revelation, I thought a brief comment might be appropriate. Wolterstorff discusses the way one person's discourse may be a medium for another person's (for example, a biblical writer's discourse a medium for God's discourse). He shows a keen awareness of problems that the biblical materials present for one who seeks to find what God is saying through the human writers. Some of these may be inseparable from using agents to say something, but others seem to arise because what God wishes to say is something other than what the biblical writers say. He describes a variety of ways in which someone may use what an agent says to convey information other than that conveyed in the words of the agent. However, he nowhere discusses why God would choose this way of discoursing to humans when, according to traditional theists, God has the power to convey the message through chosen agents (the biblical writers) in a far clearer way, such as by having them deliver verbatim the information God wishes to convey.

28. Not all religions claim a revelation. For example, though Buddhism has more sacred texts than Christianity, it is not claimed that they contain revealed truths.

CHAPTER 7

Should God's Power be Understood as Omnipotence?

In the previous chapter we discussed one possible ground that might be given for thinking that God is omnipotent: the claim that it is a revealed truth in the Bible. We found that the phenomena of the Bible were such as to give good reason to doubt that God has given any clear, divinely certified revealed truths, and therefore no good reason to think that divine omnipotence is a revealed truth even if some biblical writers believed and taught it. Our task in this chapter is to discuss and evaluate alleged grounds for thinking that God is omnipotent other than the claim that it is a revealed truth. It is important to remember that I am using "omnipotent" to refer also to the possibly more modest view that God has the power to unilaterally bring about any logically possible creaturely state of affairs.

It will be a useful preliminary to our discussion of these grounds to consider whether religious experience by itself could provide an adequate ground. By "religious experience" in this context I mean a feeling or conviction about God arising in specific circumstances that otherwise contain nothing out of the ordinary, such as a feeling, perhaps while one is in church or is praying or is looking at the starry heavens, that God is present or is forgiving one or guiding one. I raise this question about religious experience because several recent defenses of the rationality of the belief that God exists have given a prominent role to the experience of God. Though these defenders themselves do not claim that the experience of God is a basis for believing that God is omnipotent, others may not realize this, perhaps misled by the wide acceptance of divine omnipotence among Western theists. Thus, they may think that defense of veridicality of religious experience (or defense of the existence of God based on religious experience) is also a defense of the omnipotence of God.

I offer two reasons in support of my claim that religious experience does not by itself provide grounds for the belief that God is omnipotent. First, even if there were some way in which a religious experience gives us a basis for estimating God's power, our limitations as finite beings would seem to preclude concluding that the being whom we experience is omnipotent rather than just very powerful. There are limits to the range of human senses, and presumably to any analogous capacity by which humans directly experience God. Once those limits are exceeded by the object of some experience, the experience itself gives no basis for judging by how much those limits are exceeded. The second reason is based on the ways we estimate the power of some entity. We do so most often by seeing what it does; alternatively, in instances where we can study the physical structure and power sources of the entity, we can make inferences about its capacities. But neither of these seems applicable to religious experience in the sense under discussion. God does not have a physical structure that we can study as a basis for inferences about God's capacities. As for things that God is believed to have done, that God should be able to make

God's presence known to us or to affect us in some way does not entail that God is omnipotent. Nor does it even entail that God can suspend laws of nature, as I will argue in the next chapter. (In a broader sense of "religious experience," the term may be used to refer to a sense that some thing or event external to oneself that one is experiencing is the work of God; in such cases the work God accomplished may provide a basis for some inference about God's power. We will discuss this possibility later when we consider various things and events attributed to God as grounds for thinking God is omnipotent.)

Therefore, religious experience does not provide grounds for the belief that God is omnipotent. What have been given as grounds? I will consider four: the perfection of God, the belief that God is the creator of all things, miracles, and beliefs about what God will do to overcome evil.

The Perfection of God

Perhaps the most common reason, apart from alleged revelation, for believing that God is omnipotent is that it is implicit in the perfection of God. The term "omnipotence" and its cognates might be used to designate perfect power, whatever that turns out to be, or it might be used to designate a certain idea of what that power is. In Western philosophy and theology it has come to be used primarily in the latter sense, to designate a certain idea of what that power is (or any one of a number of ideas that share many common features but differ in some details). One of these common features is roughly the power to unilaterally bring about any logically possible non-divine state of affairs.[1] All traditional theists have affirmed this as part of their understanding of divine power even though some, who believe that humans possess libertarian free will, believe that God does not always exercise this power.[2] As a consequence, those who deny that God has the power to unilaterally determine any logically possible non-divine state of affairs have typically not used "omnipotence" to characterize their understanding of God's power, even though they may have believed that God has the maximum power that any one being can possess.[3] Understandably, their critics have charged them with denying the omnipotence of God. But what really matters if one is to maintain the claim that God is the perfect or greatest possible being is that one affirms that God possesses the maximum power that it is possible for any one being to possess or, more briefly, the greatest possible power. But how much power is that? As will become apparent, agreement on the general formula – the maximum power that it is possible for any actual being to possess – has not yielded a similar agreement on what that power includes.

A few thinkers, such as Descartes, have said that God's power includes the power to do what is logically impossible, but the vast majority of writers on this topic have denied this on the grounds that any logically impossible task or state of affairs is something purportedly described by a group of words that in fact does not and cannot describe anything.[4] Therefore, these writers typically would accept as a first approximation something like this formulation: the greatest possible power is roughly the power to do anything that is logically possible. However, many writers have thought that this formulation needed further clarification and/or refinement because of disagreements about what is logically possible. There is general agreement on what is called logical possibility in the narrow sense: the absence of contradiction that can be demonstrated using propositional or first-order predicate calculus. However, there is also what is called logical possibility in the broad sense; disagreement about what this includes causes different understandings of God's power.

Any broadly logically necessary propositions that a person believes to be true affect what that person believes God can do. For example, if I believe that "No one can cause the past to be different from what it was" is a broadly logically necessary proposition, then I will deny that God can change the past, but I will not regard this "limitation" on what God can do as a reason to doubt that God has the greatest possible power (or that God is omnipotent, if I accept the formulation that an omnipotent being can do anything that is logically possible). Some propositions that are alleged to be broadly logically possible are relatively non-controversial, but others have been much disputed, including some that have played an important role in philosophical discussions of God's power and other divine attributes. Under this last heading, for example, are these propositions: (1) No one, including God, can cause a person to so something freely. (2) No contingent being can continue to exist without being continually sustained in existence by a necessary being. (3) All conditionals of freedom, including those that concern persons who have not and will never exist, have definite truth-values. Theists who accept any of these propositions will say that God cannot do some things that those who deny the proposition believe that God can do.[5]

Theists who deny any of propositions 1–3 could conclude that those who accept the proposition in question do not believe that God is omnipotent, for (they might say) God does not have the greatest possible power, all the power it is possible for any being to have. But those who accept the proposition might reply that they do attribute to God all the power it is possible for any being to have, for the proposition in question states a broadly logically necessary truth, and it is no real limitation on the power of a being to say that the being cannot do what is (broadly logically) impossible. This reply holds not just for the three propositions mentioned, but for any that are alleged to be broadly logically necessary. Provided people attribute to God all the power that they believe it is possible for any being to have, it is not appropriate to criticize them for denying that God is perfect in power. I am not suggesting that it is impossible to criticize other people's understanding of God's power. But I am suggesting that, provided they attribute to God the maximum power they believe it is possible for any being to have, the criticism of their understanding of God's power will have to be directed at the allegedly broadly logically necessary proposition that grounds their denial that God can do certain things, rather than simply charging that they believe in a God who is less than perfect in power, who is limited or finite in power.

It is important not to underestimate the difficulties there may be in determining whether or not a proposition states a broadly logically necessary truth, particularly when the allegedly broadly logically necessary proposition concerns some metaphysical issue, as do propositions 1–3 above. One's convictions about the truth of broadly logically necessary propositions about metaphysical issues is grounded either on intuitions about these issues or on the fact that the propositions are part of, or entailed by, an interrelated set of metaphysical propositions (a metaphysical scheme) that one finds convincing. Unfortunately, neither of these grounds is highly reliable, though one may be at least internally justified in believing the proposition in light of other beliefs one has. Different people often have different intuitions on metaphysical issues; thus, the mere fact that one has the intuition of the truth of some broadly logically necessary proposition about a metaphysical issue is hardly good evidence that the proposition is true, particularly if the issue is a controversial one. And the inability of any one metaphysical scheme to win universal or even nearly universal acceptance shows that it is difficult to determine what is true on metaphysical matters. I have no particular advice on how to settle these disputed issues, but I would strongly recommend one principle: when the acceptance of some intuitions about metaphysical issues or the acceptance of some metaphysical scheme generates severe problems or anomalies, that should be taken as grounds to question the intuitions or the metaphysical scheme. In earlier chapters of this work, I have tried to show that traditional theism generates severe problems or anomalies that have no good solution. It is my conviction that these anomalies result from incorrect beliefs about God's power. In the final chapter, I will show how a different understanding of God's power, resting on a different understanding of what is broadly logically necessary, itself grounded in a particular metaphysical scheme, solves the problems and resolves the anomalies. Here, I wanted only to set the stage by arguing that one's conception of what a being with the greatest possible power can do depends on what broadly logically necessary propositions about metaphysical issues one accepts, and therefore that the assessment of a particular conception of what the greatest possible power includes depends on an assessment of the relevant allegedly broadly logically necessary propositions.

Though most of the issues concerning what perfect power, the power of a perfect being, includes are metaphysical, there are some primarily axiological issues as well. Though there are certainly many axiological convictions that are not disputed (for example, it is better to know than to be ignorant), some that affect how God's power should be conceived are in dispute. For example, is it better to be pure act, or to have some passive potentialities? Is it better to be in all ways independent of others, or better to be in some ways relative to and thus dependent on others, perhaps because one cares about and is affected by what others experience?[6] For God's power to be perfect, is it necessary that God exercise complete control over every detail of what occurs in the created order (as some Calvinists believed), or is this not necessary for perfect power? Differences over axiological questions such as these also contribute to the problems of defining what perfect power would be. I suspect that different answers to such questions rest on different axiological intuitions; considerations can be given for and against these intuitions, but nothing like a conclusive argument is available for them.

The upshot of these considerations is that the requirement that God must be the perfect being, the being than which no better can be conceived, does not give us an agreed-upon or non-controversial analysis of what the power attributed to God should include. For the analysis depends on one's metaphysics and one's axiology; therefore, the justification of any belief about God's powers must include a justification of the metaphysical and axiological beliefs on which the analysis depends. This conclusion applies in particular to the belief that God's power must include the power to unilaterally bring about any logically possible creaturely state of affairs; this belief cannot be assumed to be a direct consequence of the belief that God's power is perfect or the maximum any being can have.

God as Creator

Another important possible ground for an understanding what God's power includes is the belief that God is the creator of all non-divine realities. Clearly, the sort of power that one attributes to God on this basis depends on one's understanding of what the act of creation involves. The understanding of creation that seems most strongly to support a traditional understanding of God's power is creation out of nothing. On this understanding of creation, God has the power to cause something to exist out of no antecedently existing stuff. If there is no antecedently existing stuff to resist God's creative activity, then what comes to exist should be exactly what God intends. Moreover, if God has the power to cause something to exist out of no antecedently existing stuff, then God also has the power to cause it to cease to exist, to return to nothingness, and also to change it in any way God sees fit. For changing it would involve nothing more than causing to cease to exist the part or aspect that God wishes to change, and then causing to exist in its place the change God intends. Thus, the belief that God created the universe out of nothing seems at least to entail that God has the power to unilaterally bring about any logically possible non-divine state of affairs. Some other understandings of creation may not entail that the sort of power God has is sufficient to generate the problems of evil. For example, the sort of creation done by Plato's Demiurge may not entail that the Demiurge has the sort of power required to generate the problems, for Plato's Demiurge cannot completely determine what the created product will be; therefore, the Demiurge can at best influence, but not completely determine, what states of affairs occur. Thus, if the belief that God is the creator of all non-divine reality is to serve as a basis for an idea of God's power that is sufficient to generate the problems of evil, creation should be understood as creation out of nothing.

Probably the source of the idea of creation out of nothing in the Christian tradition is Genesis 1, particularly the first verse understood in a certain way. But it is far from clear that it is correct to understand Genesis 1:1 as affirming creation out of nothing. Recently, several scholars have claimed that this verse is better translated "When God began to create the heavens and the earth, the earth was void … ," rather than "In the beginning God created the heavens and the earth …."[7] Though this claim is disputed, it does indicate at least that the contrary claim is not beyond dispute, as it was taken to be throughout much of the history of Christian thought. Moreover, it is not only Genesis 1 that is unclear on this matter: a clear statement of creation out of nothing in this sense does not appear anywhere in the canonical Scriptures accepted by Jews and Protestants. The absence of clear and repeated affirmations of creation out of nothing is strange if it is so important a doctrine as its defenders usually hold. In contrast, God's role as creator is frequently and explicitly affirmed and celebrated.

In addition to the question of whether or not creation out of nothing is believed by any biblical writer or taught anywhere in the Bible, there is also the issue of what significance it should have for us today even if the answer to this question were clearly affirmative. It would have significance for us today only if we had good reason to think that the biblical writers had some very reliable way of knowing that God created the universe out of nothing. In the previous chapter I argued that the phenomena of the Bible make it very unlikely that biblical writers were the recipients of supernaturally communicated divinely revealed propositions, and also very unlikely that the Bible contains any such propositions. Therefore, even if some biblical writers believed and taught the doctrine in question, their belief would have no basis beyond the humanly accessible sources available in their day. There is no reason for us today to place any particular confidence in those sources or in the conclusions the writers drew from them. Moreover, as far as I know, apart from the doctrine of creation out of nothing itself and the support it gives for divine omnipotence, there is nothing in the Christian tradition that implies that creation should be understood as creation out of nothing.

But if there are no good reasons in the Christian tradition for understanding creation as creation out of nothing, are there other sorts of considerations available to Christians today that provide good reasons for believing in creation out of nothing? Some claim that contemporary cosmological theory supports the doctrine. For the Big Bang theory holds that our universe began about 13 billion years ago in an inconceivably powerful explosion. But this cosmological theory gives at best only weak support to creation out of nothing. For even if our universe began when and as the theory says, the theory has no implications about whether anything existed prior to that explosion. Thus, our only grounds for saying that nothing existed prior to the explosion is our ignorance about conditions prior to it. Perhaps the great explosion that generated our universe is the result of a collapse of some prior universe. Or perhaps our universe is simply a bubble on a vastly larger complex of universes.[8] Thus, while current scientific thought does not rule out the possibility that our universe came to be out of no pre-existing stuff, it also provides no good basis for affirming this rather than some other account of the origins of our universe.

If scientific thought does not adequately support creation out of nothing, are there philosophical arguments that do? Under one interpretation, the cosmological argument is thought to support the theory that the universe was created a finite number of years ago. But discussions of this argument reveal that it has not succeeded in winning general acceptance for the conclusion that the non-divine realm must have begun a finite number of years ago. Indeed, many of the most sophisticated proponents of the argument do not believe that it even attempts to show that; rather, they claim that it shows that non-divine beings all depend moment-by-moment on a divine (necessary) being for their existence and ability to do anything.[9] That is, they claim that the argument shows that non-divine beings have a continuing dependence on a divine being, but it implies nothing about whether non-divine beings originated some finite number of years ago.

However, there is a form of the cosmological argument – or perhaps another cosmological argument – that does purport to show that the non-divine realm began only a finite number of years ago. This form, called the *kalam* cosmological argument, has been expounded and defended in recent years by William Lane Craig; we will consider one of his discussions of the argument. One premise is that the universe began to exist a finite number of years ago. In *Reasonable Faith*, he gives two arguments in support of this premise.[10] The first is as follows:

1. An actually infinite number of things cannot exist.
2. A beginningless series of events in time entails an actually infinite number of things.
3. Therefore, a beginningless series of events in time cannot exist. (94)

Craig offers some considerations to support premise 1 of this argument. Using Hilbert's Hotel (an imagined hotel with a denumerably infinite number of rooms) as an illustration, he tries to show that absurd consequences result if there is supposed to exist an actually infinite number of things. For example, if all the rooms in the hotel are filled and another guest arrives, the proprietor could move all the current guests to the room with the next higher number and put the new guest in Room 1.[11] If a denumerably infinite number of new guests arrived, the proprietor could accommodate them all by moving each of the current guests to the room with double the number and putting the new guests in the rooms thus vacated. Craig claims that neither of these processes would result in a larger number of guests than before the process started (because in both cases the number of guests is denumerably infinite before and after the additional guests arrive). He mentions some other alleged absurdities as well, but they have the same features as the two already mentioned.

On reflection, it appears that there are two sorts of puzzles here. One is a physical puzzle: if all the rooms are full, how can one put in more guests? The other is a mathematical puzzle: if one adds more guests, how can the number of guests not be larger than before one added the guests? Let us consider the puzzles in that order.

I am inclined to agree with Wes Morriston that the physical puzzle shows "at most that there cannot be an actually infinite set *of a certain sort* – one whose elements are *co-existing* objects bearing a *changeable physical relationship* to one another."[12] However, the theory that the totality of beings in the history of the universe (or the series of universes including the present one) is infinite does not entail even that at any one time there is an infinity of actual things. But if there is not an infinity of things at the same time, the proprietor could not do the sort of shifting that generates what Craig calls the absurdities. To see this, change the illustration. Suppose that the universe (or the series of universes) is beginningless in time. And suppose there is one hotel (call it the Bilbert) that has always existed, but in this way: it has only one room at any one time, but at the end of each year that room is destroyed and a new one built. (I could use ten rooms at a time or any finite number, but it will be simpler to consider the illustration if I suppose that there is only one.) Then if the universe is beginningless, the series of rooms would be infinite. But any time at which the rooms were all filled, it would be impossible to add any more guests at that time. Of course, the proprietor could invite a different guest to come back next year, and in this way the proprietor might have had an infinity of different guests, but there is no obvious absurdity in what we are now supposing.

This leaves the mathematical puzzle. Here Craig is misled by thinking of the transfinite number associated with an infinite set on the model of finite numbers associated with finite sets. But transfinite numbers conform to a different set of axioms than do finite numbers. Unlike finite sets, a transfinite set does not have a greater transfinite number of members than do all its proper subsets, and no finite number properly numbers all the members of an infinite set. Thus, the mathematical puzzle also does not show that infinite sets generate absurdities.[13]

Craig has a second argument in support of his claim that there cannot be a beginningless series of events:

1. The series of events in time is a collection formed by adding one member after another.
2. A collection formed by adding one member after another cannot be actually infinite.
3. Therefore, the series of events in time cannot be actually infinite. (98)

The second premise of this argument is true only if the collection started with a finite number of members. But of course the theory that the universe is beginningless in time denies that the series of events started at some time (even a time infinitely long ago) as a finite number of events. Rather, it claims that there was always an infinity of events prior to any particular time. So we are adding a finite number of events to what is already an infinite series of events; there is no problem in supposing that the result is still an infinite series of events. Thus, the *kalam* cosmological argument as presented by Craig does not show that the universe must have had a beginning a finite number of years ago.

There is one other possible basis for concluding that the universe was created out of nothing, either in the sense that it began a finite number of years ago or in the sense that apart from the support of a necessary being it would vanish into sheer nothingness. This other basis is some metaphysical scheme. For example, Thomas Aquinas' conclusion that the universe depends on the activity of a necessary being is based on his metaphysics of act and potency and on his analysis of finite beings as composites of essences and *esse* (the act of existence). It would take us too far afield to debate the adequacy of Aquinas' metaphysics and of other metaphysical views that might be used as bases for affirming creation out of nothing in either of the two senses mentioned. Here, I can only point out again that if the doctrine is based on a metaphysics, then it is no better established than the metaphysics on which it is based, and those who are unconvinced by the metaphysics will have to find other reasons to affirm the doctrine. I have already argued that no other suggested basis is adequate. Thus, I conclude that apart from the elaboration and adequate defense of some metaphysical scheme that implies creation out of nothing in either or both of the senses, there is no reason to affirm it.

Though creation out of nothing might entail divine omnipotence (or at least God's power to unilaterally determine any non-divine state of affairs), as I claimed above, the more general idea that God is in some sense the creator would not necessarily entail it. In the next chapter we will discuss another understanding of creation, which does not entail it. Thus, we cannot look simply to the general doctrine that God is the creator in some sense as an adequate basis to affirm divine omnipotence.

Miracles

Another basis on which divine omnipotence has been affirmed is the occurrence of miracles, understood as temporary suspensions of laws of nature accomplished by divine power. (In this section, that is the only sense in which I will use the term.) Of course, their occurrence would require God's ability to suspend some laws of nature, and it would suggest God's ability to suspend any and all laws of nature. Therefore, it would also suggest that God has the power to unilaterally determine the details of worldly processes. So here the crucial question is whether we have good reason to believe that miracles have occurred.

In Chapter 4, we discussed alleged epistemic miracles (miracles whose purpose is enhancing the recipient's knowledge of God or faith in God), especially those narrated in the Bible, and we found that there is no good reason to think that epistemic miracles have occurred or do occur. But I also pointed out that some events that have been taken as miracles do not seem to have the point of confirming revelation. Instead, their point seems to have been to help people by providing them with various temporal goods, such as life, health, food, and offspring; such miracles would include curing diseases, preventing or mitigating injury in accidents, feeding someone who is hungry, and so on. The belief that miracles of this sort, which I termed "practical miracles," occur is perhaps at least as important to ordinary believers as is the belief that epistemic miracles occur. Some believers tell stories of healings (those at Lourdes are famous examples) and of other sorts of non-epistemic benefits conferred through miracles.

As we saw in Chapter 4, justifying the belief that a certain event involved a practical miracle raises somewhat different issues than justifying the belief that the event involved an epistemic miracle. I charged that there is an inconsistency in claiming that God worked an epistemic miracle that does not involve a clear suspension of a law of nature. For the purpose of an epistemic miracle is to provide evidence to confirm that something is divine revelation. But if it is not clear that there is a violation of a law of nature, then it is not clear that there is a special divine involvement in the event, so there is no clear confirmation of revelation. But practical miracles do not have confirmation of divine activity as part of their purpose, so their involving a violation of a law of nature need not be evident. But if it is not evident, then it is much harder to justify the claim that the event involves a miracle. Of course, a practical miracle *might* be such as to involve a clear violation of a law of nature, but it need not be.

Evidence for the occurrence of miracles of either type might come from material in the Bible or from extra-biblical sources. I will confine this discussion to alleged miracles in the Bible and in our time. (Other alleged miracles are too little discussed and too poorly documented to be discussed here.) One problem we face in relation to alleged miracles in either place is the lack of adequate confirmation of details that would clearly indicate that some law(s) of nature had been suspended. The biblical events that have traditionally been seen as miracles are not well attested – usually the account of the event was written a considerable time after the event by someone who was not an eyewitness, and often the account itself is sketchy. Attempts to reconstruct the oral tradition and the literary tradition (if any) behind various biblical accounts as we have them are highly controversial. Indeed, there is relatively little of significance in biblical studies today that is not controversial. Moreover, concerning many seemingly narrative portions of the Bible, many scholars doubt that the writer's intention was to present an account that is historically accurate in our sense; for example, they suggest that the Gospels are identity narratives and/or faith statements about the significance of Jesus Christ. These facts about contemporary biblical studies certainly do not prove that the details of various accounts are not accurate. But they do indicate that one cannot justifiedly simply refer to most passages as though they certainly describe the events accurately. This situation makes very problematic the prospects for using some biblical account of what we today would regard as a miracle as grounds for claiming that miracles have actually occurred. To be justified in understanding an event as a miracle, one must have an accurate knowledge of the details of the event. If one cannot be confident about at least certain crucial details, one also cannot be confident in judging that the event is a miracle.

These generalities apply to every seemingly miraculous event in the Bible, even to what is often said to be the best attested – and for the Christian, the most important – seemingly miraculous event in the Christian Bible: the resurrection of Christ. Certain experiences relevant to the claim that it occurred are mentioned by five different writers (the four Evangelists and Paul), and it is central to the faith of at least most of the New Testament writers. (The writers of the Epistle of James and of the three Epistles of John do not even allude to the resurrection; thus, its role in their faith is difficult to determine.) But even the resurrection is not as well attested as many think. One writer, Paul, did say that Christ appeared to him, *but that is all Paul says about the event; he tells us nothing about what the appearance was like.* Paul's statement, which is in I Corinthians, was written about twenty years after Jesus appeared to him. The book of Acts does contain an account of an encounter between Paul and the risen Christ, but this account dates probably thirty to forty years after Paul's statement in I Corinthians, is not by an eyewitness to Paul's encounter, and says nothing about what the risen Christ was like. In I Corinthians 15, Paul does tell us that the risen Christ had earlier appeared to others, but again he tells us nothing about what those appearances were like (and if he had, that would not be eyewitness testimony anyway). Accounts in the Gospels other than Mark do give us more detailed pictures of the appearances (and Mark does contain an account of the empty tomb), but the earliest of the Gospels with stories about appearances of the risen Christ dates at least fifty years after the crucifixion.[14] So there are reasons to doubt the accuracy of the accounts and reasons to be unsure just what the original appearances were like.

The defender of anything like traditional views has problems in addition to those noted above. We will note two here. First, if something like the traditional view is correct, one has to wonder why God did not cause a better record to be made of the event. It is true that no matter how good the record, a skeptic could ask for more. But the texts we have do not even come close to being good documents for historical reconstruction.[15] Paul could have described his experience. Even better, he and the other eyewitnesses could have recorded their experiences right away and in some detail. Surely an omnipotent deity could have assured that we had eyewitness descriptions of the risen Christ written within hours of the appearances.

Analogous questions could be raised with even greater force about the accounts of other seemingly miraculous events in the Bible: if God has the power to bring about the event as described, then God also has the power to bring about its adequate documentation. (Admittedly, some might question whether even this vastly better documentation would have been enough to make a strong case for traditional ideas about the resurrection, but it certainly would be far more nearly adequate.) Since the events are not adequately documented, God must not have wanted the events to be adequately documented. Why not?

In addition to these problems about evidence, there is the problem of justice discussed in Chapter 4. If God actually performed some obvious miracles for some people in biblical times and there are no obvious miracles or candidate events today, then God gave to certain people in biblical times an enormous benefit not matched by anything given to all other people. Thus, we have two kinds of reasons to doubt that God performed any of the obvious miracles suggested by certain biblical passages: the lack of good documentation of the details of the biblical events, and the injustice of God's performing obvious miracles for some (potential) believers in biblical days and not for all other people, such as those in our day.

In our day, we lack any obvious miracles or even candidate events. However, there are many claims about practical miracles, particularly miracles of healing. The greatest problem with believing that these events are miracles is the same as with alleged miracles in the Bible: the evidence we have simply is not adequate grounds for a justified belief that an event occurred that is inexplicable by natural processes. The inadequacy of the evidence is the result of either or both of two factors: the attestation of the details of the event is very poor, and the details of the event are not such as to warrant the conclusion that the event did not occur in conformity to natural laws. Many of the alleged miracles are reported in documents whose value as sources is open to serious question, such as tabloid journals and reports of healings in tent meetings. And even when we have good grounds for confidence that the event happened as described, such as good medical records, the details may not be sufficient to support the claim that the event is inexplicable in terms of natural laws. I will illustrate this in relation to alleged miracles of healing.

I readily grant that dramatic cases of recovery, sometimes in the context of prayer for the sick, do occur, and that some of these cases are such that each one, *considered solely in the context of its own circumstances and of certain religious beliefs*, can with some plausibility be seen as a miracle. For example, someone for whom many people prayed may recover from a life-threatening illness even though no attending doctor expected recovery. But whatever plausibility a particular case may have when considered in isolation disappears when put in the context of other similar cases. Often in medically similar cases recovery does not occur, despite an apparently similar amount of equally fervent prayer. Sometimes recovery occurs without prayer. Sometimes it occurs in the context of "positive thinking" or various self-help disciplines. Given this diversity, is miraculous healing by God really the best explanation for the cases when recovery occurs? I do not think so. Surely a more justified conclusion from such data would be something like the following. Sometimes people recover when no doctor expects them to (and sometimes people do not recover even though they are expected to). There may be several factors that contribute to the recoveries, such as religious faith, a positive outlook, and support by other people, but none of these factors guarantees recovery in every case. In general, we simply do not have enough knowledge about the natural factors that affect recovery to be confident that particular cases of recovery are not the result of the operation of natural factors. Moreover, if one claims that God did heal some and not others who were in similar situations, it would raise the problem of injustice that we discussed in Chapter 4.

The upshot of this discussion of miracles is that we have no good basis for thinking that any have occurred or do occur. Even in the case of the best-attested apparently miraculous biblical event, the historical evidence is far from what it reasonably could be and is not adequate by itself to show that something happened to Jesus' body that requires a non-natural explanation. The events of which we are reasonably sure of the details, such as certain healings, are not clearly miracles. Moreover, problems of apparent injustice arise if the miracle claims made by believers are true, as we saw in Chapter 4. Thus, not only do we lack good reasons to believe that any miracles have occurred, but we have good reasons to doubt that God performed any miracles; therefore, their having occurred cannot be cited as strong grounds for concluding that God has the power to unilaterally determine the details of worldly processes.

Overcoming Evil

Still another basis for affirming God's omnipotence is beliefs about God's eventual action to overcome evil in a final, definitive way and to provide post-mortem happiness for some or all humans. Because beliefs about these post-mortem states of affairs are so important to many of the theodicies discussed in Chapter 2, it is well worth considering what support beliefs about God's future overcoming of evil provide for the belief that God has at least the power to unilaterally determine non-divine states of affairs.

Perhaps the most important source of these beliefs is various biblical pictures and images of a future state brought about by this action. According to various accounts in the Gospels, Jesus told some parables that picture certain individuals enjoying heavenly bliss; for example, in the parable of the rich man and Lazarus, after his death Lazarus eats with Abraham. Other passages tell of Jesus' promising various people great rewards in heaven. According to Matthew 26, there will be a great judgment, after which the judge will invite the righteous to "inherit the kingdom prepared for you from the foundation of the world" (v. 34) and to go "into eternal life" (v. 45). In I Corinthians 15 Paul speaks of believers being transformed into imperishable, immortal beings. The last two chapters of the Revelation to St. John appear to describe the final state of the blessed. Christians have taken these and other images from various places in the Bible, often combined them as though they came from a single author, and elaborated on them in ways that have in turn captured the imaginations of other Christians. So we must proceed very carefully when trying to evaluate the extent to which these images provide grounds for thinking that God has the power to unilaterally bring about various creaturely states of affairs.

Perhaps the first thing to note if one shares my conclusions about the Bible and about the sort of information available to its writers is that things they wrote about future events in this world or another provide no reliable grounds for concluding that God has the power to unilaterally determine non-divine states of affairs. If inspiration does not involve the communication of truths in some supernatural way, then the biblical writers have no basis for making accurate pronouncements about a distantly future state in this world or another; what they say simply give images born of their faith. So unless one holds that God supernaturally communicated information about this future state or about God's intentions, there would be no reason to place any confidence in a biblical writer's (or anyone else's) depictions of it.

But it might be replied that New Testament writers at least had a source of information on these and other matters beyond the capacity of ordinary humans to know: Jesus. That is, Jesus knew and communicated to his disciples information that humans did not have the capacity to discover on their own, including information about a future state for humans. But we do not have good grounds to believe that Jesus possessed supernaturally known information about the future state of humans and of the world. In earlier chapters I argued that only an obvious miracle could supply such grounds, and we lack good grounds to believe that any obvious miracles occurred to confirm that Jesus had such information or to confirm any propositions about Jesus, such as that Jesus is God incarnate, that would be grounds for concluding that he had such information.

Still another reason to doubt that the New Testament contains supernaturally communicated truths about a future state for humans is that it seems impossible to put all the details together into one consistent picture. This impossibility is reflected in the fact that in the entire history of Christianity there has not emerged a detailed account of what happens after death that commands universal or even near-universal assent. In the words of Geddes MacGregor, "the supposition that there is a clear, unambiguous biblical or patristic or conciliar teaching about immortality and resurrection would be mistaken."[16] In his monumental work *Death and Eternal Life*, John Hick has an entire part (Part III) entitled "Christian Approaches" (note the plural), in which he describes something of the variety of ideas about the afterlife that were suggested by various passages in the New Testament and in subsequent Christian thought.[17] The variety, and in some cases clear inconsistencies, in these ideas strongly suggests that there is no clear, distinctively Christian revelation about an afterlife. The belief that there is an afterlife, probably sooner or later involving a body, was common (but not universal) among Jews in Jesus' day; thus, it did not originate with Jesus and his disciples, and no single consistent additional picture of an afterlife was communicated through Jesus and his disciples. On this particular issue of life after death, I ask the same question that in the previous chapter I asked generally about alleged revelation: if God wanted to communicate some information about a future state and if God is omnipotent, why is there no clear communication of information? Why should God want to *communicate* something *unclearly*, or even allow it to be expressed unclearly? If one is going to communicate unclearly, why bother at all?

If we do not accept beliefs about a future life on the authority of biblical writers, we still might ask this question: do our beliefs about what God's goodness or justice would require or incline God to do provide grounds for a belief about a future overcoming of evil in a way that would support belief in God's power to unilaterally determine non-divine states of affairs? It might seem that our belief could not provide grounds. For what God's goodness or justice could require or incline God to do is limited to options within the range of things God can do. For instance, even believers in divine omnipotence in its traditional sense generally agree that it is impossible for even God to change a past event once it has occurred. Therefore, if someone were to claim that the only just thing would be for some evil event never to have occurred, not even believers in divine omnipotence would admit that God's justice would require or incline God to make that event not to have occurred; instead, these believers would have to say either that justice does not require this, or that justice is not achievable in this situation. I suspect that they would say the former, perhaps adding the comment that the claimant wants the impossible, not justice. Analogously, other ways of understanding God's power would have other implications for what justice requires. Thus, the requirements of justice could not serve as a basis for conclusions about God's power; indeed, to think that they could would seem to be an instance of the fallacy of letting our beliefs about what *should be* the case determine our beliefs about what *is* (or *will be*) the case.

There is, however, one further response that an objector might make: regardless of what one concludes about the grounds for the belief, Christians are virtually unanimous in believing in a future life of bliss in heaven with God as a basic part of their hope for the overcoming of evil. I believe that something like this must be admitted to be a pervasive part of the Christian tradition, though not of its pre-Christian Israelite antecedents. But what its pervasiveness proves is less clear. The history of Christianity discloses more than one occasion on which what had been a pervasive part of the tradition was challenged: the unity of the Church (all churches in communion with each other) in the schism between Roman Catholics and Eastern Orthodox in 1054; apostolic succession, the role of the *magisterium* and Church tradition, and the primacy of the pope in the Protestant Reformation; and the exclusivity of Christianity as the way of salvation in our own day. Thus the pervasiveness of some part of the tradition is not a decisive indicator that the part is essential to Christianity. Instead, its being essential depends on its relation to other elements in the tradition, especially to the central elements. But which are central? The answer to this question depends strongly on one's total construal of Christianity. Each of the challenges mentioned above resulted in a reconstrual of Christianity by at least some of those involved. Thus, there is no noncontroversial construal of Christianity or list of its essential elements to which one can appeal as a standard. Rather, one must defend such a construal. Whether and what sort of an afterlife it would involve are not at all obvious. That it need not involve belief in an afterlife I will argue in the next chapter.

My purpose in the foregoing has not been to argue that Christian faith should be construed without belief in an afterlife of bliss. Rather, it is only to indicate how weak a basis we have for this belief, and what weak grounds speculations about a future state provide for conclusions about God's power.

Conclusion

Let me review what has been argued in this chapter. The concept of God as a perfect being cannot by itself provide strong grounds for the belief that God is omnipotent in the traditional sense or that God has the power to unilaterally determine non-divine states of affairs. To provide such grounds, it must be supplemented with various metaphysical and axiological beliefs, which themselves are no better established than the intuitions on which they are based or the metaphysical schemes of which they are a part. Thus, there are no good non-controversial intuitions or grounds independent of metaphysical schemes, themselves controversial, for believing that God's perfection entails that God is omnipotent in anything like the traditional sense. Therefore, the justification for any belief about what God is able to do, even on the assumption that God is the perfect being, requires justification for the metaphysical and axiological beliefs on which is based the belief about what God is able to do. The belief that God is the creator is not sufficient grounds for the belief that God is omnipotent (or has the power to unilaterally determine non-divine states of affairs) unless the former belief is glossed as creation out of nothing, and there is little support for this doing this other than taking it as a revealed truth on the basis of an one ambiguous passage in Genesis and/or its being an implications of various controversial metaphysical schemes; neither scientific theories nor philosophical arguments such as the *kalam* cosmological argument provide strong grounds to accept creation out of nothing. Though obvious miracles would provide grounds for belief that God has the power to unilaterally determine non-divine states of affairs, we have no good reason to think that any miracles have occurred. Well-supported beliefs about our post-mortem state might provide strong grounds for beliefs about God's power, but there is little reason to accept those beliefs themselves unless one takes them as revealed truths communicated via the Bible, and I have argued that there is no good reason to take any particular proposition, including a proposition about life after death, to be a revealed truth.

The conclusions reached in this chapter constitute an important result, for discussions of the problem of evil often assume that the only God worth discussing must be omnipotent in the traditional sense. Any other ways of understanding God's power that involve less than this tend to be dismissed as involving belief in a "finite god" or as not religiously adequate. No doubt some will continue to regard these dismissive comments as justified. This response by traditional Christians to non-traditional ideas of God's power is understandable *if one looks only at what the Christian tradition has explicitly said about God's being omnipotent.* But if one looks at the grounds for what it has said about God's omnipotence, as we have done, one will find the grounds to be weak. In view of the weakness of those grounds and the problems of evil discussed in this book, a reconceiving of God's power seems a worthwhile option to explore. This will be our task in Chapter 8.

Notes

1. Thomas V. Morris puts it this way: "there are and can be no independent, externally determined constraints on divine power .... God is the sole source and continuous support

of all the power there is or could be" (*Anselmian Explorations: Essays in Philosophical Theology* [Notre Dame, IN: University of Notre Dame Press, 1987], p. 71). See also the statement in note 2 of Chapter 2. It is plausible to relate this understanding of divine power to the idea of creation out of nothing, for if God creates everything else out of nothing, then nothing external to God can in any way constrain God's power (though God can refrain from exercising controlling power in relation to some creatures – those with free will – if God chooses). We will discuss the idea of creation out of nothing later in this chapter.

2. Some traditional theists who believe that humans have libertarian free will might object to my characterizing their position by saying that they believe that God has the power to unilaterally bring about any non-divine state of affairs, for they deny that God has the power to unilaterally bring it about that a person freely does various actions. However, they would say that God has the power to unilaterally bring it about that the person does the actions, though not freely.

3. John B. Cobb, Jr., makes a similar point about the meaning and use of the term omnipotence in his essay "Process Thought," *Philosophy of Religion in the 21ˢᵗ Century*, ed. D.Z. Phillips and Timothy Tessin (New York: Palgrave Macmillan, 2002), p. 258.

4. A large number of writers could be cited as examples of this line of argument. For example, Richard Swinburne, *The Coherence of Theism* (New York: Oxford University Press, 1977), p. 149, who also cites the agreement of Thomas Aquinas in a footnote; and Bruce R. Reichenbach, *Evil and a Good God* (New York: Fordham University Press, 1982), p. 155.

5. The differences should be clear for the first two propositions. As for the third, suppose that it is a true conditional of freedom that person S will do action A in circumstances C. Then though it is narrowly logically possible and causally possible for S to do not-A in C, it is not broadly logically possible for God to actualize a world in which S does not-A in C.

6. The denial that God is passive in any way and that God can be affected by anything else is central to those conceptions of God, such as those of Thomists, that affirm God's absolute simplicity. On the other hand, process theists have criticized these denials as making it impossible to affirm that God truly loves any creature; see John B. Cobb, Jr., and David Ray Griffin, *Process Theology: An Introductory Exposition* (Philadelphia, PA: The Westminster Press, 1976), pp. 44–48, and Charles Hartshorne, *Omnipotence and Other Theological Mistakes* (Albany, NY: State University of New York Press, 1984), pp. 27–32.

7. For example, E.A. Speiser, who translated and wrote the commentary on Genesis for the Anchor Bible series (*Genesis: The Anchor Bible* [Garden City, NY: Doubleday, 1964]). The relevant translation is found on p. 3, and his reasons for this translation on pp. 12–13. One of the reasons that requires no knowledge of Hebrew is this: on the traditional translation, the first result of God's creative activity is chaos ("the earth was void and without form, and darkness was on the face of the deep"). Why would/should a being who can create out of nothing by uttering a command first create a chaotic state of affairs and then make it orderly rather than simply make an orderly state of affairs in the first place?

8. These alternatives are among those discussed in John Leslie, *Universes* (New York: Routledge, 1989), pp. 6–8 and 79–85.

9. Thomas Aquinas did believe that the universe began a finite number of years ago, but he believed this on the basis of (what he took to be) revelation; he did not think it could be proved philosophically (*Summa Contra Gentiles, Book II: Creation*, trans. James F. Anderson [Garden City, NY: Doubleday, 1956], ch. 38); cf. Etienne Gilson, *The Christian Philosophy of St. Thomas Aquinas*, trans. L. K. Shook (New York: Random House, 1956), pp. 150–51.

10. Rev. edn. (Wheaton, IL: Crossway Books, 1994), p. 92. Page numbers in parentheses in the discussion of Craig's defense of the *kalam* cosmological argument refer to this work.

11. Readers not familiar with transfinite numbers might wonder where the guest in the originally highest-numbered room would go. The answer is that there is no highest-numbered room. Not having a highest-numbered member (or a lowest-numbered member if the set is infinite in the negative direction) is one of the ways in which transfinite sets differ from finite sets.

12. "Must Metaphysical Time Have a Beginning?" *Faith and Philosophy* 20/3 (July 2003): 296, italics his. My example below in the text illustrates his point, for it does not have co-existing elements bearing a changeable physical relationship with each other.

13. Morriston (ibid.: 299–300) points out that there is a sense of *greater* in which the entire Hilbert's Hotel is greater than that part of the hotel "containing rooms numbered 3 and higher," though it does not contain a larger number of rooms. In this sense an infinite set can be greater than any of its proper subsets without containing a larger number of elements.

14. The dates I am using are fairly common among New Testament scholars. For example, Howard Clark Kee, *Understanding the New Testament*, 4th edn. (Englewood Cliffs, NJ: Prentice-Hall, 1983), pp. 400–401, dates the crucifixion in the years 30–33, I Corinthians in 54–55, Mark in 68–70, Matthew in 85–100, Luke–Acts in 85–100, and John in 90–100.

15. The literature on the resurrection is vast; my own views about the documentation of the resurrection are contained in two papers: "Contemporary Christian Doubts about the Resurrection," *Faith and Philosophy* 5/1 (January 1988): 40–60, and "Response to Davis," *Faith and Philosophy* 7/1 (January 1990): 112–16. They were responses to two papers by Stephen T. Davis, "Is It Possible to Know that Jesus Was Raised from the Dead?" *Faith and Philosophy* 1/2 (April 1984): 147–59, and "Doubting the Resurrection," *Faith and Philosophy* 7/1 (January 1990): 99–111 respectively.

16. *Reincarnation in Christianity: A New Vision of the Role of Rebirth in Christian Thought* (Wheaton, IL: Quest Books, 1981), p. 22.

17. San Francisco, CA: Harper and Row, 1976. See especially pp. 171–93 on the ideas of Jesus and early Christians.

CHAPTER 8

A Process Christian Theism and the Problems of Evil

In Chapters 2–4 we explored three problems of evil, and we looked at possible responses by traditional Christian theists. In Chapter 2 we found that there are serious problems with even what I took to be the strongest type of traditional Christian theodicy (libertarian free-will theism) in its response to suffering and evil actions. In Chapters 3 and 4 we saw that certain doctrines of traditional Christian theism are in tension with the justification given for divine hiddenness and the patterns in which miracles are believed to occur. Therefore, in Chapter 5 we considered defenses of traditional Christian theism that claim that we should not expect to be able to understand why God permits many of the evils that occur. We concluded that at most this defense shows that (if there is a God who permits these evils) it is very likely that God permits (almost) all the evils that occur because God is following the general policies of (almost) never interfering with the operation of natural processes and creaturely free will, and we are unable to justifiably assess whether God has morally adequate reasons to follow these policies.

Because I intended to argue in this chapter that divine power should not be understood as omnipotence in the traditional sense, in Chapters 6–7 we discussed what grounds there are for the belief that God is omnipotent in that sense. We saw that there are no strong grounds for it. In Chapter 6 I argued that there is no reason for us today to have confidence that God revealed any particular proposition (including the proposition that God is omnipotent, or any proposition that states or entails that God has the power to unilaterally control all events). If we have no reason to believe that God has revealed any propositions, then we would have to use whatever non-revelational grounds are available to assess the proposition that God is omnipotent. In Chapter 7 I argued that unless metaphysical schemes or intuitions about metaphysical and axiological propositions provided good grounds, we had no good non-revelation-based grounds for thinking that God is omnipotent. Of course, neither metaphysical schemes nor metaphysical and axiological intuitions provide non-controversial grounds. It is beyond the scope of this work to criticize or defend any particular scheme or intuition.

In light of the foregoing conclusions about grounds for the belief that God is omnipotent and in light of the role that this belief plays in generating the problems of evil, I propose that Christian theists reconsider how they understand God's power. I will employ the understanding of God and God's power in process theism to confront the issues discussed in earlier chapters. In particular, I will show how it resolves the problems of evil discussed in Chapters 2–4, and how it leads us to expect the sort of "revelation" suggested by the phenomena of the Bible discussed in Chapter 6; I will also discuss the responses it makes possible to the reasons for believing that God is omnipotent discussed in Chapter 7. Furthermore, I will argue that process theism's understanding of God's power and God's relationship to the world justifies the conclusion that God, thus conceived, is worthy of worship. To the extent that the problems of evil present an important challenge to theistic belief, my argument in this chapter constitutes part of an argument for the conclusion that process theism is a better metaphysics for theists than any of the metaphysical schemes or intuitions that support traditional theism; however, it is beyond the scope of this work to present an argument for the overall superiority of process theism to other metaphysical schemes.[1]

Process Theism

Traditional theists typically have a two-level metaphysics. One level is the creaturely level. This typically is believed to consist basically of things that endure for some time (such as animals, plants, cells, and atoms), and causally interact with each other. God sustains all creatures in existence, and also sustains the causal laws in accordance with which they operate. What happens on the creaturely level is the result of the causal interaction of creatures operating in accordance with their capabilities and natural laws. God and other supernatural entities, if any, operate on a different level. Occasionally, God intervenes on the creaturely level to unilaterally bring about an event that is not within the natural capacities of the creatures and/or not in accordance with the natural laws relevant to the creatures and their circumstances. Such divine interventions are miracles; because they (are believed to) involve the intervention of an entity from the other level into the natural level, they are often termed supernatural events.

In contrast, process theists have a one-level metaphysics, with God and creatures both on this level. The fundamental sort of creatures are momentary events, each generally thought to occupy less than a fraction of a second (perhaps a very small fraction of a second) and a very small volume of space. Such events are called (in Whitehead's terminology) *actual occasions* or *actual entities*.[2] They are the ultimate individuals that process theists believe make up the world; they play a role in process metaphysics like that played by substances in Aristotle's metaphysics. In process metaphysics, ordinary macroscopic objects such as humans, trees, and rocks are believed to be spatially and temporally extended collections of related actual occasions; such collections are called *societies*. Each actual occasion begins with data from its past. These data have their source in past actual occasions and in God, but past occasions and God make different sorts of contributions to the new occasion. Past occasions contribute data that limit what the new occasion can become, and may also create some pressure for the new occasion to include certain features found in the past occasions. Within those limits, God provides a graded range of possibilities for what the new occasion can become. The new occasion then develops into a fully concrete thing (in a process termed *concrescence*) by "deciding" what it will become from among its range of possibilities. I put *deciding* in scare quotes because there is no implication of consciousness in the "decision." As Whitehead explains it, he chose the term to indicate that the occasion becomes one definite thing, thus cutting off all other possibilities for what it can become.[3] Its becoming that thing, within the range of possibilities allowed by its past, is entirely up to it; nothing else determines which of the possibilities it becomes. Thus, each actual occasion is partly self-determining. The contributions of past occasions constitute what we ordinarily think of as efficient causation. These contributions can greatly limit the possibilities for the new occasion. Moreover, the fact that many occasions in a new occasion's past exhibit a certain characteristic can create some "pressure" on the new occasion also to include this characteristic. The combination of these two factors is very important in process theists' explanation of the orderliness of inanimate nature. God's contributions, on the other hand, do not limit what an occasion can become, but both help to sustain the overall orderliness of nature and also provide a source of novelty within the overall order. This is an important point; let me explain it further.

Each finite (non-divine) actual occasion includes only part of its past in the determinate actuality that it becomes; thus, by its "decisions" (what it includes and excludes), it becomes an occasion that provides certain data and not others for subsequent occasions. The data it provides help set the limits of the possibilities for what a new occasion in its future can become. Therefore, subsequent occasions must concresce in relation to (what is for them) an immediate past from which that excluded material is absent. Ways of development of these new occasions that the excluded material would have made possible are thus absolutely beyond the range of possibilities for the new occasions.

For example, when the occasions in the human heart concresce in such a way as to preclude the continued beating of the heart for several minutes, it is no longer possible for occasions in the brain to concresce in such a way as to carry on the life of the person; therefore, the person dies, and other people can no longer have an ongoing relationship with that person. Even in occasions involving high degrees of freedom, any absolute control of some aspect of a new occasion exercised by past actualities is exercised by excluding possibilities rather than by forcing the new occasion to actualize particular possibilities. Thus, for example, whatever conscious thoughts occur in the next new occasion in the series that constitutes my mind will not be in Chinese because the past occasions in that series did not include a knowledge of Chinese. Since they did not, the data they pass on to the new occasion will not include a knowledge of Chinese. (Of course, even if they did, the new occasion would not have to include conscious thoughts in Chinese; whether or not it did would depend on how it freely constituted itself out of the initial data it received from its past.) For an occasion in my mind to include a knowledge of Chinese, many past occasions in that series would each have had to include data from outside the series that cumulatively produced a knowledge of Chinese. Because they did not, the possibility of thinking in Chinese is excluded from the next new occasion in the series. Thus even in occasions with a high degree of freedom such as those constituting a human mind, past actualities can absolutely exclude certain possibilities from what the new occasion can become. According to process thought, they do so by not including those possibilities in themselves.

Moreover, by including certain characteristics in themselves, occasions in the past create a pressure on the new occasion to include those same characteristics. For instance, if a series of occasions each included the characteristics that made the occasions moments in the history of an electron, then the effect of these occasions on the new one in the series would create pressure on the new one to include those same characteristics. On a human level, if the past occasions that constitute a person's mind all (or almost all) included thoughts in grammatically correct English, there would be pressure on the next occasion in this series that any thoughts in it would also be expressed in grammatically correct English, though that pressure could be resisted by the new occasion.

But according to process thought, God includes all the past. Indeed, God perfectly includes all the details of the past, so with respect to qualities derived from the world, God does not include any new or different characteristics from those exhibited in the past of the world. God's perfect inclusion of the entire past without alteration is one aspect of God's omniscience. If God did not perfectly include the past as it was, then God would not have perfect knowledge of the past. Therefore, God's decisions, unlike those of non-divine occasions, do not cut off any possibilities; nor do they alter the pressures created by the inclusion of certain characteristics in the occasions in the past. Instead, God's decisions are evaluations of what past entities have become and of what new entities can become.[4] These do influence new occasions as they begin to concresce, but they do not do so by cutting off possibilities for what the new occasions can become or by altering the pressures created by the past's including certain characteristics rather than others. God's contribution does add another pressure on the new occasion, but it is an addition to, rather than an alteration of, the effects contributed by past non-divine occasions. God's contribution creates a resistible inclination (in Whitehead's term, a *lure*) for the occasion to develop itself in a particular way. In short, God's decisions evaluate possibilities within the range established by the past, but do not further limit that range or exclude any possibilities from it.

Why God Cannot Unilaterally Control Non-divine States of Affairs

It follows from this way of understanding how the past of the world and God contribute to the beginnings of a new occasion that God cannot unilaterally determine the details of the world. Since human beings and other macroscopic objects can unilaterally determine aspects of other macroscopic objects, it might be thought strange that God cannot. Let us see how process theists explain this difference.

The non-divine occasions in the past of a new occasion limit to some extent what the new occasion can become. Within those limits, what the new occasion becomes is decided by the new occasion itself. Nothing God can do can change the effect that past occasions have on the new one nor compel the new occasion to develop in any particular way. All that God can do is to lure the new occasion in the direction God wants it to go by presenting to it the possibility God most desires for it (which Whitehead called the initial aim for the occasion). God does this by desiring that new possibility; the new occasion feels God's desires, which constitute part of the data from which the occasion begins.

If the range of possibilities allowed by the new occasion's past is very small, as is typical of occasions in inorganic entities, then the range of possibilities God evaluates for the new actual occasion is likewise very restricted. Thus, we can say that the past determines for all practical purposes[5] what each occasion will become, and not even God can *at that time and in that situation* do anything to influence it to become anything significantly different. Sometimes we can usefully identify some *part* of the past that plays a very significant role in determining some aspect of how a new occasion or group of occasions develops. This is what happens in what are often taken as standard cases of causation, such as one billiard ball striking another and causing it to move. In such a case the occasions comprising the first billiard ball unilaterally determine the development of what we call the motion of (the occasions comprising) the second billiard ball.

As the example of the billiard balls illustrates, in the realm of inanimate objects macroscopic entities often unilaterally determine aspects of the behavior of other macroscopic entities. Almost all the occasions comprising a human being, except those comprising the brain, have not much greater range of possibilities than those comprising inorganic things. Therefore, macroscopic objects (including other human beings) can unilaterally determine much of what happens to the body of a human being.

But there are occasions whose pasts leave them with a much greater range of possibilities – and thus with much more freedom. Certain occasions in the brain are of this sort, and much of the novelty that they achieve is passed on to the occasions in the brain that comprise the mind, or the "human soul" (as Whitehead termed it). The mind is a particular temporal series[6] of occasions in the brain, each of which has a very high degree of freedom – indeed, the highest of any actual entity (other than God) of which we know. These occasions inherit a rich variety of data from other occasions in the brain (which in turn get important data from occasions in the rest of the body); they also contribute data to other subsequent occasions in the brain (which in turn contribute to subsequent occasions in the rest of the body). The relations of occasions comprising the human body is such that occasions in the mind can often unilaterally determine aspects of the development of certain occasions in the rest of the body, and thereby unilaterally determine the behavior of the body. This is how the process theist explains our ability to move certain parts of our bodies (our arms or legs) "at will."

Because the occasions that comprise the human mind have significant freedom, there is a wide range of possibilities for what each one can become.[7] Thus, there is a correspondingly wide range of possibilities God evaluates for each occasion. Because its past leaves it with such a wide range of possibilities, nothing – including God – can unilaterally determine it (as opposed to unilaterally determining aspects of the body of which it is a part). Thus, we cannot expect that the possibility most positively evaluated by God (which Whitehead terms the *initial aim*) will generally be followed by the occasions in a human's mind, nor that it will not be; whether or not it will be depends on the decisions of occasions in the human mind. Nevertheless, the extent to which they adopt God's initial aim as their own aim (what Whitehead calls the *subjective aim*), by which they govern their concrescence, matters greatly. But there is no way God can force the occasions to adopt the initial aim as their subjective aim. Indeed, that is true for any occasion, but if the range of possible aims is small (as in occasions in inorganic entities), it does not matter for practical purposes which of the possibilities the occasion follows.

What God Can Do

If God cannot unilaterally determine any non-divine states of affairs, then what can God do? The fundamental activity of God in the universe is to provide each new occasion with its initial aim and other evaluated possibilities. This fundamental activity of God enables God to set the laws of nature of each cosmic epoch. Recall that I said that there is little range of possibility for what an occasion in an inorganic entity can become. For all practical purposes, in any specific situation, the range is negligible. Nevertheless, God does play an important role in preserving the laws of nature by luring each occasion to concresce in the way that will most fully conform to the existing law; apart from this activity of God, there might be a gradual drift toward chaos. Suppose, however, that God wished to change certain patterns exemplified (laws of nature followed) by occasions. If God were persistently to lure all occasions toward some new pattern of interrelations, they would tend to gradually adopt that new pattern. God could do this by using a multiplicity of intermediate forms, each only slightly different from those adjacent to it, such that those at one end were within the range of possibilities for occasions exemplifying the old pattern, and those at the other end were within the range of possibilities for occasions exemplifying the new pattern. No specific occasion would have to adopt God's new lure precisely, but there would tend to be some change in the one direction consistently presented by God. As occasions adopted new intermediate forms, they would exercise efficient causality on subsequent occasions, contributing to the likelihood that the new occasions would concresce in ways that would conform to God's wishes. The rate of change in the direction God wishes would necessarily be slow (for at each point God could desire the new occasion to exemplify a pattern only very slightly different from that of the previous occasion) and would not be predictable with certainty (for even these occasions have a very small amount of self-determination), but eventually most of the occasions would exemplify the new pattern. The process outlined in this paragraph does indicate a way in which God could bring about a new order of nature, though God's only direct activity would have been luring (but never coercing) certain occasions.

It is also consistent with process thought to believe that there is a conceivable set of conditions in which God's lures on occasions in the inorganic realm might much more quickly and completely determine the characteristics of new occasions than they can in our universe today. The relevant conditions are those in which past occasions convey no ordered influence at all. Thus, they set no limits and create no pressures on the new occasions. In these conditions, God's lure would be the only effective influence on the new occasion. Thus, new occasions could be expected to conform to a particular pattern because of the divine influence much more quickly than they do in the conditions that obtain today. However, the only time we know of when this condition of minimal order throughout the universe might obtain is at the first instants of the Big Bang. But if it did obtain then, process theism would be able to explain how God could in those first instants quickly set the fundamental characteristics of our universe.

But God does more than just create and sustain the order of nature. By contributing the initial aim, God can introduce significant, though relevant, novelty into the universe. This contributes to the emergence of new forms of living creatures and to new developments in human societies such as new ideas in the sciences and humanities, new values for human life and human communities, and new possibilities for the way an individual or a group behaves. Later in the chapter we will refer to some of these contributions by God.

Process Theism and the Problem of Suffering and Evil Actions

As we have seen, process theists claim that God cannot unilaterally determine any non-divine events or states of affairs; therefore, they also claim that God cannot unilaterally prevent or alleviate evils. Bringing about such events unilaterally would involve the unilateral determination of some event by God. Is God then powerless against evil? No, for God can and does lure creatures toward resisting, preventing, and alleviating evil, though there is no guarantee in any particular instance that the creature will conform to God's lure. However, the process theist's account does more than just explain why God does not do more to prevent and alleviate evil. It also provides a framework that leads one to expect the kinds and distribution of good and evil we find in this world: (1) Processes in nature go on in ways strongly influenced by their pasts and uninfluenced by the effects they will have on humans and other sentient creatures; sometimes these processes result in suffering by humans and other sentient creatures. (2) Suffering also occurs because creatures with differing goals compete for incompossible goods. A fox tries to catch a rabbit for food, and the rabbit tries to escape; one will suffer. (3) There is evil (usually called moral evil) because humans do not conform to the divine lure. And (4) at least some people some of the time feel an impulse, sometimes quite strong, to prevent or alleviate certain evils. Sometimes such an impulse is widespread and results in a movement that is widely effective in reducing some evil. Thus, process theism leads us to expect both the sorts of suffering we find in the world and the sorts of efforts to prevent or alleviate it that we find there.

Many traditional theists would agree with point 1 above, though they may express it differently. They would say that processes in nature operating as described by causal laws are not influenced by the effects they will have on humans and other sentient creatures. But traditional theists would still disagree with process theists on whether God could suspend the laws temporarily. Traditional theists have to admit that natural disasters and other natural evils occur only with God's permission, while process theists would insist that God cannot stop them. It seems to me that traditional theists could well accept point 2 above, though I do not think they emphasize it as much as process theists do. Traditional Christian theists would also agree with point 3 above, though they would speak of conforming to God's will and the promptings of the Holy Spirit. But again they would have to admit that God could intervene to prevent the evil (perhaps by suspending the person's free will or in some way making it impossible for the person to act at that time, perhaps by causing him to become unconscious or die), while process theists would say that God could not in any way at the time guarantee the prevention, though God could lure a human being in that direction. Traditional theists could also accept point 4 above, but process theists see point 4 in both its parts as the effect of the sort of action that they expect God to do. Traditional theists see God as capable of more. Thus, traditional theists, even when they agree with process theists on the creaturely causes of evil, face a problem that process theists do not: why God does not do more to prevent and alleviate evil.

In light of the foregoing, one can see why process theists claim to have a more satisfactory response to the first problem of evil – suffering and wickedness – than do traditional Christian theists. One cannot raise against God, as process theists conceive of God, either the guilty bystander or the defective world objections. God could not unilaterally intervene to prevent or alleviate various instances of suffering and wickedness. And God is constantly striving to make the world as good as it can be. Nor can the victimization objection be raised against God in the direct way we discussed in Chapter 2, for God cannot unilaterally prevent one individual from injuring another, and therefore God cannot be charged with permitting victimization for the sake of some good.

There is, however, a more general sense in which one might raise against God, as process theists conceive God, both the victimization objection and the animal suffering objection. For God has evoked the sort of order of living things that allows animals to suffer and humans to injure one another. If God had not evoked order that involves beings more complex than atoms, there would be no victims and no suffering creatures. What justifies God in doing this? Process theists claim that God evokes the more complex creatures because of the greater goods they can experience, though only at the risk of greater evils. This response has certain similarities to some responses by traditional theists, but there are also differences.

First, on process theists' approach, it is a package deal. God cannot unilaterally filter out some or all of the bad. Thus, in trying to decide whether evoking greater complexity is appropriate, one has to judge the whole thing. In process theism, it is at least clear that God could not immediately make this universe any better than it is (though God might evoke improvements in the future, and though God might have made a different universe with different basic features), for God is always doing all God can to make the universe (this or any other) as good as it can be. Whether this particular universe has an adequate balance of good over evil, only God is in a position to know. And as the one who feels perfectly what every creature feels and experiences fully what every creature experiences, God does know.

In process theism, there is no guarantee that no sentient creature – human or animal – will have a life that, through no fault of its own, contains more evil than good. What happens depends on the agency of too many creatures for such a guarantee to be possible. Does this entail, as some critics have charged, that process theism has an elitist view? Can one legitimately charge, for example, that for the sake of a Mother Theresa or a Gandhi, God evoked orders of complexity that allow many others to have bad lives?[8] No, for God wishes for the best life for every creature. Could God predict before sentient creatures appeared that some would have better lives than others and that some might have lives that contain more bad than good?

I certainly think so. But God could not predict what particular creatures would live, to say nothing of not predicting the kind of life each would have. Thus, God embarked on a somewhat risky undertaking. In order to give any sentient creature a chance at life and all sentient creatures a chance at a richer life, God evoked a process of development in which some creatures might have a bad life (short, painful, and so on), but no particular creatures were singled out in advance to have a bad life. The lives of some just turned out that way.[9] Now suppose that at the time when the universe contained nothing more complex than sub-atomic particles we could have been advising God whether or not to evoke greater complexity, knowing that we might come out with a good life or a bad life if God does so, and no life if God does not. If we had had to give this advice behind a Rawlsian veil of ignorance, what would we have advised? I think at least most of us would have advised God to evoke greater complexity. Consider an analogous situation. When two people decide to have a child, they know that some children, through no fault of their own (or of their parents), have lives that are short and/or (certainly seem to) contain more bad than good (at least during their life on earth). Potential parents do not know in advance whether this will happen to their child, but many who are aware of the risks nevertheless decide to have a child.[10] If so, then it is easier to accept God's doing so as appropriate. Moreover, if (as I believe but cannot prove) there is more good than bad in the experiences of the more complex creatures as a whole (though not in the lives of every one of them individually – remember the second pelican chicks mentioned in Chapter 2), then God's benevolence would also motivate God to evoke greater complexity.

Process Theism and the Problem of Divine Hiddenness

The foregoing discussion of the way the power of God is understood in process theism also enables us to understand why God is not less hidden. As we saw in Chapter 3, traditional Christian theists face the question of why God did not do more to make clear what God wanted to reveal about Godself and what the medium of that revelation is, for they believe that God could have done more to make these matters clear. But all the ways God could make Godself less hidden involve God's controlling certain details of non-divine states of affairs, such as causing human beings to hear certain words or to think certain thoughts or unilaterally determining certain details in inanimate nature in such a way as to constitute an obvious suspension of a law of nature. These are things God cannot do, according to process theists.

On the other hand, process theism leads one to expect the sort of revelation suggested by the phenomena of the Bible. As we saw in Chapter 6, the Bible contains accounts of purported divine speech and divine manifestations inextricably intermixed with human ideas reflecting the culture and issues of the writers and their communities at the time the documents were written. There is no clear divine certification of any propositions expressed in the Bible, to say nothing of the Bible as a whole. The absence of clear divine certification and the intermixing of purported divine speech and manifestations with the culture of the writers is precisely what one would expect if God's influence on individual humans and on the events of history is always only one, originally preconscious, factor out of which occasions comprising human minds develop. There is no way to separate out with certainty the part that comes from God from the part that comes from creatures. Even the direct divine influence on the occasions comprising the mind of an individual is not such as to permit the experiential isolation of the divine factor. For the provision of the initial aim is preconscious; in our conscious experience the divine influence is already mixed with creaturely factors derived from earlier occasions constituting the person's mind, the person's body, and the world beyond the person's body. People can, and do, attempt to reconstruct from their own inner experience and from events in history as accurate as possible an account of what God is like and of God's will. But these are human reconstructions, and as we have seen, none of them carries a clear divine certification. The understanding of divine power in traditional theism certainly implies that such a clear divine certification is possible, and (as I argued in Chapter 3) certain traditional Christian doctrines imply that a divine certification of genuine revelation should be expected. The absence of such a clear divine certification, while to be expected according to process theism, constitutes an anomaly for traditional Christian theism.

Process Theism and the Problem of Miracles

It is no doubt clear from the foregoing discussion of how process theists understand God's power that they cannot affirm that God performs miracles in the sense discussed in Chapter 4. In the previous chapter I said that the belief that miracles (in the traditional, supernaturalist sense) occur is one possible ground for believing that God has the power to unilaterally determine non-divine states of affairs, and I argued that we have no good reason to believe that miracles in this sense occur. But because concern with miracles has been important, not just in the reflections of philosophers and theologians, but in the lives of ordinary believers and in the Christian tradition more generally, one might wonder whether process theists can develop some concept of miracles with enough in common with the idea discussed in Chapter 4 to make it legitimate to call the concept a concept of a miracle. I think such a concept can be developed. Its development will contribute to showing that process theism is a way to understand God that is adequate for the legitimate concerns of religious people.

As we have seen, in modern discussions a miracle typically has been understood to be an occurrence willed and caused by God in which the course of nature does not conform to the laws of nature that, apart from God's intervention, describe events of that sort. This modern concept of miracle was developed in the context of an understanding of God's power like that of traditional theists. They say it may be inconsistent with God's purposes or with God's goodness to intervene in certain events in certain ways, but they believe that God nevertheless has the power to intervene to unilaterally bring about any broadly logically possible state of affairs. Thus, they believe that God has the power, for example, to stop a falling rock in mid-fall and to cause it to rise without the intervention of any creaturely agency, instantly to stop the earth in its rotation on its axis, and to heal illnesses instantly. But process theists deny that God has the power to do such things; these events are not within the range of possibilities established by the pasts of the relevant occasions. That is why only a supernatural intervention could bring them about, and process theists deny that there can be supernatural interventions.

The concept of miracles that I will delineate is analogous to the traditional supernaturalist concept of miracles in that both refer to an event in which God is supposed to be involved in a special way, but my concept differs from the supernaturalist one in how it understands that "specialness." It does not involve the suspension of any laws of nature; therefore, it will not allow a process Christian to affirm the literal correctness of all the details of certain events in the Bible and elsewhere that have been termed miracles. But it will allow a process Christian to affirm that God has been involved in certain events in a special way, and that those events involve an especially clear manifestation of God and God's will. Since it does this, I believe that it could provide a useful basis for process theists to interpret miracles in the Christian tradition rather than just ignoring or demythologizing them. However, even if it can do this, process theists may continue not to use the term "miracle" at all. For they may judge that the term is so deeply tied to the context of traditional supernaturalist theism that their attempt to use it in another sense is more likely to mislead than to be helpful.

Let us begin the delineation of a process concept of miracles by recalling my earlier claim that God can do things to increase the likelihood of certain events, though God cannot unilaterally determine that certain events will occur. Some events in the lives of people and in history have significant alternatives, and the differences between what occurs and the other alternatives are important for human life. In such moments the subjective aims in the experience of people involved may conform closely to the initial aims provided by God for these occasions. I suggest that in these cases, we may call the events miracles.

In other words, if we restrict our attention to a level of analysis concerned with the practical significance of events for human beings (and perhaps other sentient creatures), we can say that there are some events that conform to God's will, but that might not have done so. These are events in which the decisions of significantly free occasions are important in determining the outcome. If occasions with significant freedom do play a role, and if the occasions do conform to God's will, then God's will is manifested in the bearing of the event on human concerns. Among the events that include occasions with significant freedom that concresce in accordance with God's will for them, some will have a significance for human affairs that seems to some people to be a striking example of what they understand to be God's will for human affairs. Process theists may term such events miracles, not in the sense of events in which some law of nature is suspended, but in the sense of a striking event in which God's active presence in the world is (believed to be) manifest.[11] For example, God may so lure some people that they think of things or feel things that they otherwise would not. These thoughts and feelings could lead to actions that have very good but unexpected outcomes, such as some discovery or very creative action that saves human lives. Or they could result in such a change in some people's perspective on life that they live in a very different way. God might also lure a group of people to some better action. For example, after the terrorist attacks of 11 September 2001, many New Yorkers, who are often widely regarded as uncaring about their neighbors, responded with acts of self-sacrifice and caring for others. When individual and group outcomes such as these occur, some people may want to call them miracles.[12]

In contrast with events involving occasions with significant freedom, if no occasions with significant freedom play such a role, God's will is done in the sense that the event conforms to patterns of natural law that God wished, but not necessarily in the sense that the way the event affected human beings (and other sentient beings) accorded with the sort of things God wants for those beings. Thus a tornado *qua* moving air molecules conforms to God's will in moving in accordance with natural laws, but it is not necessarily God's will that certain people are killed by the tornado. Because God can offer as initial aims only possibilities within the range permitted by the pasts of the occasions in question, it may very well be that each of the occasions in the tornado conforms to God's will for that occasion, yet that the tornado kills some people, an event that God does not will nor permit and did not even foresee when the laws of nature were instituted. (To say that God permits it implies that God could have prevented the event by not permitting it, an implication that process theists deny; and God could foresee the event only if the universe were deterministic, a condition that process theists deny.) Therefore, process theists would say that events in inanimate nature that have results that God would not will are not always the result of a failure of some occasions to adopt as their subjective aim the initial aim that God offers; there was no such failure in the tornado example.

At this point my account has some similarities to aspects of the theodicies of some traditional theists (for example, John Hick and William Hasker), who argue that an orderly world is necessary for the moral development of creatures with free will. Therefore, God wills to create an orderly world, but God does not will all the specific events that happen because entities conform to these laws. But the important difference between such accounts and mine is that they claim that God *can* intervene at any time to suspend temporarily or to change permanently any of these laws of nature, whereas process theists claim that God cannot temporarily suspend any law of nature and can change a law of nature only gradually, not instantly. Thus, God's allowing the same laws of nature to hold at any moment is for these traditional theists a matter of God's will – a choice God makes – but for process theists it is something beyond God's control and not a matter of will.

In the concept of miracles I am suggesting for process theism, the distinction between miracles and non-miraculous events is a matter of degree rather than a difference in kind, because the difference between important events and non-important ones is a matter of degree, as is the extent to which occasions with significant freedom conform to God's initial aim for them. And even when occasions conform closely to God's initial aim, the outcome is within the range of outcomes established by past occasions and described by statistical laws of nature. Since the outcome conforms to relevant natural laws, a non-theist can simply ignore or deny any contribution made by God to the outcome.

It is interesting to note the extent to which the implications of this account of a process view of God's power and miracles conforms to features of our experience admitted even by most traditional Christian theists. One implication is the absence of contemporary, well-attested, clear actions by God that involve the suspension of laws of nature. This is what one would expect on process assumptions, according to which no actions of God involve suspensions of laws of nature, but it is not what one would expect on traditional assumptions. Of course, traditional Christians may assert that some such events are recounted in the Bible, but they cannot find similar events today, and we have seen that events in the Bible are not documented well enough to give us grounds for saying that an obvious suspension of a law of nature has certainly occurred. A second implication that conforms to features of our experience admitted even by most traditional Christian theists is the way God deals with evil in human beings and human affairs. Typically, Christian theists of all sorts admit that at least most of the time (that is, apart from alleged miracles, which are rare), God does this slowly and uses human beings to do it. God does not make human beings perfect overnight, nor does God defeat or punish evildoers instantly. Traditional theists may say that God will act more powerfully and more decisively in the future (at the end of the age), but for now they admit that God works this way, which is the way process theism leads one to expect. A third feature of our world is that new kinds of living things appeared slowly as the outcome of a long course of evolution. This is precisely what one would expect from the standpoint of process thought, but not necessarily what one would expect from the standpoint of traditional Christian theism. For traditional theism tends to see humankind as the center of God's interest in this world; if God's purpose does center on human beings and if God has the power to create humankind instantly and directly, the long, slow course of evolution is puzzling, to say the least.[13] These observations do not prove that process theists are correct, but they do constitute anomalies for traditional theism. At least process theists do not have to tell a story to explain why the way things appear is not a reliable indication of the power God has. With regard to the matters discussed in this paragraph at least, traditional Christian theists must hold their position despite certain features of the world, not because of them.

Thus far in this chapter I have delineated the understanding of God's power held by process theists, and I have argued that it is superior to the traditional understanding in several ways. It resolves the problems of evil, which – I argued in earlier chapters – the traditional view does not do. And it leads us to expect the sort of world in which we find ourselves: a world in which God's actions and influence are never sharply distinguishable from creaturely actions and effects, and a world in which evil seems unchecked by anything other than the efforts of creatures. But even if process theism is superior to traditional theism on these points, it still might fail to be an appropriate form of Christian theism if God, as it understands God, is not an appropriate object of worship. I wish to discuss this issue in the next two sections. In the first we will look at how process theists respond to the concerns about the overcoming of evil that may lead some traditional theists to assert that God has the power to unilaterally determine non-divine states of affairs; in the second we will consider concerns based on the belief that God is the greatest possible being, and therefore must have the greatest possible power.

Process Theism and the Overcoming of Evil

The understanding of salvation and the associated idea of the overcoming of evil are topics on which process theism differs considerably from traditional Christian theism, which has understood the salvation God provides to be primarily everlasting life in communion with God in heaven for some or all people. God's remaking the world into a permanently better place (the creation of a new heaven and a new earth) has been an important secondary sense in which salvation by God has been understood. But as I argued in Chapter 6, despite the widespread acceptance of these ideas among Christians, there is no reason to think that any of them is a revealed truth or carries a divine certification. And as I argued in Chapter 7, there is not even one consistent picture of the afterlife presented in the Bible. It is also worth noting that not all biblical writers understand salvation in terms of an afterlife, though some do. There is, for instance, no mention of a life after death in the Pentateuch, and God's promise to Abraham is that he would become a mighty nation, not that he would live forever with God. Thus, we cannot take it for granted that particular beliefs about life with God after death are an essential part of the faith of all the biblical writers.

Process theists cannot claim that there will be an instantaneous creation of a new heaven and a new earth, or even that God certainly will create a better world than we live in today. They cannot affirm the former because they deny that God can unilaterally produce any state of affairs. Because they believe that all actualities are composed of occasions that exercise some self-determination within the limits set by their pasts, they cannot affirm that God certainly will create a better world than we live in today. They do affirm that God is luring creatures toward a better world; this belief gives them grounds for hope that the world will gradually get better, though there is no reason to expect that there will be unbroken improvement, and no *guarantee* that there will be improvement at all.

Moreover, process theists' keen appreciation for the incompossibility of various goods prevents them from affirming that any creaturely state of affairs can be perfect or continue for ever. No creaturely state of affairs can be perfect (include all relevant goods) because while creaturely states of affairs certainly can be good (include important good qualities), the good qualities they include will inevitably exclude other good qualities. For instance, order in a community of humans is an important good, but so is freedom to differ somewhat from the established order. The more the former is achieved, the less the latter will be achieved, and there is no one equilibrium point that is best for every human being. Marriage is a good state of affairs, but so is being single, and the good qualities each makes possible are not wholly compossible. Being a power lifter and being a marathon runner are also both good states of affairs, but no one person can achieve excellence in both.

No creaturely state of affairs can continue forever, for the values achievable in any particular circumstances are themselves limited, and eventually boredom with them will set in, and there will be a consequent search for new values not achievable within those circumstances. This happens again and again in developments in art and in styles of clothes, as well as in the social arrangements in which human beings relate to each other. It is not just that we have not yet found the ideal arrangement, but rather that our concept of the ideal arrangement keeps changing as we approximate one ideal and see its limitations as well as its possibilities. Moreover, process theists expect that the search for an adequate understanding of God's will and the struggle to live according to it are tasks that probably will never be perfectly completed by humans. Not even God can ensure their perfect completion, because God cannot make Godself or God's will perfectly clear and because humans have significant freedom.

For all these reasons, process theists deny that there can be any perfect order or that any one good order can continue for ever. And they deny that humans ever will be in a situation where there is a guarantee that they will never choose to do something against the will of God. But process theists do believe that a better world is possible, and they seek to follow God's lure in working to bring about a better world.

What about the primary sense in which many Christians have understood salvation, everlasting life in communion with God? These Christians saw life after death as central to salvation for at least two reasons: they saw death itself, the cessation of the person, as an evil to be remedied by God; and they saw the afterlife as a time when people could achieve fulfillment and/or be compensated for evils suffered in this life.[14] On this issue, process theists are divided. Perhaps a majority deny that there is any life after death, but defenders of the actuality of life after death include some of the most prominent process theists.[15] But even those who believe that there is or may be life after death think it must end at some time rather than going on everlastingly. They rest their belief on the principle that the number of variations on the values achievable by any creature is finite. Just as there cannot be an everlasting social order, so also the significantly different values that individuals can achieve in their experience are finite. At some point all these values would have been experienced. Any new experiences would be repetitious and ultimately boring.

I am one of those process theists who are dubious about the actuality of a life after death of even limited duration, though I agree that process theism does not preclude life after death. My reasons for doubting it are more empirical than metaphysical; they are familiar to those who know the literature on this topic. The minds of human beings seem dependent on their bodies. The Cartesian idea of mind and body as two distinct substances that interact presumably somewhere in the brain seems implausible because of the difficulty in conceiving how two such different substances could causally interact. It also seems implausible because if mental activity went on in a separate substance, then one would expect that mental activity would go on even when the brain is incapacitated, but this does not seem to happen. People in a coma who recover do not remember any mental experiences they had while in a coma. (Nor does the idea that the mind could somehow emerge out of brain activity and attain sufficient independence to be preserved by God seem to me to be plausible.) And the relation of human minds to their bodies seems, as far as we can tell, similar to the relation between animal minds and their bodies, yet most traditional Christian theists do not believe that there is an afterlife for animals.[16]

While I find these reasons persuasive, this brief mention of them is far from a conclusive argument. If I am wrong and there is life after death, this would not be grounds to reject process theism, for the metaphysics of process theism does not preclude the possibility of life after death. However, the metaphysics of process theism does present problems for the idea of *everlasting* life after death, as well as for the idea of a *guaranteed* state of unending *perfection* for any creatures. But I will not discuss any further whether there is life after death. Instead, I wish to undertake the task of arguing for a reconceiving of what salvation involves based not on the claim that there is no life after death, but rather on the claim that even if there is life after death, it would not solve the problem of death and it would provide at best a limited fulfillment and/or a limited compensation for what people have suffered in this life.

Salvation and Life after Death

Hope for everlasting life is widespread in our culture and in many others. However, even if our life on earth begins (or is part of) a process that will continue unendingly, that would be irrelevant to the problem posed by the fact that we all will die. I say this because if a person is troubled about the fact that she will die, she is troubled because she – the concrete person with all the memories, desires, goals, and other characteristics that are central to her identity – will cease to exist. Life after death seems to offer a solution to this problem, for it suggests that she would not cease to exist. However, I doubt that this solution is adequate.

To see why I doubt it, it will be helpful to begin by stipulating the meaning of two terms: *person* and *self*. I will use the former to refer to a human being over his or her entire life span (including life after death, if there is one). There is a sense in which a human being is the same person throughout his or her life. That sense is recognized in legal contexts when we pay social security out of a certain numbered account of a human being who forty years earlier paid into that account, or when a human being looks at an old photograph and says that it is a picture of him or her as a child. Though I use "person" to refer to the human being throughout this period, I am not presupposing any particular analysis of what is involved in being the same person – whether it involves having the same soul or having the same body or both, or having certain causal relations between memories and/or other features of the person at various times. I will use "self" to refer to the entire mental contents, both conscious and unconscious, of a person at a particular moment. It includes such things as a person's beliefs, hopes, desires, fears, purposes, goals, intentions, memories, expectations, convictions about his or her role and importance to others, and sense of his or her body and its capabilities. One's sense of oneself is constituted by one's experience of these factors.

Given these definitions, my argument in this section can be put succinctly as follows: it is the *self* whose death we fear, but the concept of everlasting life refers to the *person* rather than to the *self*. However, the self is constantly changing; therefore, it cannot be perpetually preserved. Thus, everlasting life is an inadequate solution to the problem of death because what it offers (the perpetuation of the *person*) does not address the problem (the death or cessation of the *self*).

It may clarify my discussion of *person* and *self* if I compare it with some points in Derek Parfit's *Reasons and Persons*.[17] Parfit defines psychological connectedness as "the holding of particular direct psychological connections" (206). He mentions several kinds of direct psychological connections, including direct memory connections (X, a person today, "can remember having some of the experiences that Y had twenty years ago"); the connection "between an intention and the later act in which this intention is carried out"; the connections "which hold when a belief, or a desire, or any other psychological feature, continues to be had" (205). He points out that connectedness can hold to any degree because "between X today and Y yesterday there might be several thousand direct psychological connections, or only a single connection" (206). When there are enough particular direct psychological connections between X and Y, they are *strongly connected.* "*Psychological continuity* is the holding of overlapping chains of *strong* connectedness" (206, his italics). Though psychological connectedness is not a transitive relation, psychological continuity is transitive, as is identity over time.

Parfit distinguishes those who believe that personal identity involves something more than physical and psychological continuity and those who, like him, do not; he terms people who hold his position Reductionists. He believes that, as we contemplate things that might happen to us, what should matter to us is not the survival of that person who each of us is (who has our personal identity), but rather relation R, which is "psychological connectedness and/or continuity with the right kind of cause"; he adds the requirement that relation R must be non-branching – that is, a person at time t1 cannot have relation R with two different persons at a later time t2 (215–16). Those who believe that personal identity involves something more than physical and/or psychological continuity must believe that there is some further fact in which personal identity consists, perhaps something like a Cartesian ego. Parfit points out that on the latter understanding, being the same person over time cannot be a matter of degree; one is either entirely the same person or not at all the same person. This is the way our society tends to view personal identity. However, he presents a number of thought experiments to support the conclusion that in certain conceivable cases, being the same person would be a matter of degree or would depend on some difference between two cases that is so small as to be a highly implausible ground for a difference that is not a matter of degree.[18] For these and other reasons, he concludes that being the same person is simply a matter of relation R obtaining in a non-branching process.

Parfit also argues that what ought to matter to us as we consider our own survival is whether relation R obtains, not whether there is some Cartesian ego that survives. I agree with him, though it is not part of my argument in this chapter to support him. Instead, my claim is more radical: what should matter – and what would matter if we thought about the issues carefully – is a sense of being the same self, and that depends on what Parfit calls psychological connectedness, preferably strong psychological connectedness.

If we think of what I term a *self* as the constituent mental elements of a person at a particular time, then it seems clear that in most human lives a self will contain almost all of the same elements as a self of that same person a few seconds ago, a great many (but fewer) of the same elements as a self of that same person a few days ago, and many fewer of the same elements as a self of that same person many years ago. It seems almost inevitable that if the person endures long enough, at some point (perhaps in a very distant future) there will be no elements in common with a self very early in the life of that person. At that point, why would or should it matter to the earlier self that there will be a later self that is part of the same person? Even if there were a very few elements in common, I doubt that they should be enough to matter. Using Parfit's terminology, I am claiming that while psychological continuity may be enough for being the same person, unless there is psychological connectedness between the self at one time and the self at another, it should not (and probably will not) matter to either that they are selves in the same person. If there is no psychological connectedness between two selves, then there is no reason why the earlier should feel that what will happen to the later will represent its survival, nor is there any reason why the later should feel that it is the survival of that earlier self.

If life goes on everlastingly, eventually there would be no psychological connectedness between the self that exists in the far future and a self that existed prior to death. There would be a significant decrease in psychological connectedness in the first moments of an afterlife. For (according to the most common beliefs about an afterlife) in the afterlife either one would be disembodied or one would have a different body (at least according to all Western believers, who say that infirmities in this life would be eliminated). In either case, that part of our sense of ourselves involving our sense of our own bodies would be disrupted. Also disrupted would be our sense of what we are physically able to do and not to do. And to whatever extent our mental abilities were changed (think of a person with severe Alzheimer's who dies), that too would lessen the degree of psychological connectedness. Presumably our desires, interests, and other features of our selves would have to change to accommodate our new bodies (or lack thereof), our new mental capacities, and our new environment. (In the afterlife, are there courts for basketball players and lakes for anglers? Is our native tongue spoken, or do people communicate telepathically?) As we adjust to all these new things, much of what was important to us on earth would become irrelevant. Sooner or later we would lose memories of our days on earth. And if our memory capacity remained finite, eventually new memories would crowd out any memories of pre-mortem life. There would no longer be any psychological connectedness between any pre-mortem self and a self in the far future. Nor would it help if the transitions were gradual. That would only postpone the problem, not solve it. To be sure, at each point in the gradual process the self at that point would have strong psychological connectedness with the self a moment before; however, when we compare the concrete self far along in the process with the concrete self as she was before death, we must ask whether either would see the other as the same self.

The contrast I am describing between pre-mortem and post-mortem existence has some similarities to the smaller contrast between a person at different ages before death. In general, the self that exists at one time in the pre-mortem life of a person is neither completely identical with nor completely different from the self that exists at another time. Typically, there is some degree of psychological connectedness, but it may not be very great. The closer the selves are in time, the more similar and connected they will tend to be. Moreover, since people vary in the extent to which they remember moments in their pasts and anticipate their futures, and since people vary in the rate at which they change, two selves separated by five years in the life of one person may be more similar than two selves separated by five years in the life of another, and there will be differences in the extent to which fifty-year-olds will feel an inner connection (psychological connectedness) with the five-year-olds they once were.

There is no clear answer to the question of how long a self lasts or how many selves there are in a person's life on earth. The self at one time is different from the self at another. Sometimes the differences are so great as to prompt statements such as "I was a different person [in my terminology, self] then." But calculating the number of distinct selves is not important. What is important is noting how weak can be the felt inner connection between the self at one time and the self at another time. In some cases it can be nonexistent, even for two selves in the life of the same person on earth, typically a period of less than a hundred years.

By contrast, those who think of a life after death as involving a resurrection of the body typically conceive of this post-mortem existence as going on forever. If people's memories remain finite in capacity and if they work in a fashion similar to ours in this life, eventually people in this post-mortem state will forget their time on earth. They will cease to remember this time and to feel any inner connection with it, just as most of us do not remember and do not feel an inner connection with the person we were during our first years of life. When they have forgotten their lives on earth, it will not matter to them that the persons they now are had their origin (or spent an earlier phase of their life) on earth. And if, while they were on earth, they were to have been told that eventually there would develop out of the life they began a self who would have no memory of life on earth and feel no inner connection with a self who lived that life on earth, then I do not think they would feel that it was their life that is prolonged.

Some Objections and Alternatives

The problem with an afterlife as the solution to the problem of death is that memories and other sorts of psychological connectedness grow fewer and weaker as time passes; in an afterlife of unlimited duration, eventually all memory of, and all other forms of psychological connectedness with, life on earth would disappear if people's memory capacity and mental capacity in general remains finite. In response, it might be suggested that a person might be the same self in the sense that some elements of her character remain even though no memories do. I am not sure that there could be traces of character without any memories, but for now I will assume that there could be. Even so, this is a very thin basis for claiming sameness of self. Character traits are too generic to provide a tie to just one self, or even just one person. For example, suppose that after death a person achieves complete devotion to God by developing an element of devotion that was present in the pre-mortem person. Though that complete devotion may have some trace of having been developed from the earlier devotion, would there be anything about the trace that would identify it as that particular pre-mortem person's devotion? Presumably there would be many people who develop an element of devotion to God into post-mortem complete devotion to God. What ties each post-mortem self to a particular pre-mortem self? Memories that link the devotion with particular events in which it was expressed or developed would identify it. However, we are supposing that there are no memories of the pre-mortem existence, and I cannot conceive what else could serve as an identifier.

This line of argument assumes that in an afterlife our memory capacity remains finite and that our memories work at least roughly as they do in this life. But suppose this assumption is erroneous. Suppose that in the afterlife people have unlimited memory capacity and remember everything clearly. (This supposition is extremely implausible in relation to any being other than God, but let that pass for now.) The resulting person would remember clearly all the details of life on earth. But that person would not be human, for surely finitude of memory is a necessary condition for humanness. So it is hard to see how such a self could regard itself as the same self as the one whose life on earth forms an ever-smaller part of its total memory, for that self surely regarded itself as human. It is also difficult to think that the self on earth who contemplates this future would think of that post-mortem being as the same self as he is now on earth. Perhaps the pre-mortem self might think of himself as making a contribution to some post-mortem self, but I do not think he would see that post-mortem self as himself. Indeed, he might think of himself as being swallowed up by the post-mortem self. Thus, no matter how we conceive of memory in the life to come, it seems that an everlasting life would not solve the problem posed by death.

Some support for this conclusion comes from an unexpected source: the speculations of John Hick. This support is unexpected because Hick is well known as a defender of the idea of post-mortem existence; that idea plays a crucial role in the theodicy he has developed and defended at length. Yet when we examine his speculative description of life after death, we find striking similarities to the state of affairs that I have categorized as an inadequate solution to the problems posed by death and uncompensated sufferings. He writes: "What we can call our span of self-apprehension ... seems to be limited, so that I should not think of the person who was in some sense me fifty million years ago, or even five hundred years ago, as *me* in any personally significant or morally momentous sense.[19]

In a more recent article, Hick suggests that a person has two aspects: "an empirical or public self, formed in interaction with others within a common historico-cultural matrix" and "a basic moral or spiritual nature, or dispositional structure," which he terms the soul.[20] The empirical self is essentially related to a particular time and place; when a human being dies, this self, "with its culture-bound personality and time-bound memories, begins gradually to fade away, our consciousness becoming centred in the moral/spiritual attitudes which constitute the soul" (193). That soul then is able to be embodied again and again in different empirical selves. Hick's *empirical self* is similar to my *self*. Hick admits that this self does not survive death, at least not forever, because it is essentially related to a particular time and place (and, I would add, to a particular body). In effect, Hick is saying that the eventual fulfillment for the suffering is enjoyed by one who has no memory of the suffering. It is hard to see how this could be fulfillment for the suffering.

Hick and I also differ on the issue of whether the continuing dispositional structure that he postulates would constitute a continuing self. I hold that it does not, because, as I have already suggested, a dispositional structure simply is too thin and abstract to be a self. Moreover, as Hick admits, even this soul changes. Indeed, the point of the whole process of repeated incarnations that Hick postulates is to allow the soul to grow and develop into a religiously appropriate state. So the question arises with fresh intensity: what is it that provides the ontological basis for calling this changing dispositional structure *one self*?[21] Certainly it is not the multitude of empirical selves in which the soul is supposedly incarnated, for each of these is unrelated to the others in the contents of its consciousness. Thus, I conclude that Hick's speculations intended to defend the claim that there is in some sense a person that continues through this process actually, though unintentionally, support my claim that the self whose death (almost) everyone resists does not survive death, at least not for ever, even if something continues after death.

I have argued that an everlasting life is an inadequate solution to the problem posed by death and uncompensated sufferings. What about an afterlife of limited duration? Though it might mitigate some of the difficulties relating to the eventual fading of all memory of life on earth, it would have to face the problems raised by discontinuities between this life and the next, which would cause a discontinuity in one's sense of self; however, these discontinuities need not involve a complete lack of psychological connectedness. But clearly this sort of afterlife would not solve the problem posed by death: the cessation of the concrete self. For if the afterlife were of limited duration, then it would end, and exactly the same problem about the cessation of the concrete self would occur when it ended as is now posed by the fact that life on earth ends. Therefore, an afterlife of limited duration would not solve the problem of death.

Fulfillment or Compensation for the Sufferings of this Life in an Afterlife

The foregoing discussion of why everlasting life after death is not an adequate solution to the problem of death also enables us to understand why an afterlife does not provide a context in which one could be completely fulfilled or fully compensated for the evils suffered in this life. The basic problem is that the self in the far future has little or no psychological connectedness with the self who suffered; therefore, any fulfillment or compensation the future self enjoyed would not be seen by the self who suffered as fulfillment or compensation for that self's sufferings. Consider some examples of how that compensation might occur. One who was physically or psychologically abused as a child could experience in an afterlife some great good intended to make up for what that person suffered earlier. One who was mentally or physically handicapped in this life could have those handicaps removed and experience some great good as well. To the extent that the self who receives these benefits feels an inner connection (psychological connectedness) with the self who suffered, we could say there is compensation. And to the extent that this is adequate compensation, even an afterlife of limited duration might enable such a compensation to occur. But such compensations are not all that might be desired.

To see why, we need to consider the examples in more detail. If a person suffered physical or sexual abuse as a child and then lived many more years with the scars and memories of that abuse, his life might be very different from what it would have been without the abuse. In the afterlife (if there is one), there would be a self who has some memories and scars from that abuse. This self might experience some great good. But the self would be being compensated for the memories and scars, not for the abuse itself. For the concrete self who experienced the abuse – the frightened, tortured child – is the one who most needs compensation, and that self is gone. So are all the years lived with those scars before the compensation is received. Nor would it help for God to re-create that self, as God might have the power to do, according to traditional theists. For suppose God did. Though God might create a person with the same characteristics as the child who suffered when the child suffered, that person presumably would be re-created in a different world, and therefore might not experience himself as the same self. But even if we put that worry aside, there remains the problem that if this self were re-created and compensated and/or fulfilled, then he would have no memories of growing up and living with the scars on earth, and he would have to grow up all over again. Even if this is possible, what would happen to the person he had originally become as he grew up uncompensated and with the memories and scars of the abuse? Would the self or selves in that person (or the entire person) simply cease to exist? Would he exist as a different person from the compensated child who was growing up again? Neither answer is satisfactory. Moreover, we have discussed this as though there were only one suffering to be compensated. But in the life of most people, there would be many sufferings that should be compensated, and the same questions would arise for each one.

Similar considerations would apply to someone born with some genetic defect, such as Down's syndrome or spina bifida. If the person lived many years with this condition, her life would be very different from what it would have been without the condition. Suppose that at death the condition were corrected and the person were given some wonderful experiences. That might make the self at that time feel wonderful, but it would not help those earlier selves who lived with the condition. On the other hand, if the infant self were re-created and the condition corrected so that the person could develop from infancy without the condition, what would become of the person who developed with it?

The difficulties I have raised about post-mortem compensation also apply to post-mortem fulfillment. A self who exists after death may be wonderfully fulfilled, but that self may feel little or no connection with the self who suffered before death. However, to the extent that the post-mortem self feels connected with the pre-mortem self, we could speak of the fulfillment of that self though the one who is fulfilled would be the post-mortem self with his or her scars and memories, not the pre-mortem self who actually experienced the suffering. Of course, such fulfillment would not require an afterlife that continued for ever.

But even though the self who is compensated or fulfilled would not be identical with, but at most psychologically connected with, the self who actually suffered, nevertheless, if this compensation or fulfillment occurred, it would be a good. We ordinarily judge it to be good when it occurs in this life; there is no reason to judge it differently if it were to occur in a life after death. The experience of being compensated or fulfilled is intrinsically good; in process terms, it is rich, harmonious, and intense – the key characteristics of a good experience. And it brings to episodes in the life of a person a kind of closure that we recognize as appropriate and judge to be good. Process thinkers can recognize and value this closure because, while the primary bearers of value are individual occasions, the value attainable by any individual occasion depends on the context in which it arises. If that context contains scars or unfulfilled dreams inherited from earlier occasions – these are kinds of psychological connectedness – then having appropriate closure for these elements contributes significantly to the positive value achieved by a new occasion. But this good is not essential to the goodness of creation. There are many goods that we can imagine that do not occur. If they did, that would make the created order better, but their absence does not show that the created order is overall more bad than good. The created order is overall more good than bad, provided that the complexity that God evokes results in a net gain of good qualities over bad qualities in the experiences of all creatures; the richness and vitality of life on earth (the only life we know) certainly points to the goodness of the created order. At the very least, to borrow a point from the ignorance defense, we certainly are incompetent to judge that there not being an afterlife with compensations and fulfillment precludes the created order from being overall good.

Given creaturely freedom and conflicts engendered by incompossible goods, a complex created order will almost certainly contain significant suffering that is not compensated or fulfilled, if not that of humans, then that of some non-human animals. (I say "some non-human animals" because I do not want to presume that no animals have an afterlife if humans do.) If there is an afterlife, for which the possession of certain mental characteristics is necessary, even if some animals have these characteristics, it is plausible to think that some animals do not. The possession of these characteristics would require a certain level of complexity, and that could come to be only after lesser degrees of complexity had come to be, so there would have to be some animals that do not have these characteristics.

Let me summarize the argument so far. What I have characterized as the problem posed by death is this: the concrete self with all the hopes, goals, interests, concerns, and projects that make her the unique self she is – that self will cease when she dies or some time thereafter. It is that self which she wishes to continue, so that she can achieve her goals, complete her projects, act on her concerns, continue to experience things she cares about, and so on. I have given reasons for thinking that life after death will not solve the problem posed by death because sooner or later there will develop a self that has no sense of inner connection with the self she is now. Thus, even if something survives her death, it would be (or eventually become) so different a self from that which she now is that her present self would have no psychological connectedness with it. And uncompensated sufferings of this life cannot be fully compensated or fulfilled in an afterlife because the self being compensated or fulfilled is not the self that suffered. This may seem a disheartening conclusion. If life after death is not a solution to these problems, what is? Or is there no solution? I have a suggestion.

A Possible Solution of a Different Sort

It may have occurred to the reader that the concrete self that one now is will cease even if one does not die. Over the years, one's hopes, goals, interests, concerns, and projects will change. There is not much left in me of the five-year-old boy whom people many years ago called by my name. That self is gone. There is more, but still not much, left of the thirty-year-old whom people used to call by my name. I have no memory of the sense of self possessed by the self at that later stage of my development, to say nothing of the sense of self possessed by the five-year-old. That is, I have no recollection of the constellation of hopes, goals, interests, and other characteristics that made me at each time the distinct self that I then was. Those selves are gone, as are many others in my past. They are gone almost as completely as if they had passed into oblivion.

So let us accept, at least for the sake of argument, my conclusion that the concrete self will cease whether or not there is life after death, that even life after death offers the concrete self at most only an eventual fade into insignificance in the make-up of that being who would eventuate after a long post-mortem sequence of development. Then why have people thought that life after death is an answer to the problem of their own mortality? Perhaps because many did not realize that the concrete self would face this eventuality. Because the transition from one self to another is gradual and because one always identifies with one's current self, one does not think about the fact that any particular self will cease. To many people it may seem as though if the person never ends, there is no problem of death. But as I have argued, any self eventually ceases. To fail to note this is to confuse or equate the self and the person. But presumably not everyone does this. Perhaps some think that the passing away of particular selves does not matter, for they have the sense that the concrete selves that they now are would each have made a contribution to some future being.

I conclude, then, that to whatever extent the prospect of life after death offers a solution to the problem posed by death, it does so because that prospect offers the concrete self the assurance that it will make a contribution to some being that will exist after the concrete self ceases. Perhaps this is why some people, including some who do not believe that they will continue to live after death, are willing to die for their country (a being that will exist after the concrete self ceases). Perhaps too it is why the ancient Israelites and many other ancient peoples found immortality of a sort in their offspring and in the nation of which they were a part. Remember that God's promise to Abraham was not that he would live for ever in God's presence, but that God would make his offspring into a mighty nation in whom all the nations of the earth would be blessed (Gen. 12:2–3).

However, as a solution to the problem posed by death, the contribution made by the self to subsequent beings such as offspring or a nation has problems. These center around three factors: the significance of any one self's contribution to any of these beings will diminish over time; other than the immortal sorts of beings postulated by various forms of life-after-death theories, these subsequent beings will themselves cease; and all of these preserve only certain aspects of the concrete self, not that self in its full concreteness. Accordingly, the ideal solution to the problem posed by death would be the full preservation of the concrete self in a being who will not cease and in whom the significance of the contribution of that self will not diminish.

It may have occurred to readers that in the course of our reflections in this chapter we have already mentioned one conceivable being who would come close to meeting the requirements for what I termed the ideal solution to the problem posed by death. When discussing the qualities of resurrected persons, I mentioned the possibility that they might be everlasting and endowed with infinite memory capacity and with perfect recall of every experience of earlier stages of their development, including their pre-mortem time on earth. At that point in the discussion I criticized this proposal on the grounds that such a being would not be human and thus could not regard itself as the same self as a pre-mortem self. But now our perspective on the problem has shifted. We have seen that the self cannot be preserved as the same self. At most it can be preserved in the memory of a subsequent being, so the fact that the subsequent being would not see itself as the same self as the pre-mortem self would not matter.

There remains, however, the apparent non-humanness of the being who preserves in memory the earlier self. Our ideal solution includes the requirement that this being have infinite memory capacity and perfect recall of all experiences of previous selves. Such properties seem properly associated with a divine being rather than with non-divine beings. Moreover, since the self in which the memory is preserved cannot be same self as the one that is preserved (for the preserver must have infinite capacity, and human selves do not), there is no reason to require that it be a being in whose earlier development only one human being contributed in the unique way in which in the life of a human on earth an earlier self contributes to a later self in the same person. Thus, preservation of the self in the never-fading memory of a divine being seems as adequate a solution to the problem posed by death as we can conceive.

Before concluding, I want to discuss one possible objection to this solution. The self that is preserved in memory is not a dynamic, active self, but only a non-active copy of this self. We might say it is a frozen copy, not the true self. This objection makes an accurate comment, but it does not raise a valid criticism. For it is by acting that the self creates a somewhat different self and thereby brings about its own cessation. The self acts, and thereby puts itself in a new situation. In that situation it begins to acquire new hopes, goals, interests, memories, and so on, and thereby it becomes a somewhat different concrete self. There is no way to avoid the end of any particular self. In experiencing, in acting, in being the self that it is, any particular self brings about its own end. That self – any self – can be preserved in its full concreteness only in a frozen form, though some parts of it contribute in more or less important ways to future selves of that person.

Is what I have proposed a solution to the problem posed by death? I think so. It may help if I briefly rehearse some of the points already made, though in a somewhat different form. I began by saying that death poses a problem because it means the end of the self that exists at that time. Because that self wishes to carry out its projects, fulfill its goals, have new experiences, and so on, it wishes not to die. But as it acts to fulfill its wishes, it is succeeded by a somewhat different self that also has projects, goals, interests, and so on, and that wishes not to die so that it can fulfill them. Because there is this succession of selves, each of which wishes not to die, we think there is just one self that wishes not to die. But this is a mistake. A self that existed when a human was thirty is gone when that human is sixty, though traces of it remain in a self of sixty. (These traces comprise what Parfit calls psychological connectedness.) But because at any one time in the life of a person there is only one self, we think there is just one self throughout the life of that person, and we think that life after death will preserve that self. Indeed, it might briefly preserve some of the self that was present at death. But the self that was present at the beginning of post-mortem existence would soon also be gone, replaced by another self in the post-mortem person. In this life or after it, the concrete self must end and be replaced by another. As we have seen, even if a sequence of selves such as we are at any particular moment were infinitely extended, it would not result in the preservation of earlier members of the series. So I concluded that if a concrete self were to be preserved, it could be preserved only as an element in the experience of some being in whom the addition of more elements to the self did not eliminate or diminish the vividness of other elements, and I proposed that God would be such a being. To attribute to God infinite mental capacity and the ability to hold vividly in consciousness all items of knowledge would be fully in line with properties typically attributed to God; it would also accord well with what process thinkers claim about God. Is this sort of preservation of the self enough to solve the problem posed by death? I think so, because to ask anything more is to ask the impossible: it is to ask that the self, which is dynamic and related, both be unchanged and at the same time be dynamic and related to a changing reality.

What about the problem of unfulfilled or uncompensated suffering? The understanding of the self that I have been advocating makes it impossible to fulfill or compensate later the self that has suffered. That self is gone. When we offer some good, unless we offer it very soon after the suffering, what we are doing benefits a later, at least somewhat different, self for the traces of the suffering of an earlier self preserved in the later self. Note that we also sometimes compensate later stages of other persons for the effects on them of the suffering of a different person, as when we compensate a spouse for loss of consortium, or a child for the loss of the presence and financial support of a parent. On my analysis, compensating a person for something that person suffered earlier is often analogous to compensating another person, because even when the same person is compensated, it is often a significantly different self of that same person. Thus, the most we can expect by way of fulfilling or compensating people for the evils they suffered is to provide (or to attempt to provide) to later selves some good in their experience that will alleviate as much as possible the effects on them of the suffering of the earlier self.[22] The extent to which there are effects in later non-divine selves and the extent to which fulfillment or compensation for these effects is possible will vary from one instance of suffering to another. Clearly, there can be no guarantee of a perfect fulfillment or compensation; it may not even be clear what that would be.

However, this understanding of the sort of fulfillment or compensation that is possible fits very well with process theism. For according to process theists, God is continually working to evoke in each actual being the best experience possible within the limits imposed by its past. This would include trying to see that each self is provided with whatever is needed to alleviate in it the effects of suffering by earlier selves in the same person, so far as this is possible and consistent with a like concern for other actual beings. It is the same in the experience of God as well. As God takes into Godself the painful experiences of creatures and feels those experiences, God will supplement God's experience of these painful elements with other concepts, ideas, and memories that will reduce the painfulness for God and make the total experience as good – in process thought, as rich, harmonious, and intense – as possible. As an analogy, consider the way in which one may try to make physical pain more bearable by thinking of a good reason why one is undergoing it or what one may learn from it, and the way in which one may try to make emotional pain more bearable by thinking of some good to which the painful event contributes (for example, one comforting oneself that one's beloved died saving someone else's life).

This concludes my suggestion of a process understanding of how God overcomes evil. God's role in overcoming evil was the last of the reasons discussed in Chapter 7 why traditional theists might believe that God has the power to unilaterally determine non-divine states of affairs. My suggestion in this chapter does not require attributing that sort of power to God. It also does not rely on the assumption that there is some sort of life after death; however, if there is, that would provide some additional possibilities for what a process theist might suggest about the overcoming of evil.

The Worshipfulness of God

In this work, the final challenge to the understanding of God held by process theists is that such a God is not perfect and not worthy of worship. People whose beliefs about God have been shaped by traditional theism may raise this challenge. My purpose in this section is to show that God, as process theists understand God, is indeed perfect and worthy of worship. To do this, I will discuss the following important characteristics of God, drawing extensively on matters already discussed: God's power, knowledge, goodness, and love; and God's activity in creating the universe and providing salvation and other goods to humans.

I will begin with God's power. Traditional theists claim that they attribute greater power to God than do process theists, and they *appear* to be correct. But process theists claim that the power attributed to God by traditional theists is not possible because of what they believe to be metaphysically necessary features of individual actual creatures (actual occasions) and of God's relation to the world. According to process theists, every actual individual creature has some power of self-determination, the power to exclude possibilities from subsequent creatures by the way it constitutes itself, and the power to exert on new creatures pressures to exhibit certain qualities. If these features of individual, finite, actual creatures are metaphysically necessary features of individual finite actual creatures in any possible world, then to try to conceive of God as having the power to unilaterally determine some state of affairs in the world is to attribute to God what is metaphysically impossible and therefore broadly logically impossible (though some may not realize its impossibility, just as someone unskilled in mathematics may think it possible for God to square the circle or to calculate an exact decimal equivalent of pi).

I do not claim to be able to show that process theists are correct in their claims about what features of individual actual creatures are metaphysically necessary, but no one else has been able to show that some other understanding of the metaphysically necessary features of individual actual creatures is correct. Nor is there good reason to think that we have some sort of reliable intuitive insight into these structures or into fundamental metaphysical principles, as disagreements about these principles show. Of course, particular thinkers may reject process theism (or any other metaphysical scheme) because it is inconsistent with some metaphysical principle or scheme they already hold. But if they want to use one such principle or scheme to criticize another, then they should include a consideration of how well established their favored metaphysical principle or scheme is.

In short, process theists defend the claim that God's power is perfect (the greatest conceivable) by claiming that God has the greatest power that it is metaphysically possible for an individual actual entity to have. Though a group of occasions may in aggregate have more direct influence on what occurs in a small volume of space and time than does God, no one occasion by itself has as much influence as does God, and the aggregate itself has no influence on prior or contemporary occasions, and a vanishingly small influence on future occasions that are not near to it in time and space. By contrast, God has direct and indirect influence on all occasions (past, present, and future), and God's provision of the initial aim and other possibilities for all occasions is essential to their becoming. Therefore, God has more power than any other individual actual entity and has the maximum power any one actual entity can have if the features of process metaphysics noted earlier are correct.

The foregoing discussion of God's power deals only with God's *active* power, the sort of power with which traditional Christian theists have been concerned. But process theists also claim that God has the maximum passive power, the maximum power to receive the influence of other entities. Many traditional Christian theists have disputed that there is any passive power (or any passivity) in God. But according to process theists, God perfectly experiences everything that every other actuality experiences. This power is clearly the maximum conceivable instance of passive power.

Process theists believe that God's knowledge is perfect because God knows perfectly all the details of the past and present, and knows all possibilities for the future.[23] They believe that many propositions about the future lack a current truth-value (other than indeterminate); such propositions will acquire the value true (or false) only when the states of affairs to which they refer occur (or do not occur), or when causally sufficient conditions for their occurrence (or non-occurrence) happen. Obviously, it is no limitation on the perfection of God's knowledge that God does not know the truth-value of those propositions about the future that currently lack a truth-value.

According to process theists, God is perfectly good and perfectly loving. God's goodness is expressed in God's always luring every new occasion toward the best possible outcome for itself and its relevant future.[24] This "best possible outcome" is an experience that is as rich, harmonious, and intense as possible for that occasion and its relevant future. Being loving, though it includes being good, requires more; it requires knowing and caring about what the loved one is experiencing. If my child needs surgery, I may manifest goodness by arranging for my child to have the surgery, plus all the supportive care needed. However, being loving requires in addition that I care about what the child feels, that I sympathize and empathize with those feelings. If I do not do this, it is doubtful that I truly love the child. In process theism, God's omniscience guarantees that God knows perfectly and completely everything that every creature is feeling. But God does not know just that the creatures is experiencing certain feelings; rather, God experiences what the creature experiences.[25] God cannot know (experience) these feelings without caring about them, and thus caring for the creature experiencing them.

Process theists understand God to be the creator in at least three important senses: God gives to every actual occasion at its origin the most crucial element for its concrescence, the initial aim (as well as other possibilities); God evokes and sustains the principles of order within which actual occasions concresce; and God is the source of novel possibilities and thus is the actuality who lures into existence new kinds of beings, including different kinds of living things, and who is the source of novel possibilities for existing beings. If *per impossible* these divine activities ceased, there would be no complex world with its many kinds and not even individual actualities. Though process theists do not believe that God creates out of nothing, we have seen that there is no good reason to affirm creation in this sense anyway.

Process theists can say that God overcomes evil and provides salvation even if there is no life after death. In the previous section I argued that traditional ideas of life after death offer not a better sort of salvation, only an illusion of a better sort of salvation resting on a confusion between the self (who wants not to cease, but must, as it interacts with a changing world) and the person (whose survival of death, even if it occurs, will not preserve forever any pre-mortem self). But in God all our accomplishments and all our hopes, dreams, and struggles will be perfectly and vividly experienced and treasured everlastingly. Even our failures and shortcomings will be remembered and supplemented with divine appreciation for the efforts they involved and the opportunities they missed. Moreover, God continuously lures us to a better life, just as God lures all people toward the best. This universal action of God luring people toward the best provides grounds for hope that there will be over time a gradual, though not straight-line, improvement in the context in which human beings live.

All process theists would agree that God provides the sort of salvation summarized in the previous paragraph. Whether God also provides other sorts of salvation is, as I said in the previous section, disputed. It depends on whether or not there is life after death. If there is life after death, then process theists could claim that in the afterlife, God provides at least some of the goods traditional theists have claimed God provides: help with alleviating the problem of death and provision of a context for fulfilling or compensating people for sufferings in this life. However, I see no way process theists could claim that there could be everlasting life or a guaranteed perfect life for the individual or a guaranteed perfect society. The commitment of process theists to an inescapable element of self-determination in every actual individual seems to me to preclude any *guaranteed* ongoing perfection.

In addition to providing salvation, God also provides help to all people, not in the form of miracles in the sense of suspensions of laws of nature, but in the lures God offers every occasion. The lure of God would serve as a motivation to do what is best (divine guidance and encouragement), as a source for novel ideas (divine guidance and inspiration), as a source of motivation and inspiration to combat illness (divine healing), and as a source of solace in difficult circumstances (divine comfort). Of course, process theists would hold that God's influence in these ways is always only one of the factors that contribute to the beginning of a new occasion and that the new occasion is free not to follow the divine lure.

This concludes my presentation of process theism as a way for Christians to respond to the problems of evil and as a scheme within which Christians can rethink some of the beliefs involved in their faith. It seems to me that my proposal offers some obvious advantages: the evils of the world and the phenomena of the Bible are what we should expect, rather than problems requiring an explanation (as they are in traditional Christian theism). I have argued both that the explanations offered by traditional Christian theists have serious problems, and that one crucial factor central to generating the problems – their understanding of divine power – is something we have no good reason to accept. Nevertheless, I also recognize that some Christians will find that the understanding of divine power in process theism and the reconception of salvation it involves require too radical a change in their understandings of these matters. For these and perhaps for other reasons as well, they will not be able to accept process theism as a scheme for interpreting some aspects of Christian beliefs. Because I do not believe that there is any one set of divinely certified beliefs (including those I advocate) that all Christians must hold, I can gladly respect those Christians who continue to differ with me on these matters. But despite my respect for those who differ, I continue to think that of all the ways of thinking of God known to me, the one adumbrated by process theists is the best one for responding to the problems of evil and for making sense, from a broadly Christian perspective, of the world as we know it today.

Notes

1. It is worth noting that in a recent work, D.Z. Phillips, who represents a Wittgensteinian rather than a process approach, comes to very similar conclusions about how God's power should be understood: *The Problem of Evil and the Problem of God* (London: SCM Press, 2004). Like process theists, he concludes that God's power should be understood as persuasive rather than coercive. However, he differs from them in other ways. Process theists conceive of God as something like a non-bodied person (or a person whose body is the universe), and as knowing and being affected by what goes on in the universe, but Phillips does not. Process theists often use metaphysical concepts and schemes to explicate religious ideas, while Phillips does not. And process theists have a well-developed idea of what creation involves, while, so far as I can determine, Phillips does not. In all these ways, process theists are much closer to the positions of traditional theists than to those of Phillips, despite the general agreement between them and Phillips on how to understand God's power. The differences between process theists and Phillips are worth discussing further, but it is impossible to do so within the scope of this work.
2. In Whitehead's technical terminology, the two terms differ slightly in their extension, in that God is an actual entity, but not an actual occasion. However, this difference will not be important for our purposes.
3. *Process and Reality: An Essay in Cosmology*, corrected edn., ed. David Ray Griffin and Donald E. Sherburne (New York: Free Press, 1978), p. 43. That it is partly self-determining is, in process theism, metaphysically necessary, and the proposition that it is partly self-determining is therefore broadly logically necessary.
4. Students of Whitehead who remember his statement that "decision" means cutting off possibilities may well wonder whether the statement in the text is compatible with Whitehead's statement. I believe it is. For Whitehead's statement referred to the cutting

off of possibilities for what the concrescing entity can become. And God's decisions do constitute God as an entity who, among other things, desires certain outcomes and has aversion to others. Thus, they constitute God in one way rather than another, and in this sense they cut off possibilities for what God could have become. (God could have become an entity who desires different outcomes.) But the particular way in which God constitutes Godself does not cut off possibilities for what some subsequent non-divine occasion can become, for God does not eliminate any such possibilities in God's concrescence. The statement in the text refers to the effect of God's decisions on the range of possibilities for subsequent occasions, not to the effect of God's decision on God's self-constitution.

5. By "practical purposes" I mean those aspects of the event that affect human life, and more generally the lives of sentient creatures. Since the problems of evil are defined in relation to humans and other sentient creatures, I will often (but not always) be concerned only with the aspects of an event that I designate with this phrase.

6. A temporal series, as I am using the term here, is a series of occasions that occur one after the other in time – that is, only one occasion occurs at any time, so each occasion in the series is either in the past or in the future of any other occasion in the series. Whitehead's term for such a series is a society with personal order, or a personally ordered society.

7. Though occasions in any human mind have significant freedom, there is no reason to think that all occasions in a particular mind, to say nothing of all occasions in all human minds, have exactly the same degree of freedom. Education, experience, traumatic psychological events – all these factors and others influence the exact amount of freedom possessed by a particular occasion in a human mind.

8. John Hick makes this charge in *Philosophy of Religion*, 4th edn. (Englewood Cliffs, NJ: Prentice-Hall, 1990), pp. 52–5.

9. Moreover, God lures all creatures toward lives that are the best possible within the circumstances created by their particular pasts, and God feels perfectly, and thus shares in, the suffering of all creatures. Therefore, according to process theists, God does all that God can to give every creature the best life possible; this contrasts with the position of traditional theism, which holds that God could do more to improve the lives of particular creatures, but for various reasons God chooses not to.

10. I owe this analogy to Richard Creel's suggestion.

11. Though this sense of "miracle" is different from that employed in modern discussions, it is not totally unprecedented. It has important similarities to biblical concepts used to refer to some events that are today commonly called biblical miracles. (See note 3 in Chapter 4 for these concepts.) But though there is a similarity between the process concept of a miracle and certain biblical concepts, I am not suggesting that process theists would accept the claim that all the accounts in the Bible of events that are typically considered as miracles, if understood as literally accurate descriptions, represent events that could possibly happen in our cosmic epoch. Though suspension of a law of nature in our modern sense is not essential to the biblical concepts mentioned, some of the biblical events (as described) would involve suspension of laws of nature as we understand them. Such suspension would not be possible on the process view. Thus, my comments concern the similarity of certain concepts, not judgments about the possibility of certain events they may be used to refer to.

12. Some people may also want to speak of miracles in relation to events that involve no significant human choices, but whose outcome is good though unlikely. For example, a baby may fall into a raging river and by chance be thrown up alive on the shore rather than drowning. Though process theists can claim that God is pleased with the outcome, they can not claim that any divine influence led to its occurrence, for the occasions in the water molecules are not such as to be influenced in their concrescence by any desire that

the baby survive. While some believers may wish to call the outcome a miracle, it would not exemplify the process concept of a miracle articulated in the text.

13. I develop this point somewhat in my article "The Basingers on Divine Omnipotence: A Further Point," *Process Studies* 12/1 (Spring 1982): 23–5.

14. John Hick makes the distinction between compensation for evils, on the one hand, and fulfillment, on the other. Compensation suggests some kind of good for each evil suffered, whereas fulfillment suggests a wonderful good state whose precise quality is not dependent on the number or intensity of the evils one suffered (*Evil and the God of Love* [New York: Harper and Row, 1966], pp. 376–7).

15. For example, David Griffin defends it, most fully in *Parapsychology, Philosophy, and Spirituality: A Postmodern Exploration* (Albany, NY: State University of New York Press, 1997). Whitehead himself says that his metaphysics leaves it an open question; whether there actually is life after death is a question to be decided on "more special evidence" (*Religion in the Making* [New York: Macmillan, 1926], pp. 110–11).

16. C.S. Lewis is one of the rare exceptions. As we saw in Chapter 2, he speculates that there might be an afterlife for domesticated animals.

17. Reprinted with corrections (Oxford: Clarendon Press, 1991). I am drawing in particular on his discussion in Part III, "Personal Identity." In this discussion of Parfit's ideas, page numbers in parentheses refer to this work.

18. For example, he describes a situation in which scientists destroy his "brain and body, and then create, out of new organic matter, a perfect Replica of someone else" (he suggests Greta Garbo as she was at age thirty), but the scientists do this gradually, a few cells at a time. The scientists repeat this process again and again until there is nothing left of the original brain and body. Parfit says that the first few replacements do not create a new person, and asks where, if anywhere, in the process a new person is created. He claims that it is implausible to say that even at the end of the process it is the same person, but that it is also implausible to say that at some particular small change, the original person ceases to the be person he was and becomes a completely different person. The plausible conclusion of this thought experiment is, he claims, that one becomes a different person gradually, and that in the middle of the process there is no definite yes or no answer to the question of whether one is the same person as at the start of the process (237–43).

19. *Death and Eternal Life* (San Francisco, CA: Harper and Row, 1976), p. 410, italics his; pp. 409–11 merit careful reading on this point.

20. "A Possible Conception of Life after Death," in *Death and Afterlife*, ed. Stephen T. Davis (New York: St. Martin's Press, 1989), p. 192. Page numbers in this paragraph in the text refer to this work.

21. There may be an analogous problem about calling it "one person," but I am not discussing that sort of problem in this work.

22. My suggestion does not differ significantly from the traditional ideas of post-mortem compensation. My criticism of those ideas is not that the compensation is not as good as it could be, but that even at best it is not all that one might desire.

23. There may be some disagreement among people who generally agree on this formulation because of disagreements about how precisely future possibilities are knowable. For example, Charles Hartshorne believes that actuality always contains more definiteness than does any possibility, no matter how complex; therefore, Hartshorne thinks that God's knowledge of some future possibility is not as detailed as God's knowledge of the corresponding state of affairs will be if that possibility is realized. Moreover, some process thinkers believe that God's knowledge of future possibilities becomes more specific as the corresponding states of affairs grow closer in time. See my "Continuity, Possibility, and Omniscience: A Contrasting View," *Process Studies* 15/1 (Spring 1986): 1–18.

24. The relevant future is the future that the occasion is capable of envisioning. In occasions that constitute moments of human consciousness, the relevant future includes the well-being of other creatures; thus, the considerations that are commonly termed morality and ethics are relevant for humans. In contrast, concern about the well-being of others presumably is not something that a mosquito can envisage; thus, it is not part of the relevant future for an occasion in the experience of a mosquito.

25. Whitehead calls God "the great companion – the fellow-sufferer who understands" (*Process and Reality*, p. 351).

Bibliography

Adams, Marilyn McCord. *Horrendous Evils and the Goodness of God*. Ithaca, NY: Cornell University Press, 1999.

—— and Robert Merrihew Adams, eds. *The Problem of Evil*. Oxford: Oxford University Press, 1990.

Alston, William P. "The Inductive Argument from Evil and the Human Cognitive Condition." *Philosophical Perspectives 5: Philosophy of Religion, 1991*. Ed. James E. Tomberlin. Atascadero, CA: Ridgeview Publishing, 1991, pp. 29–67. Reprinted in *The Evidential Argument from Evil*. Ed. Daniel Howard-Snyder, pp. 97–125.

——. "Some (Temporarily) Final Thoughts on Evidential Arguments from Evil." *The Evidential Argument from Evil*. Ed. Daniel Howard-Snyder. Bloomington, IN: Indiana University Press, 1996, pp. 311–32.

Anderson, Bernard. "Signs and Wonders." *Interpreter's Dictionary of the Bible*. Ed. George Buttrick et al. New York: Abingdon Press, 1962. Vol. IV, pp. 348–51.

Aquinas, Thomas. *Summa Contra Gentiles. Book II: Creation*. Trans. James F. Anderson. Garden City, NY: Doubleday, 1956.

——. *Summa Theologiae*. New York: McGraw-Hill, 1964–.

Benn, Stanley I. "Punishment." *Encyclopedia of Philosophy*. Ed. Paul Edwards. New York: Macmillan and the Free Press, 1967. Vol. VII, pp. 29–36.

Calvin, John. *Institutes of the Christian Religion*. Ed. John T. McNeill. Trans. Ford Lewis Battles. Philadelphia, PA: The Westminster Press, 1960.

Cobb, John B., Jr. "Process Thought." *Philosophy of Religion in the 21st Century*. Ed. D.Z. Phillips and Timothy Tessin. New York: Palgrave Macmillan, 2002, pp. 251–65.

—— and David Ray Griffin. *Process Theology: An Introductory Exposition*. Philadelphia, PA: The Westminster Press, 1976.

Craig, William Lane. *Reasonable Faith*. Rev. edn. Wheaton, IL: Crossway Books, 1994.

Creel, Richard. *Divine Impassibility: An Essay in Philosophical Theology*. New York: Cambridge University Press, 1986.

Davis, Stephen T. *The Debate about the Bible: Inerrancy versus Infallibility*. Philadelphia, PA: The Westminster Press, 1977.

——. "Is It Possible to Know that Jesus Was Raised from the Dead?" *Faith and Philosophy* 1/2 (April 1984): 147–59.

——, ed. *Death and Afterlife*. San Francisco, CA: Harper and Row, 1989.

——. "Doubting the Resurrection." *Faith and Philosophy* 7/1 (January 1990): 99–111.

——. "Critique by Stephen T. Davis." *Encountering Evil: Live Options in Theodicy*. New edn. Ed. Stephen T. Davis. Louisville, KY: Westminster John Knox Press, 2001, pp. 133–37.

——, ed. *Encountering Evil: Live Options in Theodicy*. New edn. Louisville, KY: Westminster John Knox Press, 2001.

Dostoevsky, Fyodor. *The Brothers Karamazov.* Trans. Constance Garnett. *Great Books of the Western World.* 2nd edn. Vol. 52. Chicago: University of Chicago Press, 1990.

Fales, Evan. "Should God Not Have Created Adam?" *Faith and Philosophy* 9/2 (April 1992): 193–209.

Gilson, Etienne. *The Christian Philosophy of St. Thomas Aquinas.* Trans. L.K. Shook. New York: Random House, 1956.

Griffin, David Ray. *God, Power, and Evil: A Process Theodicy.* Philadelphia, PA: The Westminster Press, 1976.

——. *Evil Revisited: Responses and Reconsiderations.* Albany, NY: State University of New York Press, 1991.

——. *Parapsychology, Philosophy, and Spirituality: A Postmodern Exploration.* Albany, NY: State University of New York Press, 1997.

Hartshorne, Charles. *Omnipotence and Other Theological Mistakes.* Albany, NY: State University of New York Press, 1984.

Hasker, William. *God, Time, and Knowledge.* Ithaca, NY: Cornell University Press, 1989.

——. *Providence, Evil, and the Openness of God.* New York: Routledge, 2004.

Hick, John. *Faith and Knowledge.* Ithaca, NY: Cornell University Press, 1957.

——. *Evil and the God of Love.* New York: Harper and Row, 1966.

——. *Death and Eternal Life.* San Francisco, CA: Harper and Row, 1976.

——, ed. *The Myth of God Incarnate.* Philadelphia, PA: The Westminster Press, 1977.

——. *Problems of Religious Pluralism.* New York: St. Martin's Press, 1985.

——. "A Possible Conception of Life after Death." *Death and Afterlife.* Ed. Stephen T. Davis. New York: St. Martin's Press, 1989, pp. 183–96.

——. *An Interpretation of Religion: Human Responses to the Transcendent.* New Haven, CT: Yale University Press, 1989.

——. *Philosophy of Religion.* 4th edn. Englewood Cliffs, NJ: Prentice-Hall, 1990.

Howard-Snyder, Daniel, ed. *The Evidential Argument from Evil.* Bloomington, IN: Indiana University Press, 1996.

——. "In Defense of Naive Universalism." *Faith and Philosophy* 20/3 (July 2003): 345–63.

—— and Paul K. Moser, eds. *Divine Hiddenness.* New York: Cambridge University Press, 2002.

Kee, Howard Clark. *Understanding the New Testament.* 4th edn. Englewood Cliffs, NJ: Prentice-Hall, 1983.

Keller, James A. "The Basingers on Divine Omnipotence: A Further Point." *Process Studies* 12/1 (Spring 1982): 23–5.

——. "Continuity, Possibility, and Omniscience: A Contrasting View." *Process Studies* 15/1 (Spring 1986): 1–18.

——. "Contemporary Christian Doubts about the Resurrection." *Faith and Philosophy* 5/1 (January 1988): 40–60.

——. "Response to Davis." *Faith and Philosophy* 7/1 (January 1990): 112–16.

Kuhn, Thomas S. *The Structure of Scientific Revolutions.* Chicago: University of Chicago Press, 1970.

Leslie, John. *Universes*. New York: Routledge, 1989.

Lewis, C.S. *The Problem of Pain*. London: Collins Fontana Books, 1961.

MacGregor, Geddes. *Reincarnation in Christianity: A New Vision of the Role of Rebirth in Christian Thought*. Wheaton, IL: Quest Books, 1981.

Martin, Michael. *Atheism: A Philosophical Justification*. Philadelphia, PA: Temple University Press, 1990.

Mavrodes, George I. *Revelation in Religious Belief*. Philadelphia, PA: Temple University Press, 1988.

McDaniel, Jay. *Of God and Pelicans*. Louisville, KY: Westminster John Knox Press, 1989.

McKim, Robert. "The Hiddenness of God." *Religious Studies* 26 (1990): 141–61.

Mesle, C. Robert. *John Hick's Theodicy: A Process Humanist Critique*. New York: St. Martin's Press, 1991.

Morris, Thomas V. *Anselmian Explorations: Essays in Philosophical Theology*. Notre Dame, IN: University of Notre Dame Press, 1987.

——. *Making Sense of It All: Pascal and the Meaning of Life*. Grand Rapids, MI: William B. Eerdmans, 1992.

Morriston, Wes. "Must Metaphysical Time Have a Beginning?" *Faith and Philosophy* 20/3 (July 2003): 288–306.

Murray, Michael. "Deus Absconditus." *Divine Hiddenness*. Ed. Daniel Howard-Snyder and Paul K. Moser. New York: Cambridge University Press, pp. 62–82.

Parfit, Derek. *Reasons and Persons*. Reprinted with corrections. Oxford: Clarendon Press, 1991.

Phillips, D.Z. *The Problem of Evil and the Problem of God*. London: SCM Press, 2004.

—— and Timothy Tessin, eds. *Philosophy of Religion in the 21st Century*. New York: Palgrave Macmillan, 2002.

Plantinga, Alvin. *Warranted Christian Belief*. New York: Oxford University Press, 2000.

Reichenbach, Bruce R. *Evil and a Good God*. New York: Fordham University Press, 1982.

Rowe, William L. "The Problem of Evil and Some Varieties of Atheism." *American Philosophical Quarterly* 16 (1979): 335–41. Reprinted in *The Problem of Evil*, ed. Adams and Adams, pp. 126–37.

——. "Evil and the Theistic Hypothesis: A Response to Wykstra." *International Journal for Philosophy of Religion* 16/2 (1984): 95–100. Reprinted in *The Problem of Evil*, ed. Adams and Adams, pp. 161–7.

——. "The Evidential Argument from Evil: A Second Look." *The Evidential Argument from Evil*. Ed. Daniel Howard-Snyder. Bloomington, IN: Indiana University Press, 1996, pp. 262–85.

Russell, Bruce. "The Persistent Problem of Evil." *Faith and Philosophy* 6/2 (April 1989): 121–39.

Speiser, E.A. *Genesis: The Anchor Bible*. Garden City, NY: Doubleday, 1964.

Stump, Eleonore. "The Problem of Evil." *Faith and Philosophy* 4/2 (October 1985): 392–423.

——. "Providence and the Problem of Evil." *Christian Philosophy*. Ed. Thomas P. Flint. Notre Dame, IN: University of Notre Dame Press, 1990, pp. 51–91.

Suchocki, Marjorie. *The End of Evil: Process Eschatology in Historical Context*. Albany, NY: State University of New York Press, 1988.

Swinburne, Richard. *The Coherence of Theism*. New York: Oxford University Press, 1977.

——. *The Existence of God*. New York: Oxford University Press, 1979.

——. *Faith and Reason*. New York: Oxford University Press, 1983.

——. *Revelation: From Metaphor to Analogy*. Oxford: Clarendon Press, 1992.

——. *Providence and the Problem of Evil*. Oxford: Clarendon Press, 1998.

——. *The Resurrection of God Incarnate*. Oxford: Clarendon Press, 2003.

Tracy, Thomas F. "Victimization and the Problem of Evil: A Response to Ivan Karamazov." *Faith and Philosophy* 9/3 (July 1992): 301–29.

Van Inwagen, Peter. "Reflections on the Chapters by Draper, Russell, and Gale." *The Evidential Argument from Evil*. Ed. Daniel Howard-Snyder. Bloomington, IN: Indiana University Press, 1996, pp. 219–43.

Whitehead, Alfred North. *Religion in the Making*. New York: Macmillan, 1926.

——. *Process and Reality: An Essay in Cosmology*. Corrected edn. Ed. David Ray Griffin and Donald E. Sherburne. New York: Free Press, 1978.

Wolterstorff, Nicholas. *Divine Discourse: Philosophical Reflections on the Claim that God Speaks*. New York: Cambridge University Press, 1995.

Wykstra, Stephen J. "The Humean Obstacle to Evidential Arguments from Suffering: On Avoiding the Evils of 'Appearance.'" *International Journal for Philosophy of Religion* 16/2 (1984): 73–93. Reprinted in *The Problem of Evil*. Ed. Adams and Adams, pp. 138–60.

——. "Rowe's Noseeum Arguments from Evil." *The Evidential Argument from Evil*. Ed. Daniel Howard-Snyder. Bloomington, IN: Indiana University Press, 1996, pp. 126–50.

Index